Bounce, Tumble, and Splash!

Bounce Tumble, and Splash!

Simulating the Physical World with Blender 3D

Tony Mullen

WILEY PUBLISHING, INC.

Acquisitions Editor: Mariann Barsolo
Development Editor: Kathryn Duggan
Technical Editor: Roland Hess
Production Editor: Elizabeth Ginns Britten
Copy Editor: Sharon Wilkey
Production Manager: Tim Tate
Vice President and Executive Group Publisher: Richard Swadley
Vice President and Executive Publisher: Joseph B. Wikert
Vice President and Publisher: Neil Edde
Project Manager, I: Laura Moss-Hollister
Media Associate Producer: Kit Malone
Media Quality Assurance: Josh Frank
Compositor and Book Designer: Kate Kaminski, Happenstance Type-O-Rama
Proofreader: C.M. Jones
Indexer: Ted Laux
Cover Designer: Ryan Sneed
Cover Images: Milos Zajíc (school corridor)
Mike Pan (strawberries and milk)
Luma Studios (ClubSilo racing game)
Tony Mullen (pop bottle and boxes tumbling)
© Blender Foundation | peach.blender.org (cartoon animals)

For general information on our other products and services or to obtain technical support, please contact our Customer Care Department within the U.S. at (800) 762-2974, outside the U.S. at (317) 572-3993 or fax (317) 572-4002.

Wiley also publishes its books in a variety of electronic formats. Some content that appears in print may not be available in electronic books.

Library of Congress Cataloging-in-Publication Data

Mullen, Tony, 1971-

  Bounce, tumble, and splash! : simulating the physical world with Blender 3D / Tony Mullen. -- 1st ed.

    p. cm.

  Includes index.

  ISBN 978-0-470-19280-1 (paper/cd-rom)

  1. Computer graphics. 2. Computer simulation. 3. Blender (Computer file) 4. Computer animation. 5. Three-dimensional display systems. I. Title.

  T385.M8425 2008

  006.6'96--dc22

                    2008014650

10 9 8 7 6 5 4 3 2 1

Dear Reader,

Thank you for choosing *Bounce, Tumble, and Splash! Simulating the Physical World with Blender 3D*. This book is part of a family of premium-quality Sybex books, all of which are written by outstanding authors who combine practical experience with a gift for teaching.

Sybex was founded in 1976. More than thirty years later, we're still committed to producing consistently exceptional books. With each of our titles we're working hard to set a new standard for the industry. From the paper we print on, to the authors we work with, our goal is to bring you the best books available.

I hope you see all that reflected in these pages. I'd be very interested to hear your comments and get your feedback on how we're doing. Feel free to let me know what you think about this or any other Sybex book by sending me an email at nedde@wiley.com, or if you think you've found a technical error in this book, please visit http://sybex.custhelp.com. Customer feedback is critical to our efforts at Sybex.

Best regards,

Neil Edde
Vice President and Publisher
Sybex, an Imprint of Wiley

To Yuka

Acknowledgments

One of the most frequent things I hear from people seeing Blender for the first time is, "Wow, and this is *free*?" Of course, in the sense of *free* as in *free software*, it most certainly is. It is free for users to copy and distribute, and it is free to be developed and modified by anybody who wants to do so. But the truth is that nothing as good as Blender comes without a cost. The cost of Blender is paid in the form of countless hours donated by the dedicated and highly skilled team of volunteer developers who make Blender what it is. For this reason, I would first and foremost like to thank them, the Blender developers, and Ton Roosendaal, Blender's own "benevolent dictator for life," for all their hard work and dedication. Without them, there would be no Blender. Please visit http://wiki.blender.org/index.php/List_of_Contributors for a complete list of the current developers and the specific work they have done.

I would especially like to thank some of the developers who have been particularly helpful to me in my work on this book: Martin Poirier (theeth), Janne Karhu (jahka), Daniel Genrich (Genscher), Jens Ole Wund (bjornmose), Dolf Veenlivet (macouno), Joe Eagar (joeedh), Ramon Carlos Ruiz (RCruiz), Erwin Coumans, and Nils Theurey for their patience and responsiveness to my various questions and pestering. I'd like to give a special thank you to Tom Musgrove (LetterRip) and all those who worked to prepare the 2.46 release for placing such a high priority on maintaining a release schedule that facilitates the creation of good documentation, and also to Roland Hess for his work as technical editor of this book.

Thanks also to the Peach team of developers and artists: Campbell Barton, Sacha Goedegebure, Andy Goralczyk, William Reynish, Enrico Valenza, Brecht van Lommel, and Nathan Vegdahl, for raising the bar yet again for Blender features and artwork, and for putting up with me hanging around, drinking their espresso, and peeking over their shoulders for a week. Many other developers and users have also helped me in various ways, and I'm very grateful for all the support I've received from the Blender community. I can't begin to list all of the individuals at BlenderArtists.org whose artwork, comments, and tutorials have helped me to learn what I know about Blender, but if you spend a little time reading the forums, you will know who many of them are soon enough. Thanks also to Bart Veldhuizen and all the contributors to BlenderNation.com for their support and for the great service they provide the Blender community.

This book would not have been possible without the efforts of my editors and colleagues at Sybex/Wiley, and I'm very grateful to all of them. Thank you to Mariann Barsolo, Pete Gaughan, Kathryn Duggan, Liz Britten, Janet Chang, Joe Grasso, Kelly Trent, and everyone else who had a hand in publishing and promoting the book.

I'm also very grateful to my colleagues and students at Tsuda College for their support and encouragement of my Blender-related work.

Finally, thanks to my mom for everything and to my wife Yuka for her love, support, and patience.

About the Author

Tony Mullen is a college lecturer, animator, independent filmmaker, and writer living in Tokyo. He has worked as a newspaper cartoonist, a graphic designer, a software developer, and a researcher in natural language processing, among other things. Since discovering Blender, he has been involved in CG animation to the point of obsession, but he also maintains a keen interest in stop-motion techniques, notably as the lead animator and codirector of the 16mm film *Gustav Braüstache and the Auto-Debilitator* (winner of the Best Narrative Short award at the New Beijing International Movie Festival, 2007) and other independent shorts. He is an active member of the Blender community and one of the original members of the Blender Foundation's Trainer Certification Review Board. He is the author of a monthly series of Blender tutorials in the Japanese magazine *Mac People* and of the best-selling Sybex book *Introducing Character Animation with Blender.*

Contents

Foreword

Physics simulation is a fun and rewarding discipline. Fun, because it allows us to experiment with virtual creations that can go beyond real-world experiences, limited just by our imagination. Rewarding, because it allows us to author complex and large scale configurations that are out of reach by pure manual work.

Tony Mullen's *Bounce, Tumble, and Splash!* does a great job of stimulating our imagination, and unlocking all the simulation authoring tools of Blender. The rich 3D tools in Blender help authoring the various types of simulation, such as particles, cloth, soft bodies, and rigid bodies, useful for animations as well as real-time applications. The sheer amount of functionality and options in the Blender user interface can be overwhelming or even intimidating, but with books like this it becomes a pleasure to explore and become more familiar with all the different simulation methods that Blender has to offer. The combination of authoring, simulation, and visualization and a very fast turnaround time makes the user more productive.

Since the start of Not a Number, back in 2000, I've been involved in Blender development, mainly its interactive development. This became a great environment to try out the latest collision detection and rigid body simulation techniques, and my colleagues at Havok often looked surprised to see what Blender could do. Lacking the time to explain the custom user interface in detail, and lacking a book like this one, the others didn't have a chance to explore those possibilities. Now at Sony Computer Entertainment, with colleagues such as Craig Reynolds who is quoted in the chapter on particles for his work on flocking, the simulation capabilities of Blender proved very useful during prototyping our work on COLLADA physics export. This is a rich data standard that includes physics properties such as mass and friction, collision shapes, and rag-doll joints. With this background it is no surprise I'm fluent with the rigid body functionality of Blender, but I was unfamiliar with the other simulation methods such as particle systems, cloth, deformable objects, and fluid simulation. Until reading this book.

Visual Computing is a very active research and development area, and the gap between movie production physics simulation and real-time game physics is narrowing rapidly. I can hardly wait to see all the beautiful examples in this book becoming available in real-time applications, allowing the users to interact in real-time with cloth, rope, and soft body simulation.

Last but not least, as insider Tony welcomes the reader to the vibrant Blender community, people, forums, activities and recent projects such as the "Big Buck Bunny" open movie. This book should find its way to artists, students, researchers, developers, professionals, enthusiasts, and anyone who shares the passion to build creations using Blender.

Erwin Coumans, author of the Bullet physics library and Simulation Team Lead, Sony Computer Entertainment America

Introduction

Art and science have more in common than they are often given credit for. Although they tend to occupy far-flung corners of your typical college campus, they have always been closer in spirit than they sometimes seem on the surface. Both artists and scientists are highly creative people, and both can sometimes be a little quirky. At their best, both types can help us see the world in new ways through their work.

This book deals with what I think is a particularly interesting intersection between the worlds of art and science: the use of sophisticated computer simulations of physical phenomena for visual, expressive—that is to say, artistic—purposes. A huge amount of technical expertise has gone into the development of these tools, and in the hands of skilled and inspired creators, a lot of wonderful artwork can be created using them. I hope this book will help to bridge the gap between these tools and the people with the vision and the talent to use them most effectively.

In the last quarter of a century, the development of CG imagery has revolutionized how people think about the visible world. It is no exaggeration to say that in terms of technical methods applied to art, the recent developments in graphics are in the same league with the advances of the Italian Renaissance. It's not a coincidence that many of the same phenomena that are now central to CG are the same things that fascinated the visionaries of that era. Optics, physical laws, geometry, and material properties have always been of interest to artists, and the underlying relationships between things in the world have always been the true raw materials from which art is created.

There's another common point between art and science: the way that even the most astonishing new ideas and methods become accepted and even commonplace over time. The technical innovations of the Renaissance, once found only in the work of the most brilliant artists of the era, are now so accepted and accessible that perspective drawing is routinely taught as part of grade school art classes. Advances in the sciences, likewise, begin by being comprehensible only to a few brilliant minds, and wind up being taught to school children. Newtonian physics, one of the themes in this book, is a perfect example.

An analogous thing is happening now in the world of CG. For years, the tools and technologies for creating high-quality CG artwork have been expensive and inaccessible to most people. Recently, however, this has begun to change rapidly, and

Blender is a big part of the change. Now, students, hobbyists, freelancers, and studios alike have access to a powerful, extremely versatile 3D content-creation tool with no restrictions on using, distributing, or modifying it to suit their needs. Casual users can dip into Blender to see whether it suits their needs at no expense at all, and serious users can keep up with every upgrade, fix, and new feature patch even between official releases, all entirely for free.

It still requires effort, skill, and resources to create top-quality work, and it always will. However, the availability of a free resource such as Blender has begun to lead to a considerable increase in the number of people who can entertain the thought of creating CG artwork. One of the artists who created work for this book began creating artwork in Blender at the age of 12. Few 12-year-olds can afford high-quality proprietary CG software.

To say that it's an exciting time in the Blender world is an understatement. It's hard to know where to begin when listing recent milestones. Releases have been coming frequently, with exciting new features being implemented at a steady clip. The recently completed Peach project, the creation of the new open movie *Big Buck Bunny* to follow 2007's *Elephants Dream*, has pushed Blender forward once again. Blender is the most widely installed 3D modeling and animation application in the world, and has been making steady inroads into the CG industry. The perennial need for documentation and learning materials has also begun to be addressed, with a spate of commercially released books and training material including the Blender Foundation's *Essential Blender*, an excellent series of tutorial DVDs, my own book *Introducing Character Animation with Blender*, which has been translated into Spanish and Japanese, and several other books and videos in the works to cover various aspects of Blender's functionality.

Who Should Read This Book

Ton Roosendaal, lead developer of Blender and chairman of the Blender Foundation, is fond of saying, "Blender is for Blender users!" Everything about Blender is designed with the goal in mind of enabling the most efficient workflow for experienced users who have put in the time and effort to learn the software. Likewise, this book is for Blender users. To the best of my knowledge, in fact, this book is the first Blender book that is explicitly *not* targeted at beginners. To get the most out of this book, you should already know your way around the interface, and you should be reasonably well versed in the basics of modeling and animation in Blender. I won't be telling you how to split desktop windows or extrude faces or keyframe Ipos in this book. Beginners should start with the Blender Foundation's *Essential Blender* and my own previous book, *Introducing Character Animation with Blender*, both of which contain information that I will assume you know if you are reading this book.

This book is for people who are ready to move beyond the basics and get a deeper understanding of some of the advanced features that Blender offers. Some of the features discussed in this book are features that some other 3D applications lack, and I realize that some readers of this book will be mainly hoping to take advantage of those features and export the results for use in another environment. The fluid simulator is a good example of this. I have tried to describe all the steps necessary to use these features in sufficient detail that fairly casual users of Blender can follow along, but I highly recommend that those users save themselves some headaches by getting familiar with the basics of Blender before diving into this material.

What You Will Learn from This Book

This book is concerned with how to represent physical phenomena in Blender. As I did in *Introducing Character Animation with Blender,* I am casting the net wide in terms of what I cover here. Traditional physics simulations are covered, such as fluid simulation, soft body simulation, and rigid body Newtonian physics. In addition, the book covers such topics as the recently rewritten Blender particle system (including hair and fur), and the use of algorithms that simulate the growth of plants. Although the book's main objective is to cover these sophisticated simulation features, in practice artists also need to know how to get similar and related effects quickly and with as little computational overhead as possible, so I've devoted one chapter to general-purpose methods that I think will be of use to anybody interested in the material in this book. I've made an effort to cover material that is not thoroughly and accessibly documented elsewhere.

How to Use This Book

For the most part, you can work through this book in whatever order you choose. Each chapter addresses a different area of Blender's functionality and so can be read independently of the rest of the book. In some cases, reference is made to material covered previously, but in general this is not crucial to understanding the subject at hand. Chapter 4, "Hair Essentials: The Long and Short of Strand Particles," is a bit of an exception in that it assumes a basic familiarity with the subjects of the previous two chapters: the particle system in general and soft bodies. Even in this case, however, most intermediate Blender users should have no trouble diving directly into the chapter.

Hardware and Software Considerations

Blender has a very small footprint and is exceedingly light to run, so in general, you should have no trouble running Blender on any current machine. Some graphics processors are known to have trouble with OpenGL, which is a necessary graphical component of Blender. I have had problems with Blender graphics only on Windows Vista running on certain laptop PCs. Usually, these problems can be solved by updating your graphics drivers. Hopefully, after a few Windows service packs, these problems will diminish.

Although Blender itself is light and fast, the brutal truth is that some simulation methods can still be time- and memory-intensive. Although most Blender users will have hardware that can handle much of the simulation functionality, there are a few examples in this book that may try your patience or max out your RAM if you attempt them at high resolutions. Running some of these simulators will remind you of another practical reason to use free software: It leaves more money to upgrade your *hardware.* Builds of Blender are available for 64-bit capable operating systems, but nevertheless, it helps to have a wide palette of tools from which to choose when approaching any simulation effect. In this book, I've made an effort to indicate where things might get resource intensive and to give suggestions for how to work around this and get what you want accomplished in the most efficient way possible.

As an intermediate or advanced Blender user, you are no doubt accustomed to upgrading from one version to another, but it bears repeating that Blender is a constantly evolving thing. Official releases come frequently, and for those interested in using development builds, new features become available even more quickly. To truly learn Blender is to become comfortable with the pace of development. Still, changes from one release to the next are incremental, and documentation usually has a fairly long shelf life. This book is written to be accurate to the 2.46 release, the official release of the Peach project. Much of the functionality described in this book is new or has been recently updated and will not change drastically in the near future. Most changes will likely be intuitive for anyone who learns the material in this book. For example, 2.50 may see the fluid bake system replaced by a system more in line with the caching functionality of the current particles and soft body systems. If you have worked through this book, you will find it straightforward to keep abreast with such developments.

I recommend that you study the material in this book with the Blender version on the accompanying CD, and refer to the official online release notes for the latest Blender version to find out where there might be updates. Release notes are available for all versions on the official Blender website, at www.blender.org. If you are interested in exploring new features, unofficial executable builds are available at www.graphicall.org. Because installing multiple copies of Blender is no problem, you can always keep a stable version and an experimental version installed. However, be careful if you choose to do this. Stick with stable versions for important projects, and always be sure to back up your work and to test thoroughly if you plan to upgrade in the middle of a project.

How This Book Is Organized

Each chapter of this book deals with a specific topic related to physical simulation in Blender. The exception to this is the first chapter, which is a bit of a hodgepodge, covering a variety of general-purpose methods, tricks, and tools. The material covered in each chapter is as follows:

Chapter 1, Re-creating the World: An Overview, introduces the themes that will come up throughout the book, and provides tutorials on a variety of useful features and techniques that have not been extensively covered in print. The chapter covers using the Wave, Displacement, and Array modifiers, working with node-based materials, and using animated textures in interesting ways. It also touches briefly on the use of PyDrivers. The goal of the chapter is to provide information about techniques that I think will be of interest to most readers of this book, but that are not covered elsewhere in print.

Chapter 2, The Nitty-Gritty on Particles, explores the possibilities of Blender's powerful new particles functionality. You'll learn all the details of how to set up and control any of several types of particle systems, how to make objects appear to shatter into bits with the Explode modifier, and how to simulate swarming behavior with boids.

Chapter 3, Getting Flexible with Soft Bodies and Cloth, shows you how to get the most out of Blender's soft body simulation functionality and the new cloth simulation. You'll look in detail at how soft body simulation operates on meshes, lattices, and curves, and how soft body objects and cloth interact with forces, deflection objects, each other, and themselves. Several common mistakes are pointed out, and related topics such as the popular Demolition Python script are also covered.

Chapter 4, Hair Essentials: The Long and Short of Strand Particles, builds on the previous two chapters to introduce strand particles for hair and fur. In this chapter, you'll learn how to set up particle hair and create convincing hairstyles by using Blender's powerful new styling tools. Portions of this chapter assume an understanding of soft bodies, and discuss using soft body simulations with hair. Some other uses of strand particles are also touched on.

Chapter 5, Making a Splash with Fluids, dives into Blender's fluid simulation functionality. You'll learn how to set up fluid domains and to control inflows and outflows, how to make fluids interact with other objects, and how to use fluid particles. The chapter also contains in-depth discussion about obtaining the level of quality you need for the effect you're after, and how to think about the memory and time demands of your simulation.

Chapter 6, Bullet Physics and the Blender Game Engine , covers the basics of working with the Blender Game Engine, with a focus on using it to create rigid body physics simulations for use in your animations. You'll learn how the Bullet Physics library works with rigid body objects, hinges, and forces. Using rigid body objects to control an armature ragdoll is also covered.

Chapter 7, Imitation of Life: Simulating Trees and Plants, is devoted to methods of simulating plants and foliage. This chapter takes a step outside Blender's built-in functionality to introduce several useful scripts and external open source software that can be used to create convincing flora quickly and easily.

Throughout the book, I've included brief personal profiles of Blender artists and developers whose work is especially pertinent to the material I cover. Some may find this to be a little bit unusual for a book like this one, but Blender is an unusual piece of software; the community is truly its lifeblood. Without the talent and enthusiasm of volunteer developers and users who share their work and their knowledge with others, none of what has been accomplished with Blender would have been possible. I've included these profiles to help put some faces to these contributors to the community. Some of the individuals I've profiled are already well known among Blender users for their artwork or their contributions to the software, others less so. In any case, I hope you will get some inspiration from learning a little more about some of your fellow Blenderheads. As usual, I encourage you to think creatively about how you too can contribute to Blender and the Blender community. After all, it's your software.

What's on the CD

This book comes with an accompanying CD that includes Blender 2.46 installers for Windows and Macintosh and a source tarball for users of Linux and other flavors of Unix. You will also find a variety of .blend files intended to support the text.

How to Contact the Author

If you run into trouble at any point in reading this book, or if you have any insights or tips you would like to share, the first place I recommend to turn for quick responses and knowledgeable feedback is to the community itself at www.blenderartists.org/forum, where I post regularly under the handle bugman_2000. You can also contact me directly at blender.characters@gmail.com.

Re-creating the World: An Overview

In this chapter, I introduce some of the main themes that come up throughout the book, and give a brief description of what you can expect in later chapters. Then I move on to some important general-purpose tools in Blender that can be of great use in modeling and animating certain physical phenomena. Some of the features covered here, such as node-based materials, are things you will use in conjunction with advanced physical simulations. Other features will come in handy when full-fledged physical simulations would be unnecessary or inappropriate. Some of the techniques I describe here use common tools such as textures and modifiers in ways you might not have thought of.

1

Chapter Contents
Re-creating the physical world with Blender
Using materials and textures
Faking physics with general-purpose tools

Re-creating the Physical World with Blender

If you're reading this book, you probably already know that Blender is a powerful tool for creating 3D imagery and animation. You probably also know that it can be difficult to find good documentation on a lot of Blender's advanced functionality. There is of course the official Blender wiki, which is an invaluable resource, and numerous excellent online tutorials. Nevertheless, getting good, thorough information about many of these features can be a challenge. Unfortunately, this means that many of Blender's most exciting features tend to be underused; artists want to create, not spend their time searching for tutorials and documentation.

I'd like to change that with this book, by giving a complete introduction to Blender's intermediate to advanced functionality. I hope that this book will help artists become familiar enough with this functionality to comfortably incorporate these features into their creative workflow. Unlike in my previous book, *Introducing Character Animation with Blender* (Sybex, 2007), which has readers model, rig, and animate a character over the course of the book, there's no single, overarching goal here. This book, like the physical world it aims to simulate, is a bit of a hodgepodge. Each chapter addresses a specific aspect of Blender's functionality. There's not much dependence between chapters, so you don't need to read the chapters in strict order. Regardless of the order you choose to approach it in, I hope that this book helps unlock some of the mysteries of Blender's advanced functionality and gives Blender artists some powerful new tools to create their worlds.

Blender's Physical Simulation Functionality

Blender has a variety of tools for simulating physical phenomena. For Blender users who have not yet had the opportunity to study these tools closely, some of them can be a bit confusing. Not all the effects discussed in this book are located in the same place in Blender, and not all are activated in the same way. Getting them to interact in the ways you want them to requires a certain degree of understanding what's going on. In particular, this book is geared toward animators who want to incorporate physics simulations into actual animated scenes. This is not at all difficult to do, but it may sometimes require stepping out of your comfort zone. For example, although the Blender game engine and its integrated Bullet physics engine is widely used by Blender game creators, that area of Blender's functionality remains unexplored by many animators. One of the things you will learn in this book is how to access the various physics-related tools in Blender and put them to work to create the animations you are after.

The main focus of this book is on the features found in the Physics Buttons area (Figure 1.1) and the Particles Buttons area (Figure 1.2), and on the Bullet physics engine, which is accessed through the Blender game engine. The parameters for the game engine are set mostly in the Logic Buttons area (Figure 1.3).

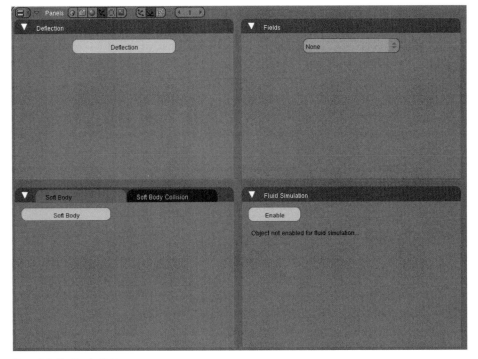

Figure 1.1 The Physics Buttons area

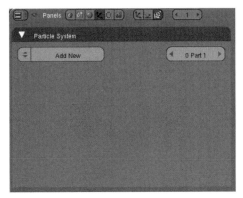

Figure 1.2 The Particles Buttons area

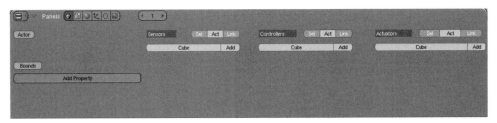

Figure 1.3 The Logic Buttons area

The simulation features available in the Physics Buttons area are the following:

Particles Particles are used to simulate very small real-world objects whose collective behavior can be calculated by the simulator. Particles are often used to simulate smoke and fire, by assigning translucent halo materials to each particle. Particles can also be used to simulate swarm behavior—for example, in the case of insects—and Blender 3D objects can be treated as constituents of a particle system by use of the Duplivert tool. Parameters relating to the speed, direction, life span, and other traits of particles can be set. Using "static" particles, the trajectory of each particle from the emitter is also modeled in the 3D space, to simulate strandlike real-world objects such as hair. Numerous options exist for controlling the behavior and appearance of static particles. In this book, both ordinary and static particles are covered.

Soft Body This simulates the behavior of materials that are flexible, and are visibly deformed by the forces acting on them, such as friction, gravity, and others. In Blender, soft bodies' vertices can move relative to each other, but their underlying structure does not change. Depending on settings, soft body simulation may be appropriate for modeling rubber, gelatin, sheet metal, cloth, and other materials. As you will see in Chapter 4, soft bodies can also be used with static particles to control hair, which also exhibits soft body behavior.

Fields and Deflection These settings are pertinent to both particles and to soft body simulation. Fields are options for external forces that can be made to act on other objects that have soft body properties or particle systems active. Among the fields available are curve guide fields, wind, vortex, and spherical fields. Each of these field options is discussed throughout the course of this book.

Fluid Simulation The Fluid Simulation panel contains settings pertinent to fluid simulation, and any objects that will play a roll in the fluid simulation, including any obstacles, inflow or outflow objects, and the object that acts as the domain for the simulation and marks off the spatial area in which the simulation will take place.

These features are all in some way connected to the internal structure of objects. In soft body simulation, the mesh structure is affected; in fluid simulation completely new meshes are constructed on the fly; and in particle simulation mesh structure is bypassed entirely in favor of a different approach to calculating the location and relationship between points.

For forces that operate on objects and enable rigid bodies to interact as they would in nature, with mass, gravity, friction, and collisions accurately modeled, it is necessary to use the Bullet physics engine, a component of Blender's game engine.

In this book, I show examples of all of Blender's various physical simulation functionalities, and give examples that I hope will encourage you to come up with creative and innovative approaches to using the simulators to get the effects you want. Particles, soft bodies, fluids, and rigid bodies are all included, as are the various deflection properties and forces that enable other objects to interact with these simulations. These topics make up the lion's share of what this book is about. Although numerous tutorials and examples can be found online for most of this functionality, these features have not been well documented in book form until now, and I hope to provide a coherent overview of all of Blender's physical simulation functionality. To take advantage of Blender's rigid body physics capabilities, it is necessary to do some work in the game engine environment. Because this book is written primarily with animators in mind, I don't assume that you have experience with that, and include a brief overview of how to get what you need out of the game engine.

The Science of Simulation

The main objective of this book is to give CG animators a complete understanding of the various physical simulation tools available in Blender, to enable them to realize their creative ideas. For this reason, the book is "artist-oriented" and is intended to be only as technical as is necessary for artists to understand what is possible and how to achieve it with the available tools. Nevertheless, Blender being an open source project as it is, there is another audience I would like to reach with this book, and that is the audience of technically-oriented readers who may be inspired to take an interest in the area of physics-based animation research or, if already engaged in such research, may be motivated to use Blender in their work or to contribute to Blender's code base. For those people, I hope that this book can serve as a way to become quickly familiar with the Blender approach to physical simulation, and as a demonstration of what Blender is capable of at present. People who are aware of recent developments in physical simulation will quickly identify numerous areas in which Blender could be extended and improved.

Physical simulation for 3D animation is an active field of research. Although it is a subfield of general physics simulation, the requirements and objectives of 3D animation are different from those for other kinds of physics simulation. Simulations used for engineering purposes, for example, must be able to compute real-world effects of physical situations with great accuracy, and they don't have to be especially fast. When planners of a skyscraper use fluid simulations to evaluate how the structure will hold up to wind, it is worth a considerable amount of time and money to ensure that the results in terms of forces and stress are as physically accurate as possible down to very small details, and at the same time the visual aspect of this simulation is likely not to be of interest at all. An example of a powerful open source package for computing these kinds of simulations is the OpenFOAM tools from OpenCFD. On the other hand, simulations for animation must be visually convincing, and computationally efficient enough to be carried out in a reasonable time frame on an appropriate budget, whereas very little depends on precise accuracy.

As Kenny Erleben and his coauthors amusingly observe in *Physics-Based Animation*, another difference is that the "artists and creative people" who use these simulations have "very little respect for the real world." Animators are constantly creating situations that would be impossible or highly improbable in the physical world, and it's important that the tools they use offer them the ability to create what they want to create, regardless of its physical authenticity. This is why CG armatures for character animation are so different from human skeletons; in Blender it's possible to stretch, bend, and swivel bones into any kind of position you like. A physically accurate representation of a human would not allow this. In the area of physical simulation for CG animation, the line between flexibility and robustness on the one hand and verisimilitude on the other is a key consideration. As in other areas of Blender, very high levels of accuracy are not the objective. In the same way that Blender's modeling functionality is not oriented toward advanced computer-assisted design (CAD) work, the approaches taken to physical simulations are intended to be useful to artists, not aeronautics engineers. Not to say that CG animators are not rocket scientists, but indeed, their needs in terms of fluid dynamics simulations are quite distinct!

If you're interested in the technical underpinnings of the physical simulations described in this book, a good place to start reading more is the home page for the Bullet Physics Library, at www.bulletphysics.com. In the forum area of that website you'll find a special area dedicated to links, research papers, libraries, demos, and discussions of Bullet and other physics software. For technically inclined readers, the previously mentioned book, *Physics-Based Animation* by Kenny Erleben, Jon Sporring, Knud Henriksen, and Henrik Dohlmann (Charles River Media, 2005), provides an excellent overview of many of the main methodologies used in physics simulation for CG. The book goes into considerable detail about kinematics, interaction of multiple rigid bodies, soft body and fluid simulations, and collision detection, among other subjects.

Nonsimulation Tools and Techniques

As you'll see throughout this book, there are cases when physical simulation can be demanding in terms of time and computing resources, and cases when the results are not exactly what you have in mind for your effect. For these reasons, it is important to have a solid understanding of your other options for creating physical effects. Even without dipping into sophisticated simulation methods, you'll find that there is an awful lot in the toolbox of Blender's standard features. A good understanding of materials, textures, and modifiers will enable you to think creatively and to approach each simulation challenge with freedom and flexibility. The remainder of this chapter is a tour of tools and techniques that have not been covered in much depth in print in the past. None of the techniques touched on in this chapter are crucial to understanding the rest of this book, but I think that people who want to get the most out of Blender will find them well worth checking out.

Using Materials and Textures

This book is about approaches to simulating physical phenomena. To do this, you can use a variety of tools to calculate the internal and external forces that are acting on objects and that determine the movements and the structural behaviors of the objects. But modeling the movement and deformations is not the whole story. No matter how realistically the objects in your scene collide, and no matter how convincingly the liquid in your fluid simulation flows and splashes, no one will be convinced if everything is the same opaque, dull, gray material. Blender has a powerful system of materials and textures that can be used to create stunning effects such as the mountain in Figure 1.4. Because this book is for intermediate to advanced users of Blender, it's assumed that you know the basics of using materials and textures, but there are a few techniques and functions that are either relatively new in Blender, or else are specific enough in use to be worth describing here in detail.

Figure 1.4 *Mount Reckon* by Robert J. Tiess is an excellent example of the potential of Blender's procedural textures.

Hot Lava with Material Nodes

The nodes system greatly increases Blender's power and flexibility in creating materials. By using nodes, it is possible to mix materials with different qualities in a wide variety of ways. In this example, I demonstrate how to use the system to combine two materials to achieve a simple but effective lava effect.

A notable feature of flowing lava is that it is composed of two very different main "materials" (of course, in reality, the material is the same, just in a different state). There is the flowing, molten part of the lava, which is liquid and glows from heat, and there is the portion of the lava that has been exposed to cold air and hardened, which is a dark-colored rocky crust. In Blender, it is possible to create these two materials separately and then combine them by using nodes. To create this material, follow these steps:

1. Delete the default cube and add a UV sphere with default values (32 segments, 32 rings, radius 1). Set it to have an active material called Material.

2. Select Nodes in the Links And Pipeline tab of Material, as shown in Figure 1.5. This makes Material a node material. If you are not used to working with node materials, it is easy to get confused, so it helps to keep track of which materials need to be node materials and which materials do not need to be. In most cases, materials that you use as inputs into node materials should not be node materials themselves. You can always tell which materials are node based and which are the basic kind in the material list, because each node material has an *N* before its name. Open a nodes window now and you will see the setup in Figure 1.6. What you're looking at are two nodes: an Input material node and an Output node. The Output node represents the final appearance that Material will take on. At present, the Input node is not linked to any material, as indicated by the red Add New button. Click Add New to create a new material node. The node's header bar will now read MatNode.

Figure 1.5 Activating Nodes on Material

3. Add a second material node to the node setup. Do this by pressing the spacebar while in the Nodes Editor window and choosing Add > Input > Material, and then selecting Add New from the highlighted drop-down list on the node. The new node will be connected to the previous node by default. Hold the left mouse button (LMB) and drag your mouse across this connection to sever it, as shown in Figure 1.7. Rename MatNode and MatNode.001 to **Rock** and **Magma**, respectively, and rename the main node material from Material to **Lava**.

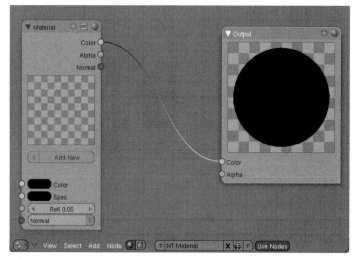

Figure 1.6 Nodes window

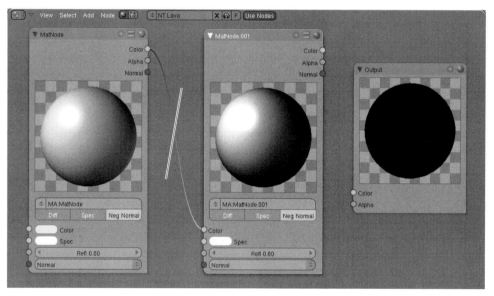

Figure 1.7 Two new input materials

4. Select the Rock material node and set its material values by using the Material buttons as you would for any ordinary non-node material, as shown in Figure 1.8. Note that when you select an input material node in the Nodes Editor, the settings for that material appear in the Material buttons window. Add a Clouds texture set at a very small noise size, as shown in Figure 1.9, and map the texture to Nor on the Map To tab as a bump map to give roughness to the surface of the rock. Then select the Magma material node and edit the material settings as shown in Figure 1.10. Note the high Emit value for the glow. For the orange color texture, use a soft Clouds texture with default parameter settings.

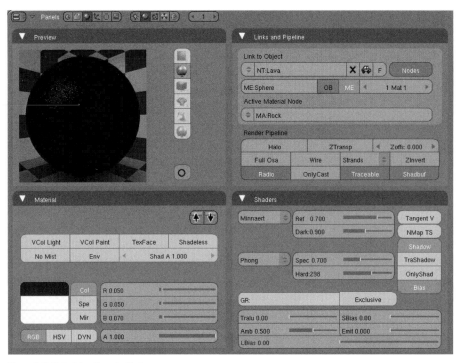

Figure 1.8 Material settings for Rock

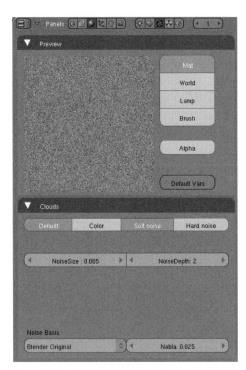

Figure 1.9 Roughness texture for the rock

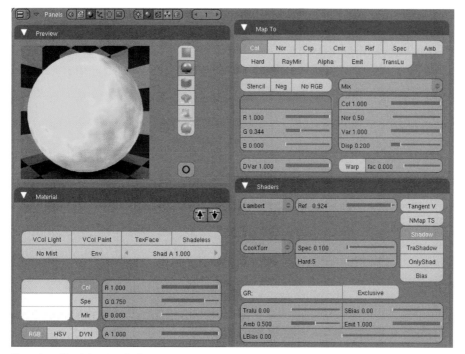

Figure 1.10 Material settings for Magma

5. You now have the two basic materials completed in your node setup. What remains is to mix them. To do this, add a Mix node by pressing the spacebar while in the Nodes Editor and choosing Add > Color > Mix. Create connections between nodes by LMB-dragging your mouse from one node's socket to another socket. To mix the two materials, draw a connection between Rock and the Color1 socket on the Mix node, and a connection between Magma and the Color2 socket. Draw a connection between the Color sockets on the Mix node and the Output node, as shown in Figure 1.11. As you can see, the output material is now a mixture of the two input materials. The mix factor of the Mix node is 0.50, which means that the two materials are mixed at a uniform level of 50/50 across the entire object. It is necessary to input a mix factor that will give a more-appropriate mix effect.

6. Add a new Input node in the same way you did for the previous two material nodes, except this time select Texture instead of Material for the node type. In the drop-down menu on the node, select Add New to create a new texture, and name the texture **Mix**. Make this texture a hard Clouds texture with the values set as shown in Figure 1.12. This texture will provide a pattern of black-and-white (that is, 0.0 and 1.0) to replace the uniform 0.50 that's the default for the Mix node.

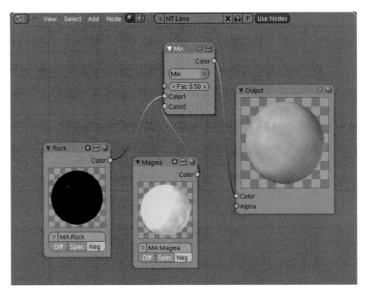

Figure 1.11 Mixing the materials

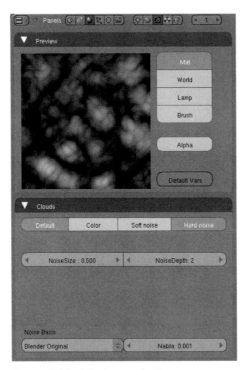

Figure 1.12 A hard Clouds texture for Mix

7. Add an RGB Curves node by pressing the spacebar and choosing Add > Color > RGB Curves. This will enable you to tweak the contrast and brightness of the factor value going into the Mix node. Connect the Mix node to the RGB Curves node, and the RGB Curves node to the Fac connection point on the Mix node, as shown in Figure 1.13. All that remains is to tweak the RGB curve to yield the mix pattern that looks best. To get the correct black-and-white pattern, reverse the direction of the RGB curve so that it goes from upper left to lower right, and then edit the shape of the curve itself. The more gentle the curve, the smoother the transition between the two materials will be. Points can be added on the curve simply by clicking the LMB, and deleted by clicking the button on the node itself marked with an *x*.

8. Finally, add a Displace modifier to the object with the settings shown in Figure 1.14. Type **Mix** in the Texture field to use the texture you just created to determine the displacement. After you've done this, set up your lights and take a render. The finished material should look something like Figure 1.15.

If you have trouble getting the object lit the way you see it here, check the file lava.blend on the CD for the book to see how I've done the lighting.

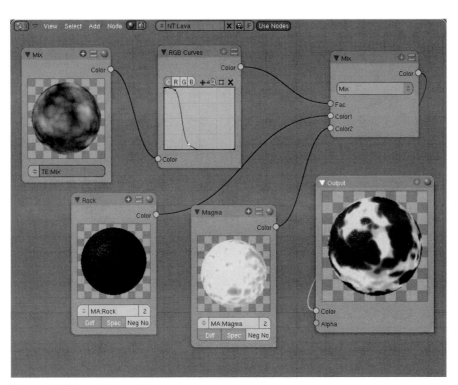

Figure 1.13 Finished node setup for lava

Figure 1.14 Displace modifier

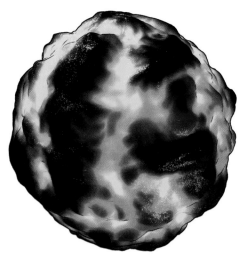

Figure 1.15 Finished render

As you can see, being able to mix different materials and textures in this way is a powerful way to create complex materials that more faithfully represent the complexity of nature.

Transparency and Subsurface Scattering

In Blender, there are three kinds of transparency: Z transparency, ray transparency, and the environment (Env) material setting. In fact, only the first two are true transparencies in terms of the Blender 3D environment. The Env setting creates an area of alpha 0 transparency in the rendered image itself and is used primarily for compositing. In Figure 1.16, you can see an example of the three types of transparency together. The knight piece on the left has the Env option selected, as shown in Figure 1.17, and the area defined by its outline is alpha 0, with the world background visible in the render. This material does not have any transparency option selected, and its true material alpha value is 1. The Env option is not gradated in any way; if it's on, the object and everything behind it will be cut out of the final render. Note that things that are in front of the object are not cut out, such as the middle horse's nose in the image. This option is useful for compositing.

The middle knight uses Z transparency, with the settings shown in Figure 1.18. Z transparency takes two values into consideration: the material's alpha value and the Z values of the points in the scene. The alpha value of a material is a measure of how opaque the material is. A 0 (zero) alpha means the material is completely invisible; a 1 alpha means that the material is entirely opaque. The Z value is the distance of a point in space along the camera's local Z axis; that is, the distance from the camera. Z transparency works very much like layer transparency in a 2D image-manipulation program, using the Z value to determine the ordering of the layers. In the image, the middle knight's alpha value is set to 0.2.

Figure 1.16 The knight piece on the left has the material setting Env selected. The piece in the middle has ZTransp selected, and the one on the right has RayTransp selected.

Figure 1.17 The Env option

The knight on the right also has an alpha value of 0.2, but with ray transparency, with values shown in Figure 1.19. As you can see, the effect is very different from the middle knight. Whereas the middle knight looks ghostly, the third knight looks like it is made of a real-world transparent material. The difference, as you can see, is mainly in the way the light from the background is distorted as it passes through the object, as it would be in real life. This distortion depends on the index of refraction (IOR) of the material. Denser materials have higher IORs. Air has an IOR of approximately 1 (1 is the IOR of a perfect vacuum), water has an IOR of about 1.3, glass has an IOR of somewhat higher, between 1.5 and 1.8, and diamond has an IOR of about 2.4.

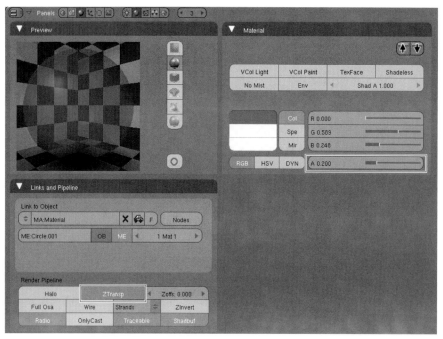

Figure 1.18 Z transparency values

To represent a material's IOR, it is necessary to use ray tracing to follow the path of the light. Using ray tracing will make render times longer, but in cases like these it is necessary. The Depth value on the Ray Transp panel is set at 2 by default. This means that the ray calculation will pass through two surfaces. If there are more than two transparent surfaces for the light to pass through, the subsequent surfaces will appear black. To calculate ray information passing through more surfaces than this, you must raise the Depth value. Again, this will increase render times, so it should be done only when necessary.

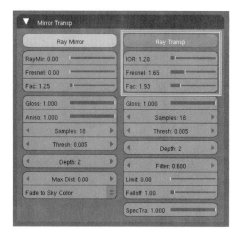

Figure 1.19
Ray Transp values

Transparent Shadows

Ray shadows cast by transparent objects are transparent. However, in order for them to appear as they should, the material on which they are cast needs to be set to take transparent shadows. This setting is found on the shaders tab, as shown in Figure 1.20. You can see how this affects the shadow that falls on the checkerboard material in Figure 1.21.

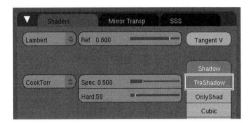

Figure 1.20 TraShadow option for receiving transparent shadows

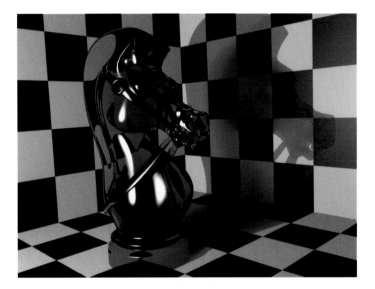

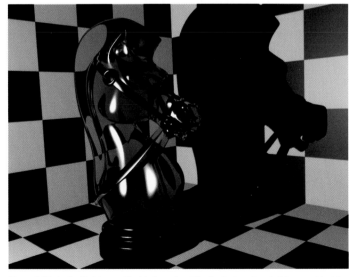

Figure 1.21 In the first image, the black- and- white checkerboard materials are set to take transparent shadows; in the second, they are not.

If you want to avoid ray tracing, transparent shadows can also be produced by using a spotlight with the Irregular shadow buffer type and setting a <1 value for Shad A in the shadowing object's Material tab. In upcoming versions of Blender, the new Deep Shadow Maps functionality coded by Joe Eagar as part of the Google Summer of Code will offer significant speed and quality benefits, as well as transparence, to non-raytraced shadows.

Subsurface Scattering

When light strikes an object, it can be reflected in a variety of ways. Mostly, the way it reflects depends on qualities of the surface of the object. In Blender, the diffuse and specular shader settings determine how a material reflects light (other settings, such as ray mirroring, may also play a part). With some materials, however, calculating how light behaves on the surface only is not enough. For materials such as wax, skin, most vegetation, jade, milk, and many others, a very small amount of surface translucency influences the way light reflects. Although most of the light reflects back from the surface, some of the light penetrates the surface of the material and is reflected back through the material in a scattered state, diffusing some of the light. Although this effect is subtle, it is present on many of the things that humans are best at recognizing, such as food, animals, and other people. For this reason, a lack of subsurface scattering can be a dead giveaway that an image is CG. When used well, it can enable you to achieve extremely realistic organic materials, as in Enrico Cerica's image in Figure 1.22.

Figure 1.22 Enrico Cerice used subsurface scattering to achieve photorealism in this image.

To enable subsurface scattering, click the Subsurface Scattering button on the Subsurface Scattering (SSS) tab in the materials buttons area, shown in Figure 1.23. There are a handful of preset materials: skin (two different ones), marble, whole milk, skim milk, potato, ketchup, cream, apple, and chicken. (I guess the developer who set up the presets was eager to get to lunch!) You can select one of these and then modify the values to create a Custom setup.

The settings for subsurface scattering are as follows:

Scale indicates the scale of the objects that the material is applied to. It is used to calculate the size of the blurring radius for the material. To calculate the scale you should use, divide 1 by the number of millimeters you want a single Blender unit (BU) to represent. If you want a Blender unit (BU) to represent a meter, the Scale value should be $1/1000 = 0.001$. If you want a BU t to represent 2 centimeters, the scale is $1/20 = 0.05$. If a BU is a millimeter, the scale is 1.0. It is important to pay attention to this, because correct scale is the most important factor in getting your materials with SSS to look realistic.

Radius R, G, and B are the blurring radii for Red, Green, and Blue. These values determine the distance that different colored light scatters under the surface of the material. If you've ever shone a flashlight through your hand in the dark, you have seen that the red in your hand scatters more than the other colors.

IOR is the index of refraction, or the degree to which light is bent when it travels through the material. As mentioned in the previous section, higher IOR values indicate higher density. In the case of subsurface scattering, the effect is subtle, because no actual rays pass through the material. In most cases, you can get away with setting the IOR to approximately the value of water, 1.3.

Error controls the precision of sampling. Higher error values will speed up rendering but can result in visible artifacts. You can set it as low as 0.02.

Col determines how much the base color of the material is affected by the diffuse color set in the color picker above the Col field.

Tex controls the degree to which textures on the material are also blurred. 0 will leave the textures unaffected by the scattering.

Front is the weighting factor for front scattering. Front here means pointing toward the camera. Front scattering shows as diffusing of the light and blurring of shadows on the surface of the material.

Back is the weighting factor for back scattering. Back scattering shows up as light passing through from behind the material.

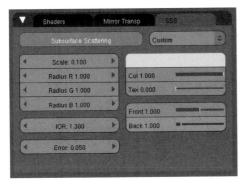

Figure 1.23 The SSS panel

Figure 1.24 shows three objects with materials that differ only in their subsurface scattering. The knight on the left has no SSS, the knight in the middle has strong front SSS with weaker back SSS, and the knight on the right has strong back SSS with weak front SSS. Of course, for more-convincing materials, you would also want to adjust the shader values appropriately; wax has a different specularity from jade. This example is mainly to highlight the differences in the subsurface scattering effect itself.

Figure 1.24 Three materials: no SSS, strong front SSS, strong back SSS

The algorithm used in Blender for subsurface scattering was originally presented at SIGGRAPH '02 in the paper "A Rapid Hierarchical Rendering Technique for Translucent Materials" by Henrik Jensen and Juan Buhler. You can find the original paper at http://graphics.ucsd.edu/~henrik/papers/fast_bssrdf.

Sky Maps

If you want to make outdoor scenes, you need to create a sky background. There are a variety of ways to go about modeling clouds and other features of skies. Mostly, though, it is enough for the sky to be a background, and in this case the simplest and most common approach to making skies is to use an image texture called a sky map. I won't discuss how to make sky maps here. You can make them by taking photographs, or by using sky and landscape creation software such as Terragen. Blender user M@dcow has created a fantastic repository of free sky maps at http://blenderartists.org/forum/showthread.php?t=24038 that you can use in any way you like. The sky maps used in the various examples in this book were taken from that resource.

The two sky maps shown in Figure 1.25 are included on the CD accompanying this book as files angmap12.jpg and sky_twilight.jpg. As you can see in the figure, sky maps can come in several forms, which require different mapping methods to accurately fit into a scene. The rectangular sky map shown in the figure is intended to be mapped onto the top half of a sphere. Angular maps appear as highly distorted sphere-shaped reflections, and represent the entire visible background in all directions.

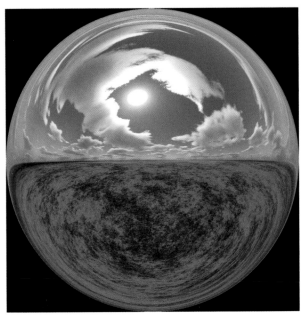

Figure 1.25 A sphere map and an angular map

Using these sky maps is simple. The sky map is added as an image texture to the world in the same way that an image texture is added to a material. The texture buttons panel should look something like Figure 1.26. The world buttons should look like Figure 1.27. Make sure the options Hori, Real, and AngMap are selected. Hori is the option for mapping the image with respect to the horizon. Real means that the actual 3D space horizon is used, as opposed to the center of the camera's current view. Selecting this option ensures that the view of the sky will shift correctly as the camera moves or rotates. AngMap maps the coordinates of this specific type of image to the 3D world. When you use a spherically mapped image, select the Sphere mapping option, as shown in Figure 1.28.

Note that in the case of the Sphere mapped image, only the top half of the background space is mapped with the image. The remainder is the default blue. The spherical mapping describes a hemisphere extending from the horizon to the zenith in the 3D space. Because this map is all sky, it is assumed to end at the horizon. If you use this mapping, you must set up your world to include or conceal the horizon, just as in real life. If you want to have the horizon in view, it may be better to map the sky image onto a mesh dome or tube, so that you have more control over where the horizon is in the camera view. It is also possible to turn the camera's clipping value up very high and extend a plane so that it nearly meets the horizon, and then to match the gap of background color to the color of the plane. The AngMap option is necessary if you want the entire background, ground and all, to be included in the sky map. For example, if you are animating an airplane dogfight, you want your camera to be able to move freely and have an accurately mapped image background visible from any angle. It should be noted that the motion of the "ground" part of the image will not necessarily match up with the motion of real 3D objects on the ground if the camera is moving, making them appear to slide across the terrain, so this is most useful as a backdrop for flying objects. As with everything, remember that different shots may have different setup requirements.

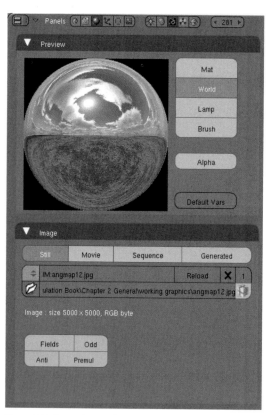

Figure 1.26 Texture buttons for a sky map image texture

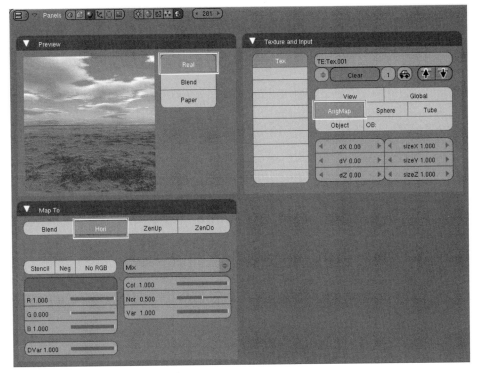

Figure 1.27 World buttons for an AngMap sky map

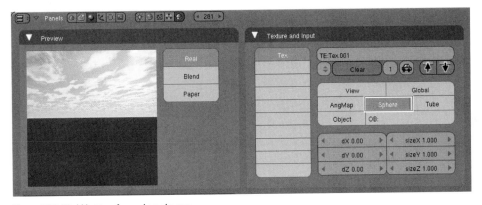

Figure 1.28 World buttons for a sphere sky map

Faking Physics with General Tools

In this section, I describe techniques I've come across for achieving various physical effects without using actual simulations. Some of these techniques are based on methods that can be found in some form or another on personal websites or in threads on BlenderArtists.org, but they are all approaches that I think deserve a wider audience. Not only are the methods themselves useful, but the tools you'll use to set them up are generally applicable.

Robert J. Tiess

The artist who created *Haiku* and *Mount Reckon*, Robert J Tiess has been a Blender user since he discovered the software in 2003, and has gained a reputation in the Blender community for his stunning, thought-provoking images. His lush, richly textured character illustrations were featured in *Introducing Character Animation with Blender*. His work covers a wide variety of styles, and he is constantly exploring new ways to use Blender to the fullest in expressing his own artistic vision. His enthusiasm for Blender comes through clearly in his comments about the software and its community. He writes, "Blender's thriving community, amazing artists, gifted and generous coders, supporters, forum moderators, and documentation writers, all make it so much less a piece of a software and far more of a generally positive and empowering phenomenon that is truly global in scope and as universal in appeal, adaptability, and usability as it gets in the technology world."

Modeling Bodies of Water by Using Modifiers and Textures

In Chapter 5, "Making a Splash with Fluids," you'll see how to work with the Blender fluid simulator. It is a common misconception that this is the best way to represent water and liquids, and in many cases this is not the most direct way to get the effect you want. Other methods for creating fluid effects include displacement textures, as used in Figure 1.29 to excellent effect.

In this section, I show you an approach for representing the behavior of large bodies of water in a way that animates convincingly. I also show a simple way to make the surface of the water interact with an object floating in the water. The methods I present here draw on several methods described in Colin Litster's excellent ocean tutorials, which you can find at his web page, at www.cogfilms.com. The method I present here is somewhat simplified, but it will give you a good sense of the main ideas of the approach. I highly recommend a visit to Colin's website to see the rest of his tutorials.

To create this effect, follow these steps:

1. Delete the default cube and add a plane in the top view (NUM7). Scale the plane to 30. Press the W key, select Subdivide Multi, and subdivide by 70 subdivisions. The result is a subdivided plane, as in Figure 1.30. With the whole mesh selected, click Set Smooth in the Links And Materials tab.

Figure 1.29 *Haiku* by Robert J. Tiess uses displacement textures to model the wave pattern on the surface of water.

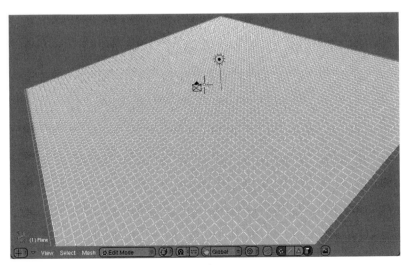

Figure 1.30 A subdivided plane will be the ocean surface.

2. Give the plane a material, as in Figure 1.31. Choose a base color for the water similar to the one shown, and increase the specularity slightly from the default. Set up your lights and camera along the lines shown in Figure 1.32. The camera view should be filled by the water surface. I have one lamp placed off to the left of the camera and one placed over the far corner of the plane in front of the camera. Place your lamps in similar positions. Turn off shadows for the lamps.

3. With the plane selected, add two Wave modifiers, with the settings shown in Figure 1.33. The first wave will move along the Y axis, from one edge of the plane to the other. The other wave will move along the Z normal of the plane, creating a swelling effect. Using the two Wave modifiers together will help make the motion less obviously regular. Note that each modifier can be set to display in render, 3D, and edit mode view. For now set the modifiers to display in render and 3D views. Throughout the tutorial, I've switched the 3D view display on and off. Also, add a Subsurf modifier with the settings of Levels: 2, Render Levels: 3. Make sure that the Subsurf modifier is at the bottom of the modifier stack. The Wave modifiers should be acting on the subsurfaced mesh, not the other way around. I've set the start time for the waves at –200, so that the waves will be in full effect by frame 1.

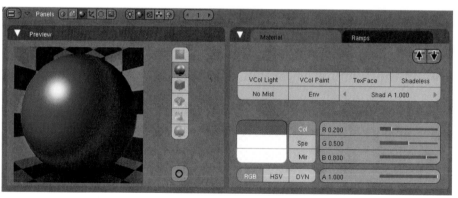

Figure 1.31 A base material for the water

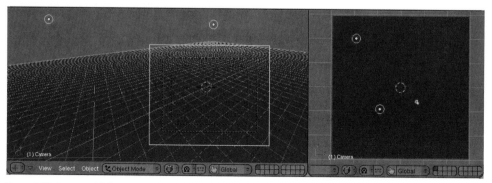

Figure 1.32 Camera and lights setup

Figure 1.33
The modifier stack

4. Everything else to be done for the ocean surface effect from here on involves adding textures and texture effects. First, add an Empty object at the center of the plane. Snap the cursor to the plane by pressing Shift+S and selecting Cursor To Selected. Add the empty by pressing the spacebar and choosing Add > Empty, and then press Alt+R to clear the rotation of the empty (this is not necessary if you add the empty in top view). Create the first texture for your ocean surface material and map it by using the Empty object. Make the texture a soft noise Clouds texture with settings as in Figure 1.34 and name it **Displacement**. Map it to Nor and Disp with the values shown in Figure 1.35, and set the Disp value in the texture to 0.3. This will add one more level of displacement waves to make the movement of the surface even more uneven. Scale the Empty up a factor of 3 by pressing the S key and 3. Run a test render and make sure your surface looks something like Figure 1.36. If not, back up a bit and figure out where yours is different.

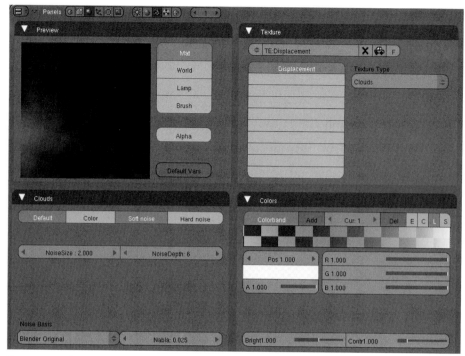

Figure 1.34 Displacement texture

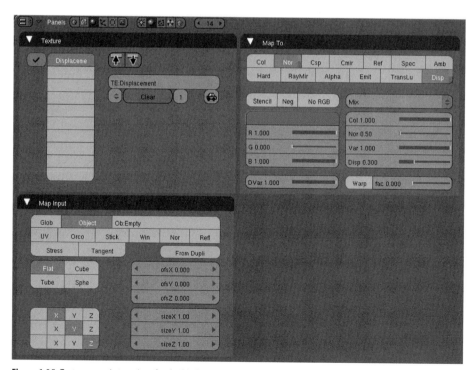

Figure 1.35 Texture mapping settings for the Displacement texture

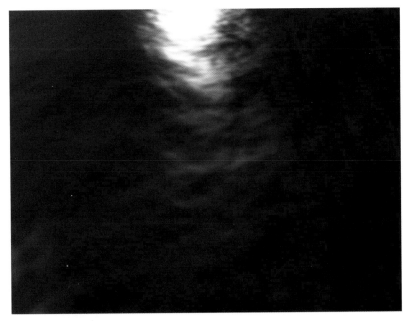

Figure 1.36 Test render

5. These texture-based waves will be animated by keying the movement of the empty. Key two points for the empty and set the empty's Ipos as shown in Figure 1.37. Select the curves, and choose Curve > Extend Mode > Extrapolation in the header menu to make steady slopes. The empty should move along X and Y axes only, and be sure to keep the slopes gradual so that the empty doesn't move too fast.

6. Make a texture to represent the small wavelets on the surface of the water, and call it **Small-waves**. This texture will be a hard noise texture, as shown in Figure 1.38. The mapping values for the texture are shown in Figure 1.39. Note that Size is set to 10.0 for all dimensions, to make these wavelets small. The Map To value is Nor. Change the Nor value in the Map To panel to 3.0. When you take a test render, you should see something like Figure 1.40. Once again, the placement of the lights will make a lot of difference in exactly how your render turns out. Experiment a bit with this.

If you find yourself having difficulty getting things to look as I have them, study the lighting setup in the corresponding file ocean.blend on the CD.

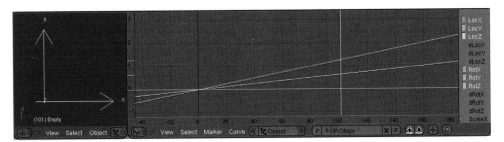

Figure 1.37 Ipos for animating the empty's movement

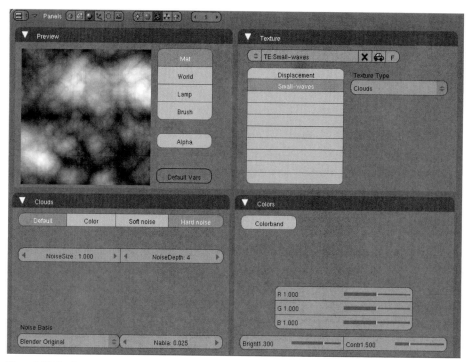

Figure 1.38 Small-waves texture

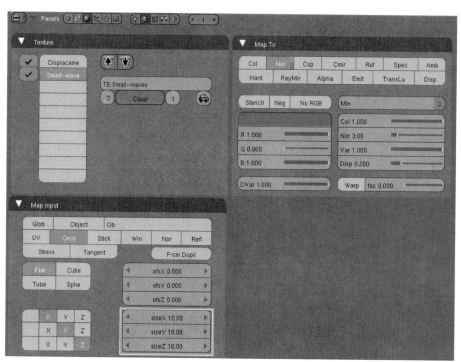

Figure 1.39 Small-waves texture mapping

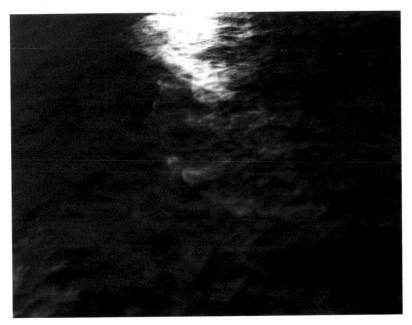

Figure 1.40 Test render

7. For the foam on the waves, use the same texture as you used for the displacement. Do this by selecting channel 0 (the top channel) and pressing the Copy To Clipboard button (the left-hand button of the two highlighted buttons in Figure 1.41). Then select channel 5 (the sixth one down, as shown in the figure) and press the Copy From Clipboard button. Map this texture to color, and make sure the R, G, and B values are turned to white. A test render yields something like Figure 1.42.

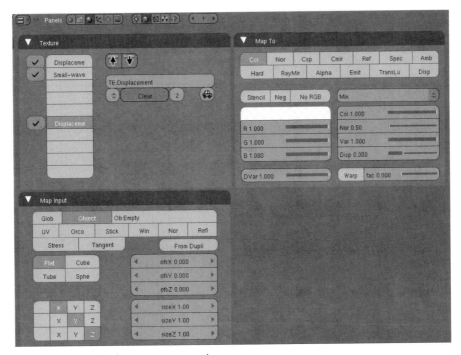

Figure 1.41 Using the Displacement texture as a color map

Figure 1.42 Test render

8. Following the same procedure as step 7, copy the Displacement texture from channel 5 to channel 6. With channel 6 selected, go into the texture buttons. This time, you will create a separate texture by pressing the 3 highlighted in Figure 1.43 to make this texture a single- user texture. The 3 represents the number of "users" of the texture, which in this case means the number of channels that the texture is associated with. Clicking this button separates the texture you are working with from the texture associated with the other channels, creating a new, identical texture. You can edit this texture now without affecting the other channels. Rename this texture **Crests** and adjust the brightness, contrast, and colorband as shown in Figure 1.44. Map this with the Empty object also, but select Emit as the Map To value. Set DVar to about 0.359, as shown in Figure 1.45. This texture channel will give a faked translucency to higher points of the textured displacement.

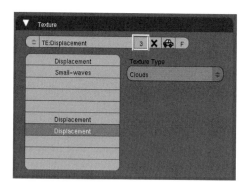

Figure 1.43

Press the button displaying the number of users to make a single-user copy of the texture.

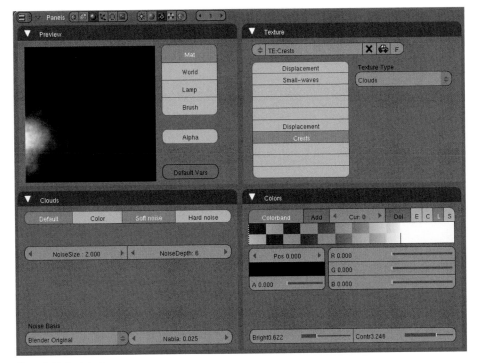

Figure 1.44 Crests texture

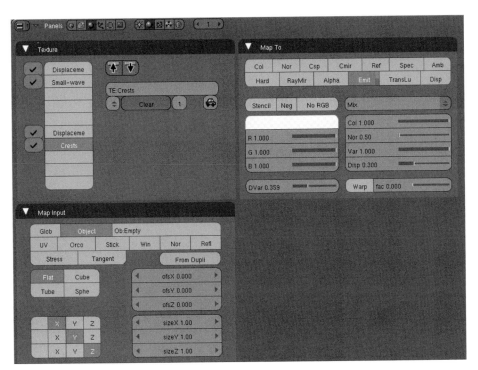

Figure 1.45 Crests texture mapping

9. Select channel 4 in the Texture tab of the Material buttons and click Add New to add a new texture. Name this texture **Stencil** and set its values as shown in Figure 1.46. Select Stencil in the Map To tab. This will prevent the foam and crest textures from matching the displacement too perfectly. A test render should look like Figure 1.47.

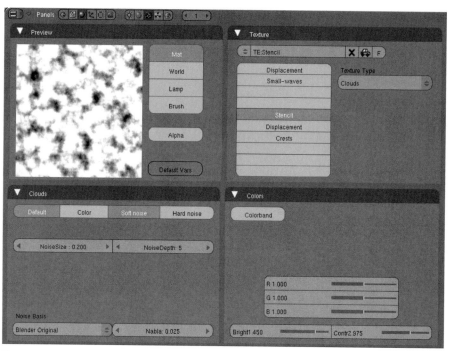

Figure 1.46 Stencil texture

Figure 1.47 Test render

10. Key the movement for the small waves as shown in Figure 1.48. Note that this is a Material Ipo and that the index of the Ipo to the right of the drop-down must match the channel of the texture, counting from top to bottom and beginning at 0. The second channel down, therefore, is channel 1. This wraps up the water itself. If you like, render out a few seconds of animation to see how the movement looks. You might want to do this without oversampling by deselecting the OSA button and at a small size, such as 25 percent, to make it quicker.

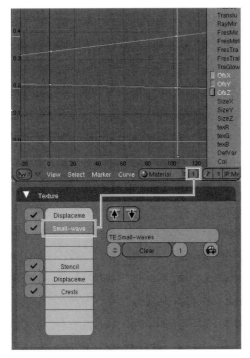

Figure 1.48 Keying the offset for channel 1

11. When you're satisfied with the water, set the modifiers on the plane not to display in the 3D view mode, as shown in Figure 1.49, so that the plane appears perfectly flat. Snap the cursor to the plane again, go into top view, and add a torus by pressing spacebar and choosing Add > Mesh > Torus. The default settings and size are just fine as they are. Add a white and a red material to the object, as shown in Figure 1.50, to make a simple life ring.

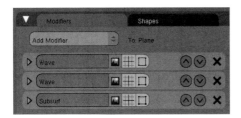

Figure 1.49 Modifiers set to display only when rendered

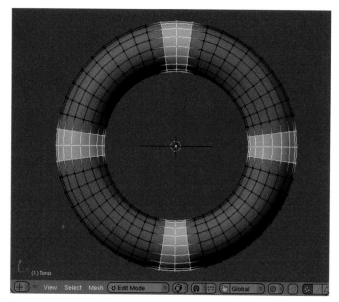

Figure 1.50 A life ring

12. In Object mode, move the torus up slightly, as shown in Figure 1.51. With the torus selected, Shift-select the plane and enter Edit mode with Tab. Select three vertices in the plane in places that correspond to points on the ring, as shown in Figure 1.52. Press Ctrl+P to make the vertex parent. Set the modifiers on the plane to display in the 3D view again and preview the animation by pressing Alt+A. The life ring should follow the motion of the displaced surface, floating gently on the waves.

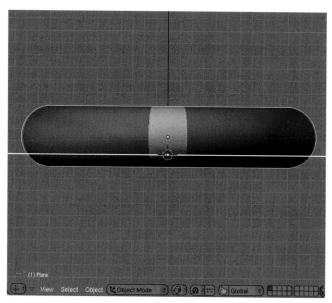

Figure 1.51 The life ring's basis floating position

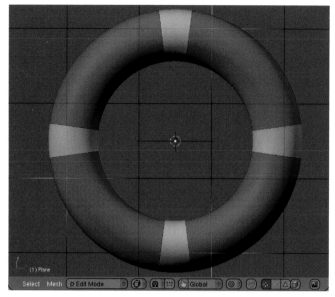

Figure 1.52 Three vertices selected for vertex parenting

13. Run another test render. This time you should see something like Figure 1.53. The water and the ring look okay individually, but the point where they meet is not convincing at all. The line is too abrupt, and there is no sign that the ring is having any effect on the water. Water should deform slightly at the points where it touches an object, as a result of surface tension.

Figure 1.53 Test render of the life ring

14. Add another texture in channel 2 called **Tube**. The Tube texture will be a Sphere Blend type texture. You will also need to add an extra index to the colorband by clicking Add. Make the new color black with alpha 0 and arrange the colorband as shown in Figure 1.54. Set the Map Input value to Object and type **Torus** in the field, as shown in Figure 1.55. This will make this texture follow the movement of the life ring object. Also, adjust the size values in the Map Input tab to 0.50 in all dimensions. In the Map To tab, select color and RayMir. Push the R, G, and B values up to make white. Setting the texture to map to RayMir will enable ray mirroring on the surface of the water, but only in the area directly around the life ring. Using ray tracing will slow down your renders, so you can disable this if you want to speed things up, but it looks good. To enable the ray mirroring, be sure to select Ray Mirror in the Mirror Transp tab, but leave its RayMir slider value at 0.00.

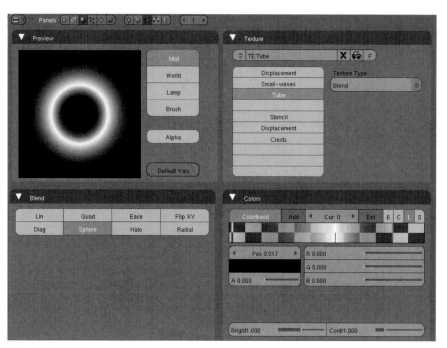

Figure 1.54 The Tube texture

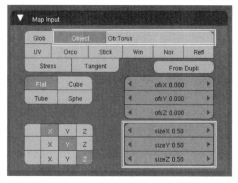

Figure 1.55 The Tube texture Map Input tab

15. Finally, create the displacement texture for the surface tension on the life ring. Duplicate the Tube texture and place the copy in texture channel 3 by using the Copy To and Copy From Clipboard buttons as you did previously. In the Texture buttons, click the 2 next to the TE drop-down to make the texture a new single-user texture, and rename the texture **TubeDisp**. Set the values as shown in Figure 1.56. Set the mapping values as shown in Figure 1.57. The Map Input values are the same as they were for Tube.

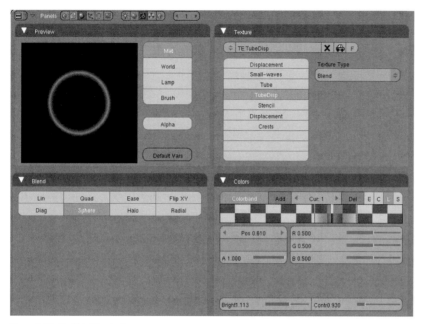

Figure 1.56 The TubeDisp texture

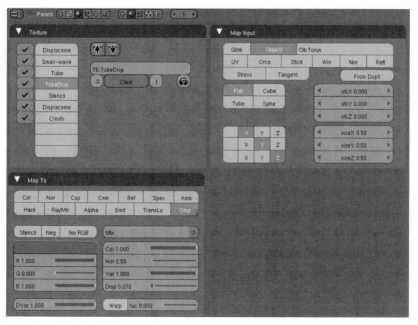

Figure 1.57 The TubeDisp texture mapping

16. To see what's happening to the surface of the water, try a test render with the torus placed on a separate layer, out of view. You should see results along the lines of Figure 1.58. Placing the life ring back in the picture where it belongs will give you a final rendered effect like that in Figure 1.59. Render out an animation to see the effect in motion.

Figure 1.58 Surface tension displacement without the life ring

Figure 1.59 The full effect with surface tension and reflection

Faking a Cloth Flag by Using a Displacement Modifier

In Chapter 3, "Getting Flexible with Soft Bodies and Cloth," you'll see how to use soft bodies and how to achieve convincing cloth effects. For animating a flag waving in the wind, there is a simple approach that does not require any actual simulation, but rather uses Blender's displacement modifier. To create the effect, follow these steps:

1. Model the flag and the flagpole. The flagpole can be a simple cylinder scaled appropriately. The flag is a plane, scaled to the appropriate dimensions and subdivided to about the level shown in Figure 1.60. You can press the W key, select Subdivide Multi, and set a factor of 45 to get a good level of subdivision. Activate a Subsurf modifier and click Set Smooth. Create materials for the pole and flag and set the material settings for color and specularity to whatever you think looks good.

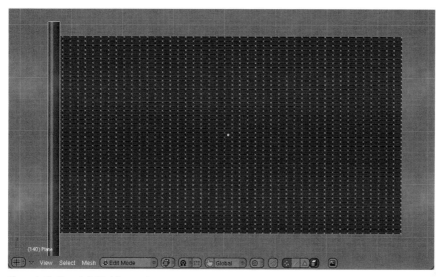

Figure 1.60 The subdivided flag mesh

2. In the Texture panel of the Material buttons, click Add New to add a new material. This will create a new texture in the topmost texture channel in that panel. As I mentioned previously, this is channel 0.

Add an image texture with the logo image (logo.png) from the CD, as shown in Figure 1.61. You need to UV-map this texture to the flag, or else the texture will not behave correctly when the surface of the flag displaces. To do this, access UV Face Select mode with the flag selected, select all faces by pressing the A key, and then open a UV/Image Editor window and unwrap the flag by pressing the E key. Open the logo image in the UV/Image Editor and position the flag and logo appropriately, as shown in Figure 1.62. Map the texture to the Col value in Map To, and in Map Input make sure that UV is selected.

Figure 1.61 The blender-logo texture

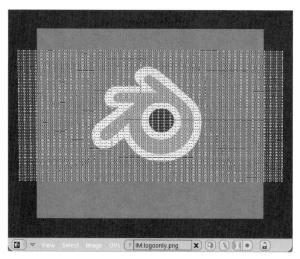

Figure 1.62 UV Mapping the blender-logo texture

3. Create a vertex group for the flag mesh by clicking New in the VertexGroups buttons, and name the vertex group **PoleDamp**. In a moment, you'll use this vertex group to determine the intensity of the displacement modifier that will produce the flag's ripples. Because the flag should be fixed at the pole, the intensity of the ripples will be zero at the pole. You can assign the vertex group weights by hand in Edit mode, or you can do this by weight painting, as shown in Figure 1.63. The part of the flag that meets the pole should be weighted 0, and most of the flag should be weighted 1. The yellow and green transition area in the figure indicates where the weight should be gradated.

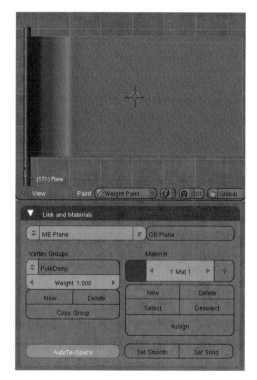

Figure 1.63
Weighting the vertex group

4. Create the texture that will be used to displace the ripples in the flag. Select channel 2 (the next channel down, below the channel with blender-logo) and click Add New. Name the texture **wood-ripple**. This texture will not be used directly on the material, but will be used to control a Displace modifier, so make it inactive on the material by deselecting the channel as shown in Figure 1.64. For the ripple pattern, select a Wood texture type and set the values shown in Figure 1.65.

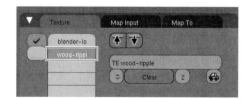

Figure 1.64
Deselect the second texture channel

5. The Displace modifier will be animated by means of an empty. Snap the cursor to the Flag object and add the empty. Clear the rotation on the empty by pressing Alt+R and scale the empty up by a factor of 3.5, so that it looks as shown in Figure 1.66.

6. Now it's time to add the Displace modifier for the flag mesh in the Modifiers tab, with the settings shown in Figure 1.67. For VGroup, type the name of the vertex group you set up in step 3, and select Object from the texture coordinates drop-down menu at the bottom of the panel. Type the name of the empty from step 5 in the Ob field. Leave Midlevel at 0.5, and set the Strength at around 0.2. You can see the effect of the modifier in the 3D window.

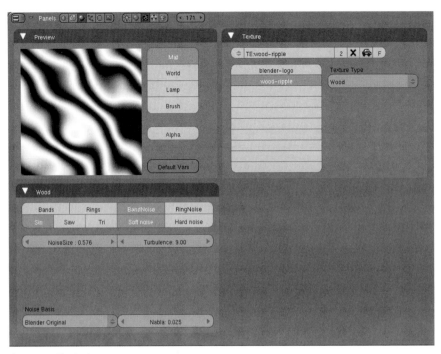

Figure 1.65 The ripple texture

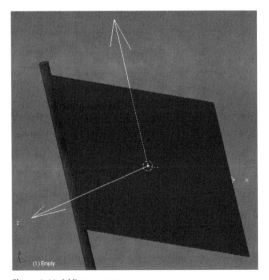

Figure 1.66 Adding an empty

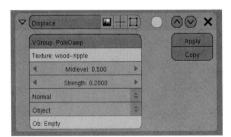

Figure 1.67 The Displace modifier

7. The last thing that needs to be done is to add motion by animating the empty. Add a LocRot keyframe at frame 0 with the empty at its original position by pressing the I key. Advance 50 frames and translate the empty along its X axis to about the edge of the flag (it doesn't need to be perfect), and then add another LocRot keyframe. Select the LocX Ipo in the Ipo Editor and change its Extend mode to Extrapolation by choosing Curve > Extend Mode > Extrapolation in the header menu. The Ipos should look as shown in Figure 1.68.

8. If you render a still now, it should look something like Figure 1.69. (As you can see, I've added a sky map for the background here, as discussed previously in this chapter.) Render a test animation to make sure that the level of displacement is right and the speed looks as you want it. If you need to adjust the speed of the flapping, adjust the LocX Ipo for the empty.

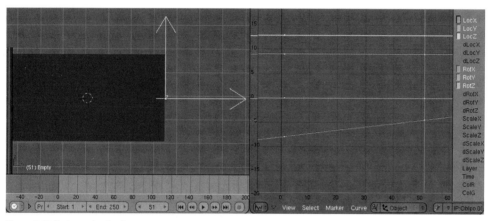

Figure 1.68 Keying an Ipo for the empty

Figure 1.69 Flag with displacement texture

Creating a Poseable Spring by Using an Array Modifier, Shape Keys, and PyDrivers

A recurring concept in the area of physical simulation is the behavior of springs. Springs are designed to be flexible and to extend a certain distance relatively easily. As a spring extends, internal forces build up that compel the spring to compress. Eventually (assuming the extending force does not break the spring), the spring bounces back into a compressed position. A spring has a natural point of equilibrium, and if it is pushed by an external force in either direction out of this position, its internal forces will push back and forth with decreasing energy until the spring returns to its position of equilibrium. Many physical forces can be well described as behaving analogously to springs.

Several of Blender's various simulators model something like spring behavior, and later in the book I discuss how this results in the physical effects that you use in your animations. But what about an actual spring? Aside from the issue of simulating the internal forces of a spring, there is the question of how to model, rig, and deform the 3D object itself. It is not entirely trivial to do this, and the approach I describe takes advantage of a variety of useful features of Blender and shows how these can be used together to achieve a simple and elegant solution for a rigged spring. First, I show how to model the spring itself by using the Array modifier in conjunction with driven shape keys (thanks to Blender user mexicoxico for his post on BlenderArtists.org, outlining this approach). Next, I'll show how a simple armature can be added that uses a PyDriver to control the deformation of the spring in an intuitive way.

Later, in Chapter 3, this spring will also come in handy as a nice example of the basic mechanics of soft bodies and one of the ways they can be used to control the movements of non-soft- body objects.

Modeling the Spring Mesh

Begin in front view (NUM1). Make sure the cursor is exactly in the center. To do this, first select the default cube, press Shift+S, and select Cursor To Selected. Then delete the default cube, add a plane by choosing Add > Plane, and subdivide once, as in Figure 1.70.

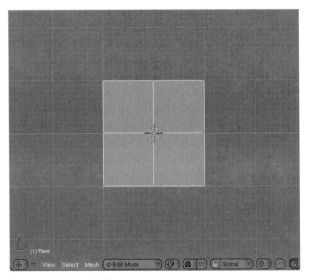

Figure 1.70 Subdivided plane

Select the leftmost and lowermost vertices as in Figure 1.71 and delete them, to result in a square exactly one Blender Unit high, as in Figure 1.72. In Edit mode, select all by pressing the A key, and move the square 3 Blender Units in the positive direction along the X axis (that is, to your right). You can do this by pressing the G key followed by the X key, and holding Ctrl while you move the square. Looking at the situation from top view (NUM7), it will look like Figure 1.73. It's important to do this in Edit mode, so that the object center remains where it is.

Press the period key to toggle the rotation pivot to the 3D cursor (you can toggle it back to the median point by pressing Shift+comma). In top view with all the vertices selected, press the E key and select Region to extrude the face, followed by the R key to rotate the extruded face. Press the Z key once to force rotation around the global Z axis, and input the value −30 so that the extruded face rotates as in Figure 1.74.

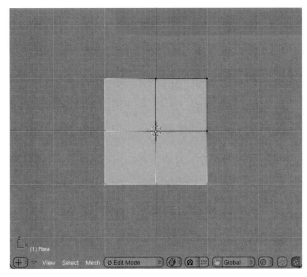

Figure 1.71 Select and delete these vertices.

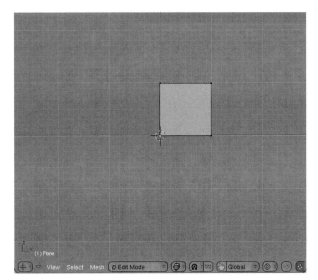

Figure 1.72 A one-BU-high square, in front view

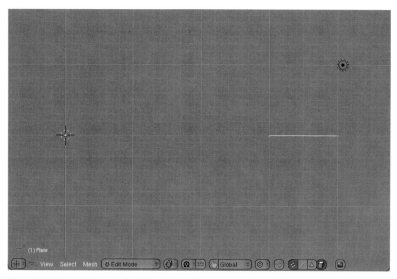

Figure 1.73 Moving the square in Edit mode, top view

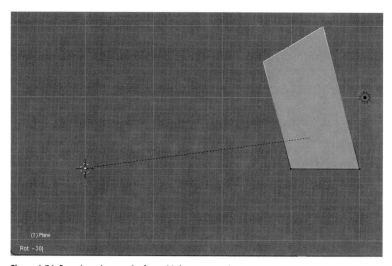

Figure 1.74 Extrude and rotate the face −30 degrees, top view.

Enter Face Select mode either by using the header menu or by pressing Ctrl+Tab+3. Press Z to go into transparent view and select and delete the faces shown in Figure 1.75.

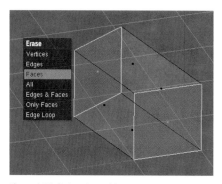

Figure 1.75 Delete the end faces.

In top view, enter Object mode and once again ensure that the cursor is on the center of the object. Press the spacebar to add an empty. Select the mesh, and press Ctrl+A to apply the current scale and rotation to the object, as in Figure 1.76.

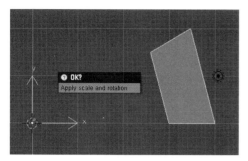

Figure 1.76 Add an empty and apply the scale and rotation to the mesh object.

Now things begin to get interesting. With the mesh selected, in Object mode, go to the Modifiers panel in the Edit buttons and select an Array modifier. The Array modifier creates a sequence of copies of the original object that can be manipulated in various ways. One of the ways to manipulate the array is to use an object to determine how the coordinates of each instance of the object in the array differs from the previous instance. To do this, deselect Relative Offset and instead select Object Offset. This will make the offset between instances of the array dependent on a separate object. The object to use for this is the empty, so fill in the Object Offset Ob field with the name of the empty, which is **Empty**, as in Figure 1.77.

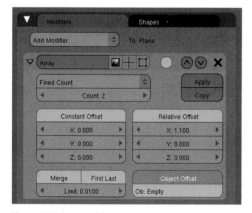

Figure 1.77 Array modifier

Select the empty in top view, rotate it by pressing the R key, and input the value –30 degrees. Rotating in this way means that each subsequent instance in the array will be offset from the previous instance by a –30 degree rotation. At the moment, because Count is set at 2 by default, there are only two instances in the array, so you should be seeing something like Figure 1.78.

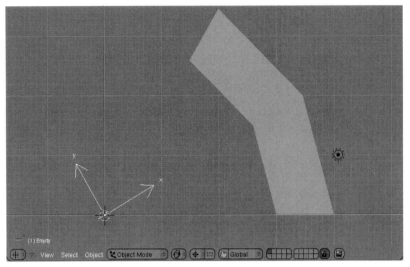

Figure 1.78 Rotating the empty

Setting Up the Shape Keys

This offset will account for the shape of the spring around its central axis. However, the spring also needs to be offset upward in the direction of the axis. Furthermore, simply offsetting the mesh with the Array modifier will not result in an unbroken coil, but in a lot of small chunks stair-stepping around the axis, which is not right for a spring. In addition to this, the deformation of the spring along the Z axis must be possible to animate.

In Blender, deformations that can be animated as increasing and decreasing linearly in intensity are easy to achieve with shape keys. To set up the necessary shape keys, follow these steps:

1. By pressing the G key and then the Z key, and holding Ctrl to constrain the movement to discrete increments, translate the empty exactly one Blender Unit up along the Z axis. This will cause the second instance of the array-modified mesh to offset upward along the Z axis also, as shown in Figure 1.79.

2. With the mesh object selected, go to the Shapes tab in the Edit buttons, and click Add Shape Key. This creates the basis shape key. Click Add Shape Key one more time to create a deform shape key called Key 1.

3. With Key 1 selected in the panel, enter Edit mode. The idea is to create a shape key such that the end of one array instance meets the beginning of the next, creating an unbroken coil. To do this, it is necessary to select only the vertices shown in Figure 1.80, and translate them directly upward along the Z axis one Blender Unit (hold Ctrl while translating, to constrain the movement), as shown in Figure 1.81.

4. In the Modifiers tab, toggle Merge on in the Array modifier panel, select Set Smooth on the mesh, and add a Subsurf modifier set to Levels: 2 and Render Levels: 3. As you can see in Figure 1.82, the spring is taking shape.

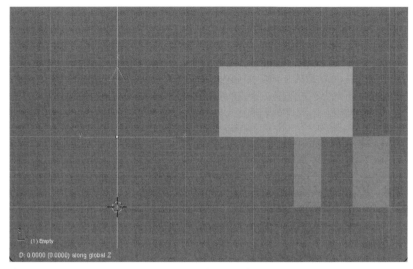

Figure 1.79 Translating the empty one BU up along the Z axis offsets the array.

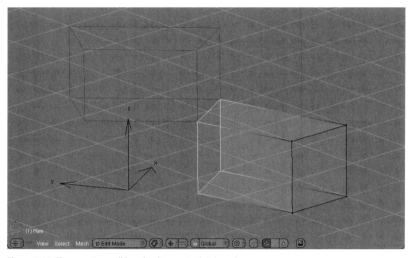

Figure 1.80 These vertices will be edited to create the shape key.

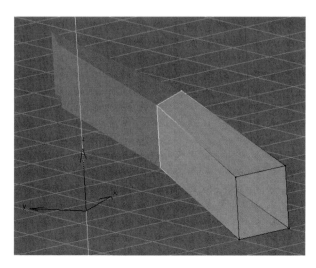

Figure 1.81
Translate the vertices straight up to meet the bottom vertices of the array-modified instance.

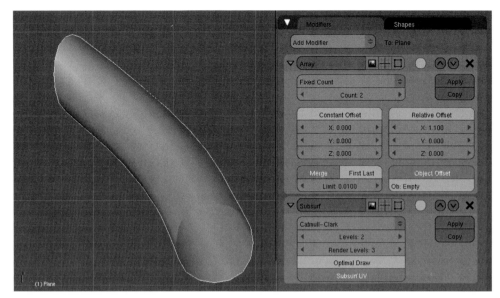

Figure 1.82 Adding a Subsurf modifier

5. The shape will be driven by the location of the empty. To set up the shape key driver, open an Ipo Editor window with the mesh selected and choose Shape from the header drop-down list. Press Ctrl+LMB to create an Ipo curve, and then again to add another vertex on the Ipo, along the lines of Figure 1.83. It doesn't really matter where the vertices are located; you'll be adjusting them manually in a moment.

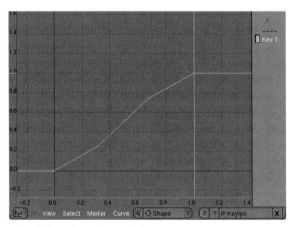

Figure 1.83 Placing vertices on the Ipo

6. Press the N key to bring up the Transform Properties dialog box in the Ipo Editor. Click Add Driver and type **Empty** in the OB field. In the drop-downs to the right of this field, select Object and LocZ. In Edit mode, select the control points on the curve one by one and make sure that they are set at Vertex X: 0, Vertex Y: 0, and at Vertex X: 1, Vertex Y: 1, as shown in Figure 1.84.

7. Tab out of Edit mode, and from the header menu choose Curve > Extend Mode > Extrapolation. This results in the Ipo becoming a straight diagonal line.

8. Go back to the Array modifier on the mesh. Set Count to 250. Your spring is now fully formed, and you can control its degree of extension by translating the empty along the Z axis, as shown in Figure 1.85. The most natural range is to have the empty between the 0.1 and 1 points on the Z axis. You can see and set the Transform Properties for the empty in the 3D viewport by pressing the N key.

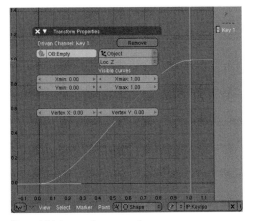
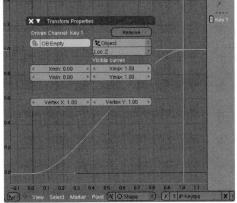

Figure 1.84 Ipo transform properties

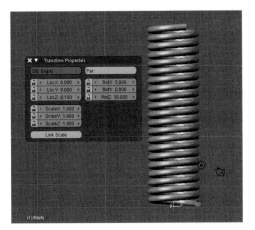
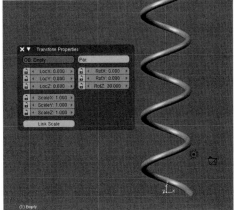

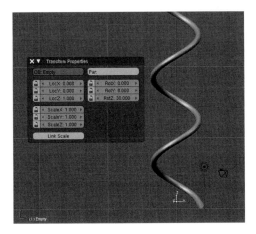

Figure 1.85
The extension of the spring is controlled by translating the empty.

Rigging the Spring

Although it is now possible to control the position of the spring by using a combination of object transforms on the spring itself and on the empty that is driving its deformation, doing so would be unnecessarily complicated. Intuitively, for a spring like this, it is desirable to simply have two control points, one at each end of the spring, that can be used to pose the spring directly. This can be done by using a simple armature to control the position and rotation of the objects, and to drive the movement of the empty by means of a PyDriver.

To create the armature, once again go into Object mode and ensure that the cursor is snapped to the location of the original mesh's center, which should also be the location of the empty. Press the spacebar to add an armature. Select X-Ray in the Editing Options area in the Armature tab of the Edit buttons. Press the G key and the Z key and hold Ctrl to move the tip of the bone directly up the Z axis 25 Blender Units, as shown in Figure 1.86. Extrude by pressing the E key and draw the tip of the second bone another 25 Blender Units up along the Z axis, as in Figure 1.87. With this bone selected, press Alt+P and select Clear Parent.

Figure 1.86 Adjusting the size of the first bone

Go into Pose mode. Select the top bone, whose name is Bone.001, and then Shift-select the bottom bone, called Bone. Press Ctrl+I to add an inverse kinematics (IK) constraint to the selected bone. The bottom bone, Bone, should turn yellow.

Now bone-parent both the spring mesh object and the empty to Bone. To do this, select the mesh, Shift-select the empty, and then select the armature, which will appear in Pose mode. Select Bone, press Ctrl+P, and select Make Parent To Bone.

To make the armature's appearance more intuitive, it will be useful to create a custom bone shape to represent the ends of the springs. I used an extruded 12-vertex circle for this.

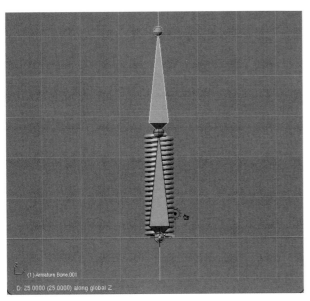

Figure 1.87 The second bone

With the armature selected in Pose mode, go into the Armature Bones tab in the Edit buttons and type **Circle** into the OB field for each bone. Then go to the Draw tab in the Object buttons and select the Wire draw type.

You'll want to adjust the size of the Circle object so it displays sensibly. When you change the size or rotation of the object, press Ctrl+A to apply the scale and rotation, to have the object display with the new values in the armature. Your rig should look something like Figure 1.88.

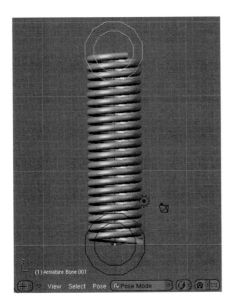

Figure 1.88
The rig so far

The Circle object itself you can hide in the Outliner by toggling the visible, selectable, and renderable icons off, as in Figure 1.89.

Figure 1.89 Controlling visibility, selectability, and renderability in the Outliner

Setting Up a PyDriver

You can now pose the armature, and the spring and empty will rotate around to follow the endpoints of the armature as they ought to. However, the spring does not extend to follow the endpoints, because the empty is not being translated along its Z axis.

You might consider using a stretch bone in some way, but this is likely to add undesirable side effects of distorting the mesh. Using some combination of copy location constraints with very small or precisely adjusted influence values may also be possible, but it is not practical in this case. The most simple and straightforward approach is to use a PyDriver to drive the Z location of the empty as a small fraction of the vector distance between the two bones' roots.

If you have some experience with Python scripting in Blender, you will find PyDrivers straightforward. If not, it is probably best to study some Python programming and familiarize yourself with the basics of Python scripting in Blender before diving into PyDrivers. The remainder of this section assumes that you have some basic knowledge of this. Unfortunately, it's beyond the scope of this book to go into depth on this background information. The information I present here won't be crucial to anything else in the book, though, so feel free to skip it if you don't feel ready for it.

Unlike with ordinary scripts, you are limited to a single line of code. Also, PyDrivers can use a shorthand form that is not available for ordinary scripting to access several common data types. These shorthand forms are as follows:

- ob('name') to access the object named name

- me('name') to access the mesh named name

- ma('name') to access the material named name

In this case, the values we're interested in are found in the Armature object, so the first of these shorthand forms will come in handy to access that object.

An object of class Armature has a Pose object associated with it, accessed by the .getPose() method, which in turn has a set of PoseBones corresponding to the bones of the armature. The .bones attribute of the Pose is a dictionary keyed on the name of the bone, which returns a PoseBone object. These PoseBone objects, intuitively, represent the bones of the armature when it is being posed. The location of the PoseBone is the location of the bone in Pose mode. Furthermore, each PoseBone has an attribute head and a tail, and each has a set of coordinates associated with it. The location of the base of the bone is the head, so this is the value of interest here.

Python in Blender has access to a math utilities library that enables it to do vector math simply, so finding the distance between two 3D points is simply a matter of subtracting one from the other.

Finally, because the rest position of the spring has the empty at location 0.1 BU and the distance between the bones at 25 BUs, and the empty's location should change proportionately to the distance between the bones, it is possible to calculate the position of the empty as the distance between the two bones, divided by 250.

Putting all that together yields a single line of code that will serve as the PyDriver for the local Z axis location of the empty:

```
(ob('Armature').getPose().bones['Bone.001'].head-
ob('Armature').getPose().bones['Bone'].head).length/250
```

Setting up the driver is simple. Select the empty and select Object from the header drop-down in the Ipo Editor. Select LocZ from the list of Ipos along the right side of the Ipo Editor window. Press N to show the Transform Properties dialog box. Click Add Driver, and then click the Python snake icon to the left of the OB field. In the new field that appears, type the preceding code in a single unbroken line, as shown in Figure 1.90.

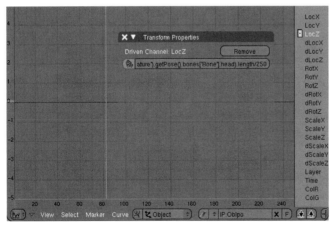

Figure 1.90 PyDriver

After this is done, the spring is fully rigged. You can play around with posing it by moving either end of the armature and seeing how it behaves, as in Figure 1.91. In Chapter 3, you'll revisit this rigged spring to see how a simple soft body simulation can be used to control the spring's behavior.

PyDrivers

Blender uses the Python language for scripting, and a great deal of additional functionality can be implemented by using Python scripts. Another way that Blender uses Python is in PyDrivers, which enable an Ipo curve to be driven by any value that can be expressed in a single line of Python code with access to the Blender Python applications programming interface (API). This means that rather than having a one-to-one correspondence with the value of another Ipo, as ordinary Ipo drivers do, an Ipo can be driven by much more sophisticated operations on multiple input values. In the example in the text, an Ipo is driven by an operation on the vector distance between two bones.

It is beyond the scope of this book to give a thorough introduction to Python or to object-oriented programming (OOP), but people who have some experience with the ideas behind OOP will find PyDrivers fairly easy to pick up after a bit of studying the Blender Python API.

Accessing an object's attributes or calling class methods on an object is done by appending the name of the attribute or the method to the end of the name of the object, separated by a period. In the case of calling a method, the method call ends with a set of parentheses enclosing the arguments. If there are no arguments, as in the case of most getter methods, the parentheses are empty.

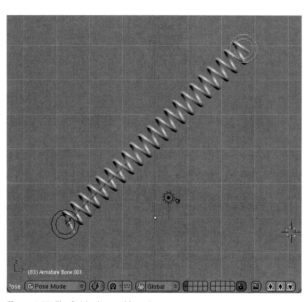

Figure 1.91 The finished, poseable spring

In this chapter, you saw several interesting ways to use general-purpose tools in Blender to represent various physical phenomena. Some of the tools you may have already been familiar with, but I hope that you've had your imagination stimulated to think of new and creative ways to use these tools to achieve the effects you want. In the next chapter, you'll look at Blender's powerful new particle system, and the discussion of physical simulation will begin in earnest.

The Nitty-Gritty
on Particles

In preparation for the Peach project, Blender underwent a complete recoding of its particle system, introducing a host of fantastic new features. The particle system is now much more powerful than before, and if you are accustomed to the old particle system or have never used particles before, all the new functionality may seem intimidating at first. In this chapter, you'll learn how to use the new features to create a variety of dynamic particle effects. In Chapter 4, "Hair Essentials: The Long and Short of Strand Particles," you'll pick up where you left off and learn about using static particles for hair, fur, and other effects.

2

Chapter Contents
Introducing particles
Working with dynamic particles
Using boids

Introducing Particles

In CG, the behavior of very small things acting in groups is animated differently from the way ordinary-sized objects are animated. Many programs, including Blender, deal with these kinds of effects by using *particles*. As you can imagine, effects such as smoke, dust, or granules of some substance are often best handled with particles, but as you will see in this chapter, the potential of particles extends beyond these uses. Whether something is "very small" depends on the perspective you want to take in the animation. A bird, for example, is clearly big enough to warrant being animated in a traditional way in certain cases. A flock of birds, on the other hand, behaves in a way that may be better simulated by using a particle system, as demonstrated later in this chapter.

Blender's particle functionality enables you to define groups of particles called *particle systems* by setting how they animate and render. You can create multiple particle systems with different parameters and have them interact in a variety of ways. There are two fundamentally different ways in which particles are usually used. The particles used for simulating tiny moving objects such as dust, smoke, insects, or the like are called *dynamic particles*. This chapter covers dynamic particles. In Chapter 4, you'll learn about other cases, in which particles are used to simulate long, slender objects such as hair or grass that are anchored to a surface.

Setting Particle Parameters

All particle systems are set up in the Particles subcontext of the Object Buttons area, which is accessed by clicking the button shown in Figure 2.1, or by clicking F7 to enter the Object Buttons area and then twice more to cycle through to the correct subcontext. When you enter this area with a Mesh object selected, you will see the panel shown in Figure 2.2. Only a Mesh object can act as a particle emitter. If you have any other object type, or no object selected, you will not be able to add a particle system.

Figure 2.1 The Particles Buttons icon

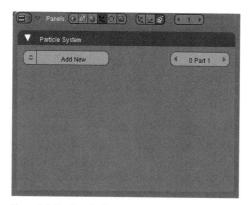

Figure 2.2 The Particles Buttons area

This Particle System tab enables you to select which particle system you are working with and add and delete particle systems. The drop-down menu on the left enables you to select which particle system is associated with the current particle system index, or add a new system to the particle system index. The field on the right has two values. On the left side of the field, the number of indices with associated particle systems is shown. When you first begin in a fresh .blend file, no particle systems are set up, so the number shown is zero. On the right side of the field, the active index is shown. This value begins at one, and can always increment as far as the first empty index.

To create a new particle system at the currently active index, click Add New.

Particle System Tab

When a particle system has been added, the Particle System tab displays the basic information about the system. The first thing to decide is what type of particle system it is. This can be selected in the particle Type drop-down menu shown in Figure 2.3. The options here are Emitter (the default value), Reactor, and Hair. Hair, the option for static particles, is discussed in Chapter 4. This chapter focuses on Emitter particles and Reactor particles.

Figure 2.3
The particle Type drop-down menu

Emitter particles are particles that emit from the Mesh object that they are associated with. Their emission is controlled directly by the various parameters set in the particle system. *Reactor particles* are particles that react to other particle systems. They can be set to emit from a mesh, or they can be set to emit from other particles, and their emission depends on the behavior of their target particle system.

In the example shown in Figures 2.4 and 2.5, Emitter particles are set to emit from a Sphere mesh, and a separate Reactor particle system is set to emit from the particles of the first system upon their deaths. The Emitter particle system is shown selected in Figure 2.4, visualized as circles. The Reactor particle system is selected in Figure 2.5, visualized as lines (the first frame in Figure 2.5 is the same frame as the last frame in Figure 2.4). Emitters and Reactors can be used together in a variety of interesting ways, and several of them will come up throughout this chapter. The Enabled button toggles the whole particle system on and off.

The rest of the buttons on the Particle System tab determine the general characteristics of how the particle system behaves. Some of these values are only applicable to Emitter particles, and some apply to both Emitters and Reactors. The Basic buttons include the following:

Amount determines the total number of particles that will be emitted over the course of the particle system's duration.

Sta sets the start frame for emission.

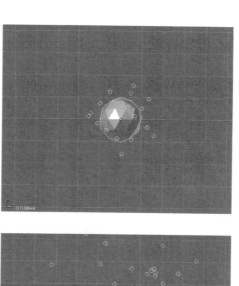

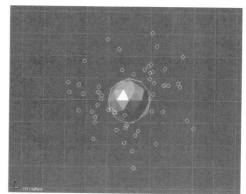

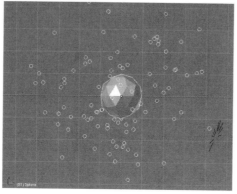

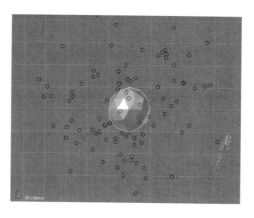

Figure 2.4
Emitter particles

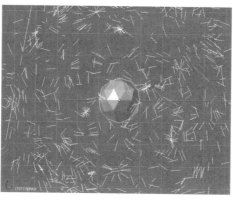

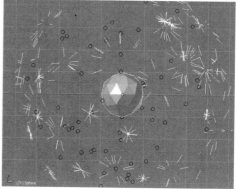

Figure 2.5
Reactor particles

End sets the end frame for emission. The number of particles set in the Amount field will be entirely emitted between the start and end frames.

Life determines the number of frames that each particle will persist between the time it is emitted (birth) and the time it disappears (death).

Rand sets the range around the Life value in which the life span of each particle can vary randomly. A Rand value of 0 will constrain all particles to last exactly as long as the Life value.

All of these values taken together influence the density of the particles. The density of the particle system often plays an important part in creating a convincing effect, so it is important to be aware of this. For example, if you increase the number of frames that your particle system is active without changing the Amount value, the resulting particle output will be sparser.

The Emit From button values determine how the particles emit from their emitter mesh or, in the case of Reactor particles, from their target particle system. The Random button controls whether particles are released from the mesh in a set order or whether the ordering is randomized. For example, if 800 particles are set to be emitted from a cube's vertices, 100 particles will be released from each of the cube's 8 vertices, in a fixed order, if Random is toggled off. The Even button sets the emission of the particles to be calculated based on the size of faces and the lengths of edges in order to yield a more uniform distribution.

There are two drop-down menus among the Emit From buttons. The topmost menu enables you to select where on the mesh the particles emit from. By default this is set to Faces, so Emitter particles will emerge from the mesh's faces. The other two options for Emitter particles are Vertices and Volume. Obviously, when Vertices is selected, particles emit from the mesh's vertices. In the case of Volume, the particles originate from points within the mesh. This can be useful when you do not need the shape of the mesh itself to play as much of a role in the particles' emission—for example, in explosions. In the case of Reactor particles, this menu also includes an option for Particles, which causes the Reactor particles to emit directly from their target particle system's particles.

Volume vs. Faces emission is also significant when Grid is chosen from the Distribution drop-down menu, which is the second drop-down menu in the Emit From buttons. This menu enables you to choose how the particles are arranged with respect to the surface they are emitting from. The default value is Jittered, which means that the particles are slightly offset from points subdividing the surface they are emitting from. The degree to which they are offset depends on the Amount value in the field directly below the menu. The other values for this menu are Random and Grid. Random creates a patternless distribution of emission points over the surface.

The Grid option in the Distribution drop-down menu does something a little bit different. When this option is selected, the top field in the Basic options changes from Amount to Resol, with a default value of 10. The Grid option creates a three-dimensional, volumetric grid in the bounding box area of the Mesh object, with a resolution of the value in the Resol field. If the Emit From drop-down menu selection is Volume, the shape of the mesh is filled with particles positioned on the grid. You can see an example of particles positioned inside a Sphere mesh in Figure 2.6, where the particles are visualized as 3D axes. The Invert option below the drop-down menu reverses which points on the grid have particles; as shown in Figure 2.7, the bounding box's negative space is filled with particles and the shape of the mesh is empty. If Faces is selected from the Emit From drop-down menu, with a Grid distribution, then the grid particles will conform to the shape of the mesh shell of the object, rather than to the shape of the object. With the Invert option, the empty space inside the mesh will also be filled with particles. This is a way to make particles take a specific shape. This can have a variety of potential uses. For example, you can target a Reactor particle system on a grid system in order to make the Reactor particles react to the shape of the mesh.

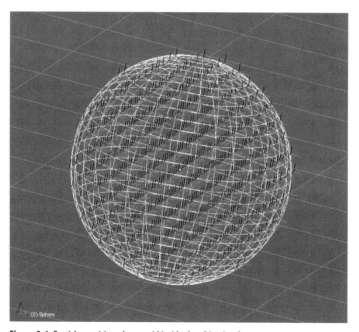

Figure 2.6 Particles positioned on a grid inside the object's volume

Baking

It is possible to store the calculations for the particle simulation, so that the animation can be sped up in subsequent viewings. To do this access the Bake tab in the Particle buttons area, by default located behind the Particle System tab. To bake the simulation, simply enter the start and end frame values for the time segment you want to bake and click the Bake button. Once baked, the basic particle properties for the system will no longer be editable. If you want to adjust these properties, you will need to click the Free Bake button that replaces the Bake button on the same tab.

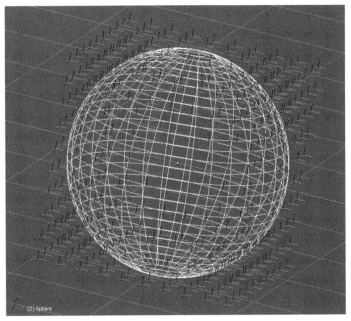

Figure 2.7 Particles positioned on an inverse grid

Using the Physics Tab

The Physics tab contains the fields that most directly influence the way the particles interact with the forces in the world. There are four options in the Physics drop-down menu: Newtonian, Keyed, Boids, and None.

Newtonian Physics

Newtonian physics is the default physics option for particles. With Newtonian physics selected, the particles are subject to gravity, acceleration, and force fields defined on other objects. Newtonian physics enables particles to interact with deflection objects and is also necessary in order to use soft body simulations on a particle system. Most of the cases described in this chapter and in Chapter 4 use Newtonian physics.

With Newtonian physics selected, you can set the physics parameters in the panel shown in Figure 2.8. You can determine the initial velocity of the particles in a number of directions. These directions include the following:

   Object indicates the direction that the emitter object is moving. If this value is set as an initial velocity, particles will move in the direction that the object is moving at the time they are emitted. If the object's direction or velocity changes, the particles will maintain the impetus of the movement the object had when the particles were emitted. Smoke trailing a rocket is a good example of this kind of movement.

Normal indicates the direction of the surface normals of the emitter mesh. With this value set, particles will emit from the surface of the mesh directly outward. This is good for sparks and explosions and, as you will see in Chapter 4, it is useful for working with hair.

Random indicates velocity in a random direction. When this value is set, particles move in a random direction outward from the mesh.

Tan sets velocity tangential to the surface of the object. This indicates velocity perpendicular to the surface normals of the object's faces. The exact direction of the velocity is indicated by the Rot value.

Rot indicates which direction, perpendicular to the surface normals of the object's faces, the Tan valued velocity actually moves in.

In the case of Reactor particles, there are two more possibilities for initial velocity values:

Particle indicates the velocity of target particles. With this value set, Reactor particles will get their velocity from the velocity of their target particles.

Reactor gives Reactor particles a velocity away from the target particles at the time of emission.

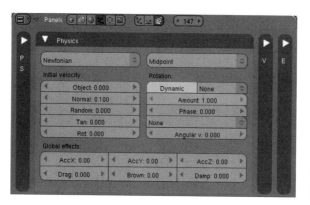

Figure 2.8
Newtonian physics parameters

You can set the angle and degree of rotation of individual partners in the Rotation area of this tab, and set the angular velocity in the Angular v field. Above this field is a drop-down menu with the default value of None shown. This menu enables you to select characteristics for the angular velocity of individual particles. The options are Spin, Random, and Velocity.

Finally, you can set acceleration values along each of the three axes X, Y, and Z (–9.8 in the Z will simulate the effect of Earth's gravity) as well as setting values for Drag (to simulate air friction), Brown (to simulate Brownian motion, the random movement of particles in nature), and Damp (to diminish the effect of acceleration values).

Keyed Physics

Keyed physics makes the movement of one particle system dependent on the movement of another particle system. A particle system with keyed physics needs a target object and particle system defined in the red-highlighted field shown in Figure 2.9. It is possible for the target system to also be a keyed system. However, a nonkeyed target system is necessary at some point to initiate the motion of the keyed systems.

It is possible to chain several keyed particle systems together to get a high degree of control over the flow of particles, as shown in Figure 2.10. In this example, the particle system emitting from the sphere labeled 1, shown as white points, is a standard Newtonian physics system with a slight downward acceleration applied. The particle system on sphere 2 is keyed on that system. The particle system on sphere 3 is keyed on the one on sphere 2, and so on, with each particle system keyed on the previous one.

In Figure 2.10, all the keyed particle systems have the First button toggled on, meaning that the objects emit particles directly. In Figure 2.11, First is toggled off for all objects except sphere 9. In this case, the other objects act analogously to control points for the curve of the particle flow. The curve will change if the objects are repositioned, but no particles emit directly from the objects themselves. It is necessary to have at least one keyed particle system set as First; otherwise, no particles will be emitted at all.

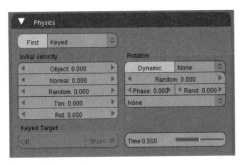

Figure 2.9 Keyed physics parameters

Other Physics Options

Boids physics is another special case of physics designed to simulate the behavior of large numbers of living organisms. You'll read more about boids later in this chapter. The None option turns off physics. With None selected, particles will stay where they are emitted and will not respond to any forces.

Setting Visualization Options

As you've seen already in previous examples, there are various options for visualizing particles, both in the 3D view and in the final render. Some of the visualization options are useful mainly as ways to visually distinguish separate particle systems when more than one are active. Some of the options enable extended functionality and require further parameters to be set. These are managed in the Visualization tab. The options available in the Visualization drop-down menu are shown in Figure 2.12 and are as follows:

Point displays particles as simple points. This is the default for dynamic particles. In previous versions of Blender, this was the only option available for dynamic particles. Point visualization renders as halos.

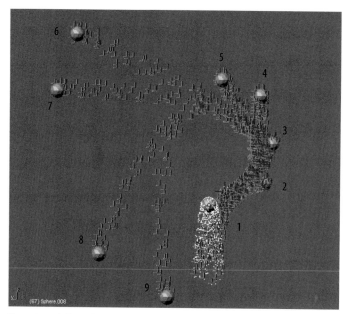

Figure 2.10 A chain of keyed physics systems, all set to First

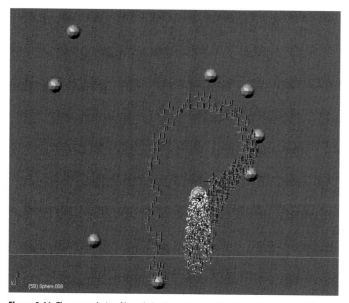

Figure 2.11 The same chain of keyed physics systems, with only number 9 set to First

Circle displays particles as small circles. Circle visualization also renders as halos.

Cross displays particles as six-pointed, three-dimensional crosses. Cross visualization also renders as halos.

Axis displays particles as local X, Y, and Z axes in red, green, and blue, respectively. Axis visualization also renders as halos. This is a good visualization option if you want to see particles' rotation.

Line displays the particles as lines representing the direction the particles are moving. Line visualization renders as solid lines of the material active on the particle system. Lines can be textured by using strand mapping.

Path displays particles as continuous strands from the emitter mesh. The Path option is available only for Hair type particles or particles using keyed physics. In other cases, selecting Path will result in default point visualization. In the case of keyed physics in Path visualization, the ends of the path particle strands follow the movement of the target particles, as shown in Figure 2.13.

Object displays particles as duplicates of a specific object. In Figure 2.12, the specified object is a purple Suzanne mesh.

Group displays particles as duplicates of objects in a group. In Figure 2.12, a purple Suzanne mesh, a green torus, and a red sphere are all members of the specified group.

Billboard displays particles as two-dimensional panels called *billboards* that are set by default to face the camera at all times (this setting can be adjusted). The panels can be textured with images as shown in Figure 2.14 (for example, to create trees in a forest), or with procedural textures to simulate volumetric effects (as in the flames example shown in Figure 2.49).

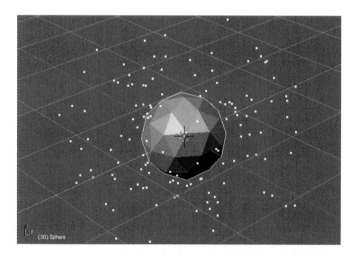

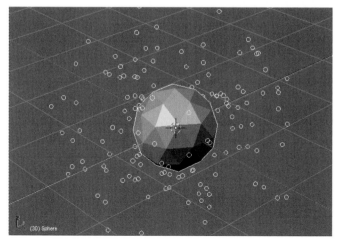

Figure 2.12 Visualization modes: Point, Circle, Cross, Axis, Line, Path, Object, Group, and Billboard

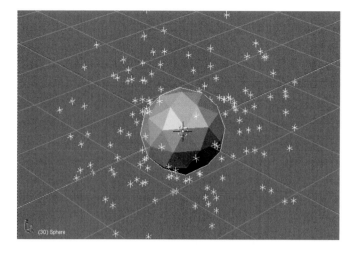

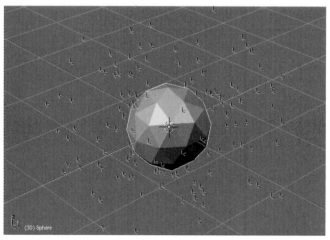

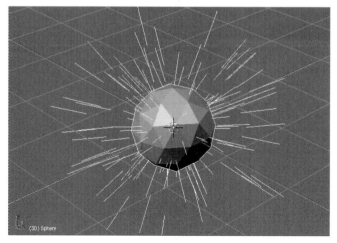

Figure 2.12 *(continued)*

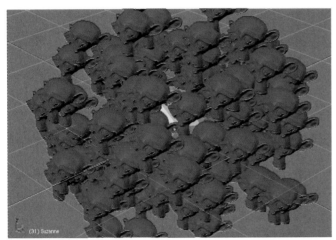

Figure 2.12 *(continued)*

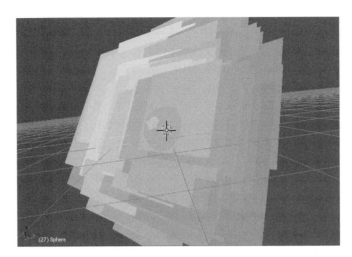

Figure 2.12
(continued)

The Draw buttons determine what information about the particles is shown in the 3D view, including information about velocity, size, and number. There are also fields to input the size of the particle visualization in the 3D viewport and the percentage of the total number of actual particles that will be displayed in the 3D viewport. Setting the Disp value to less than 100 may make it easier to work with large particle systems that require large amounts of RAM.

The Render options in the Visualization tab determine what material the particles are rendered with according to the material index of the emitter object. You can also determine here whether the emitter itself will be rendered, whether parent particles will be rendered, whether unborn particles will be rendered, and whether particles will be rendered after they have died, all by toggling the corresponding buttons in this area.

Using the Extras Tab

The Extras tab contains a variety of further settings. In the Effectors area, you can set parameters relating to harmonic effectors discussed in the next section. With the GR value, you can restrict the effectors that influence the particle system to objects of a specific group. It is a good idea to manage your effectors (force fields, and so forth) with groups rather than relying on layers, because it is easy to have forgotten effectors inadvertently messing with your particle systems in complex scenes. Size Deflect enables the particles to bounce against deflection objects based on the particles' own size, which is set on the Size control on the right side of the panel, rather than bouncing at the center of the particle, as is the default. Die On Hit makes the particles die upon coming in contact with a deflection object, and Sticky makes the particles stick to the surface of an deflection object.

The Time settings enable you to choose whether the particles are calculated in Global time or whether they can be affected by the object's Time Ipo (Object time). Absolute time affects how Ipos that influence particles are calculated. The default is for them to be calculated relative to the life span of the particle. Loop sets the particles to be emitted again after their life span runs out. With the Instantly button toggled on, the particle will be re-emitted immediately after it dies, even if it dies before its life span runs out, as it might do if it is set to die on hitting an effector.

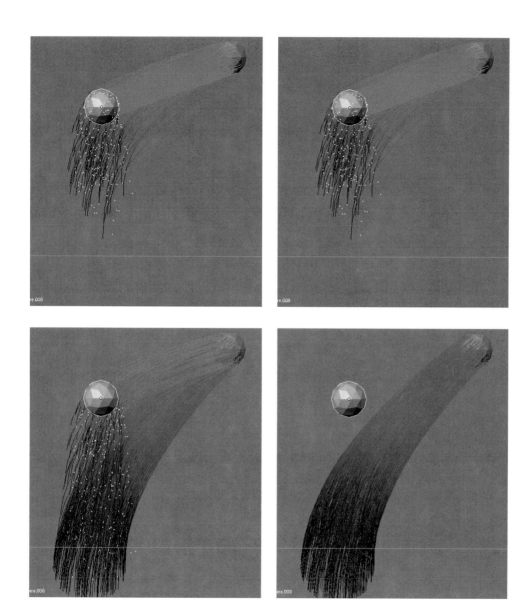

Figure 2.13 Keyed particles with Path visualization

Using Force Fields and Deflection

Objects can influence the behavior of particle systems in two main ways, by using force fields and deflection, which can be found in their respectively named tabs in the Physics Buttons area.

Force Fields

Force fields can be activated on an object to produce forces that act on particle systems. It is common to assign force fields to empties, although they can be assigned to other objects as well. In order for a force field to act on a particle system, the force field object must be on the same layer as the object with the particle system and within the Group designated in the Effectors controls, if one has been specified.

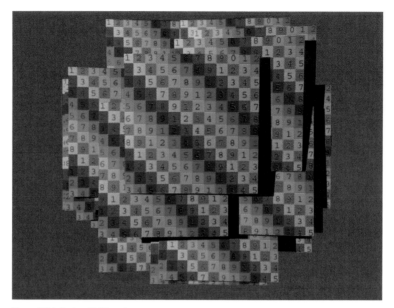

Figure 2.14 Textured billboards

There are six types of force fields that you can use:

Texture force fields exert directional forces based on the values of a texture. Higher texture values have higher strength.

Harmonic force fields use the center of the force field object as the median point for a harmonic loop, causing the particles to pass back through their starting point again and again over the course of their life span. The effect of a harmonic force field can be seen in Figure 2.15.

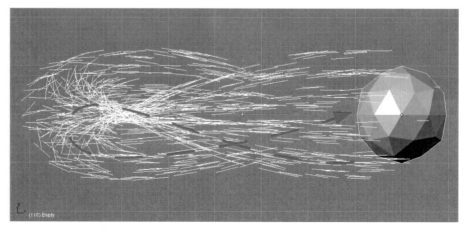

Figure 2.15 A Harmonic force field

Magnetic force fields cause particles to move in a way that mimics the behavior of magnetic fields, as shown in Figure 2.16. If you were an inquisitive child in a hobby-minded household, you might be familiar with similar patterns from the time you accidentally wrecked the family television with the rare-earth magnets that your father kept lying around in the garage. This force field is excellent for creating the kind of swirling, chaotic patterns that you might see in a blizzard.

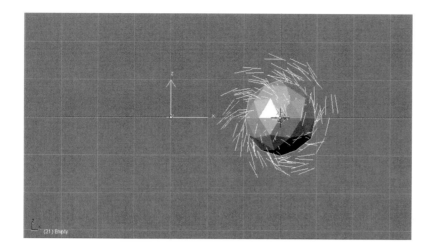

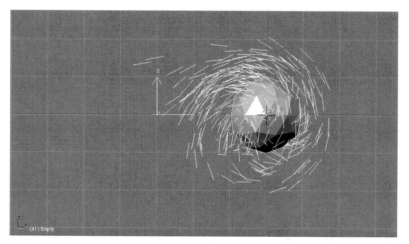

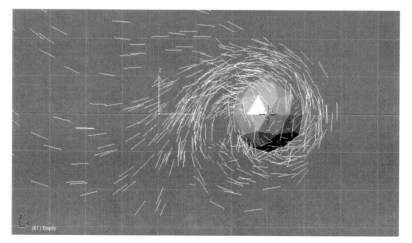

Figure 2.16 A Magnetic force field

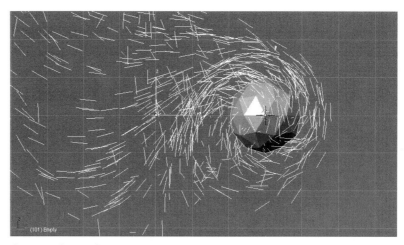

Figure 2.16 *(continued)*

Vortex force fields cause particles to swirl around the axis of the force field object's center like a tornado or a whirlpool, as shown in Figure 2.17.

Figure 2.17 A Vortex force field

Wind force fields produce a force in a single direction, depending on the orientation of the force field object, as shown in Figure 2.18.

Spherical force fields produce a force that emanates spherically from the center of the force field object, as shown in Figure 2.19. Negative force values on Spherical forces will attract the particles toward the center of the force object.

Although any single object can have only one force field active on it, it is possible for multiple force field objects to operate on a single particle system at the same time. Force parameters are keyable, so you can control the strength of the force with an Ipo in the same way you would control other keyable values. This enables you to create effects such as gusty winds, or to change the direction of a vortex force.

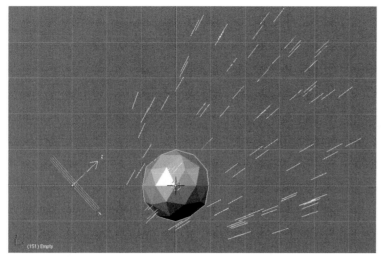

Figure 2.18 A Wind force field

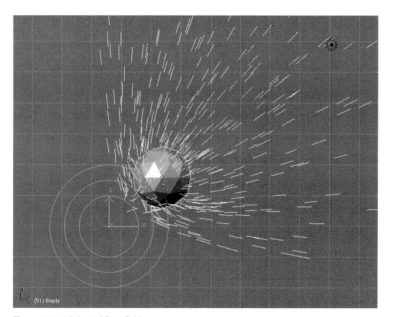

Figure 2.19 A Spherical force field

Deflection

Particles can be made to bounce off an object rather than penetrate it by toggling on the Deflection button in the Deflection tab for the object. The deflection values for particles are as follows:

Damping controls how much energy is lost by the particles when they bounce off the deflection object. Figure 2.20 shows a particle system with a negative Z (downward) acceleration bouncing off a deflection object with a Damping value of 0. Figure 2.21 shows the same particle system bouncing off a deflection object with a Damping value of 0.5. If the Damping value is 1, the particles will not bounce at all; they will simply cling to the deflection object (if there are forces or acceleration on them parallel to the surface of the object, they will slide along the surface).

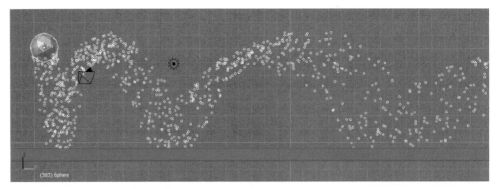

Figure 2.20 Bouncing particles with 0 Damping deflection

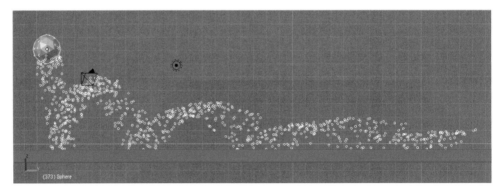

Figure 2.21 Bouncing with 0.5 Damping deflection

Rnd Damping adds a random component to the Damping value, so that some particles are more dampened than others.

Friction reduces the particles' acceleration parallel to the surface of the deflection object when the particles come into contact with the surface. Figure 2.22 illustrates the difference between particles bouncing with no friction and the same particles, with the same acceleration values, bouncing with maximum friction.

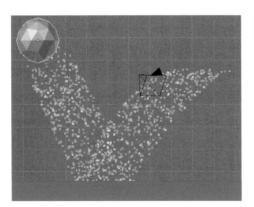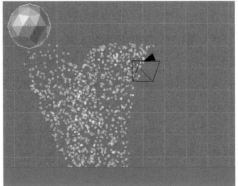

Figure 2.22 The same particles bouncing on a surface with no friction and with maximum friction

Rnd Friction adds a random component to the Friction value, so that some of the particles are more affected by friction than others.

Permeability determines how many particles penetrate the surface of the deflector object. The default value of 0 means that all particles will bounce off the surface. A value of 1 means that all the particles will pass through the object. As Figure 2.23 shows, a value of 0.5 will result in half of the particles passing through the object while the other half bounce off the surface. Permeability, like several of the deflection parameters, can be keyed so that the value changes over time.

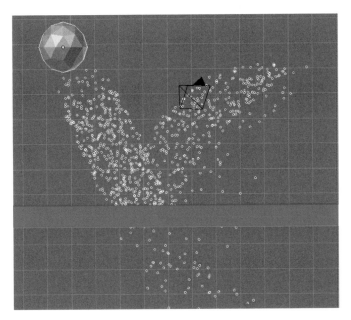

Figure 2.23
A deflection object with
Permeability set to 0.5

Kill can be toggled on or off with the Kill button. If it is toggled on, particles will end their lives upon coming in contact with the deflector object, regardless of what their life span is set to. Reactor particles set to react on death will also be triggered. By default, particles disappear on death, but they can be set to be visible after death in the Render section of the Visualization tab.

Force fields and deflection objects also interact with soft bodies similarly to the way they interact with particles. You'll read more about using force fields and deflection with soft bodies in Chapter 3, "Getting Flexible with Soft Bodies and Cloth."

Working with Dynamic Particles

As mentioned before, one of the primary uses of particles is to simulate the behavior of large groups of very small, point-like objects such as specks of dust or snowflakes. Particles that move independently and are not connected to their emitter are called *dynamic particles*. Previous versions of Blender used the contrasting term *static particles* to refer to strandlike particles that remained connected to their emitting mesh, but this term has been replaced by the Hair option in the new system, which you will read about in Chapter 4. There are many similarities in how particles behave, whether dynamic or not, so it helps to have a good idea of how to work with dynamic particles.

Creating Fire and Smoke

A classic use of particles is to create fire and smoke effects. The technique I describe here is a straightforward approach to creating rising flames and smoke. The basic methods can also easily be extended to create fiery explosions, by adjusting the way the particles move and tweaking some of the textures.

This approach to making flames takes advantage of the fact that Blender's procedural cloud textures are actually 3D textures projected onto 2D surfaces. By projecting the same texture onto many different 2D surfaces and setting their alpha values so that they are all visible at once, it is possible to obtain convincing 3D textural effects, even without a full volumetric simulation. Blender's particle simulation system provides an ideal 2D surface to use for this: the Billboard visualization option generates 2D panels that are set by default to track to the camera and can be textured and adjusted in a variety of useful ways.

The key to making convincing fire effects with particles is to conceal the particle nature of the effect as much as possible. A number of sources of localized randomness help to obtain this effect. In general, using more particles with lower alpha values will make the effect more convincing by reducing the flicker that occurs when individual particles are born and die, but very large numbers of particles can slow down rendering and demand a lot of hardware resources.

To set up a particle flame simulation, follow these steps:

1. Start a fresh Blender session with the default cube. This is as good an object as any to serve as the emitter mesh for this simulation. Select the cube, go to the Particle System tab in the Particles Buttons area, and click Add New. Caching is activated only after the file is saved, so don't forget to save the file after creating it.

2. Click Random as shown in Figure 2.24, and set the Life value to 70. The Random option causes particles to be released from different points on the mesh in random order. If Random is not selected, the particles will be emitted from the mesh's structure in a strict order and will not appear organic at all.

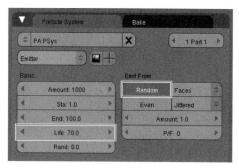

Figure 2.24 Setting Particle System values

3. Smoke and flames are good examples of a case where Newtonian physics is called for. The particles should interact with forces in a natural way. Leave the Physics drop-down menu as it is, with the default value of Newtonian. Give

the particles an initial velocity of 0.55 in the Normal direction, and 0.5 in the Random direction, as shown in Figure 2.25, and give them an AccZ value of 2.50 to make them rise. In the Visualization tab, choose Billboard from the drop-down menu shown in Figure 2.26. In the Extras tab, set the Size value to 2 and the Rand value to 2, as shown in Figure 2.27. If you press Alt+A now over the 3D viewport, you will see how the billboards emerge from the emitter mesh. Figure 2.28 shows two views of the billboard particles. Note how they all face the camera. This is usually what you want, and it's the default. The orientation and target of the billboards can be adjusted by using the fields on the right side of the Visualization tab.

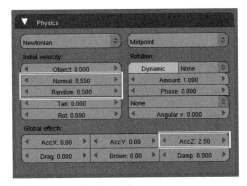

Figure 2.25 Particle physics values

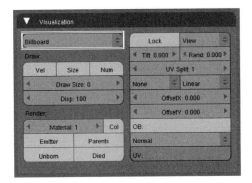

Figure 2.26 Visualization

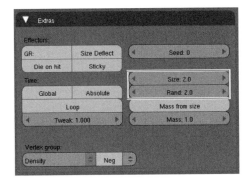

Figure 2.27 Extras

4. Move the current frame back to 1 to clear the particles from the viewport. It is going to be necessary to map some textures to a moving object, and a good option for this is an empty. Add an empty by pressing the spacebar and choosing Add > Empty. Press Alt+R and Alt+G to clear the rotation and the location, which will send the empty to the same location as the default cube, as shown in Figure 2.29.

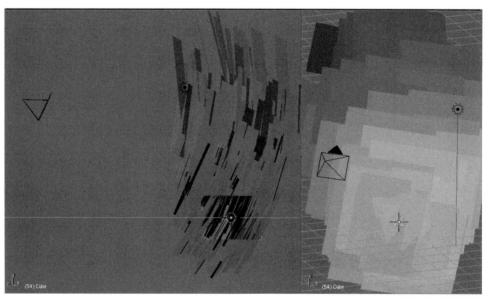

Figure 2.28 Billboards facing the camera

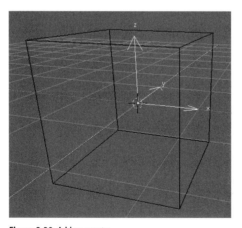

Figure 2.29 Add an empty

5. Materials are the heart of this approach to making flames. Add a material to the emitter object as you normally would, and name the material *Flame*. Set the ZTransp, Traceable, and A (Alpha) values as shown in Figure 2.30. As mentioned previously, alpha values will be governed by textures. It is important to turn off ray traceability (Traceable) for several reasons. For one thing, ray tracing a large number of transparent objects would be very resource-intensive and would render extremely slowly. For another thing, flames are not supposed to cast shadows, give off reflection, or exhibit other behaviors typically accomplished by ray tracing. Even if the rest of the scene is ray-traced, it won't yield any benefit to have this material ray-traced.

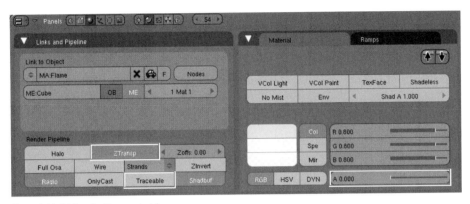

Figure 2.30 Adding the Flame material

6. Add a texture. Call it *FlameTex* and choose Clouds from the Texture Type dropdown menu, with a Hard Noise setting, a Noise Size of 1.20, and a Noise Depth of 6, as shown in Figure 2.31. On the Colors tab, click the Colorband button to activate the colorband. The colorband for this texture should consist of three colors, shown in Figure 2.32, so click Add to add another color (by default it will be gray) to the colorband. You can switch between colors by clicking the triangular arrow icons on the right and left of the Cur field in the middle of the colorband widget. Edit the colors and their alpha values by using the appropriate sliders, and adjust the gradations by dragging the bars in the colorband with your mouse.

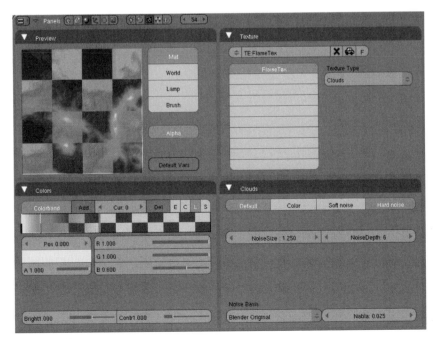

Figure 2.31 Flame texture

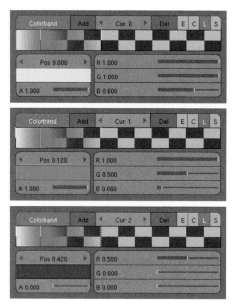

Figure 2.32 Colorband

7. The texture mapping and shader values for the Flame material are shown in Figure 2.33. In the Map Input tab, set the mapping to Object and type **Empty** (the name of the Empty object you added in step 4) in the field. Set the Map To options to Col and Alpha, so that the material will get its color values and alpha values from the texture. In the Shaders tab, deselect all the option buttons along the right-hand side of the tab. These are concerned with shadow casting and receiving, and should be turned off for something like a flame. Finally, turn the Spec (specularity) down to 0 and Hard (hardness) as low as it goes. Fire isn't shiny.

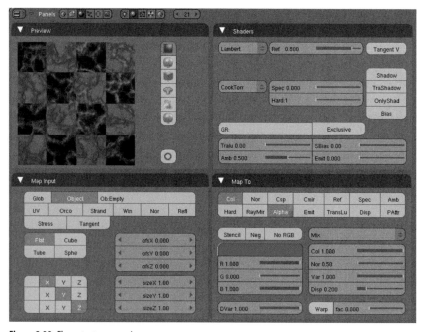

Figure 2.33 Flame texture mapping

8. If you advance a few single frames to emit some particles and render now, you'll see something along the lines of Figure 2.34. It's a start, but obviously it doesn't look much like a flame. For one thing, the flame seems to be composed of a collection of straight-edged panels. This should come as no surprise, because that's exactly what's happening. So far, nothing has been done to conceal the shape of the billboards. The other problem with this material is that it's dingy. Fire emits light, so it won't do to have it looking as dark as this. It is possible to deal with both of these issues simultaneously by using another texture. First, move the Flame texture to channel 2 in the Texture tab of the Materials buttons, as you saw how to do in the ocean tutorial in Chapter 1, "Re-creating the World: An Overview." The new texture will need to be above the Flame texture, so add a new texture in channel 1. Name the texture *Stencil* and set its values as shown in Figure 2.35. Choose Blend from the Texture Type drop-down menu, and select Sphere in the Blend tab. Activate the colorband and set it as shown in the figure, with a gradation between a white alpha 1 color and a black alpha 0 color. Return to the Edit buttons and add a UV texture to the object, as shown in Figure 2.36. Finally, set the mapping values of the texture on the material as shown in Figure 2.37. In Map Input, select UV. This will map the full sphere blend texture onto each individual billboard panel. In Map To, set the texture to Stencil, and select the Emit value to be affected by the texture. The stencil value hides textures that are located on lower channels, so that the Flame texture appears as a soft-edged circle. Selecting Emit makes the material emit light in proportion to the value of the texture.

Figure 2.34 Rendering the material so far

Figure 2.35 The Stencil texture

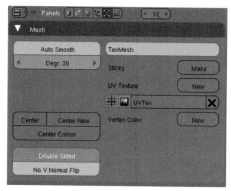

Figure 2.36 Adding a UV texture

9.   If you render now, the result looks like Figure 2.38. This is an improvement, but it's not finished yet. For one thing, there's that hazy dim glow where many low-alpha values are adding up to become a rather dull color. To counter this, add one more blend texture in the topmost channel of the material's texture channels. Make the texture look as shown in Figure 2.39, with a Lin (linear) blend type and white, yellow, and red-orange colors. In the Materials buttons, map the texture as shown in Figure 2.40. In Map Input, select Object, type **Cube** into the field, and set the topmost mapping axis to Z rather than the default X. In Map, set the Col value to 0.75.

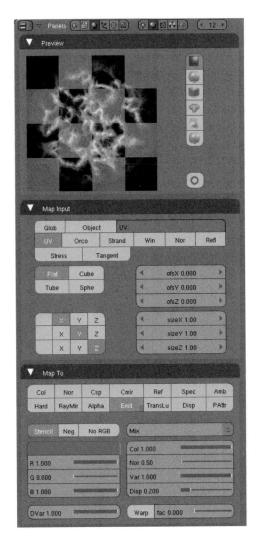

Figure 2.37
Stencil texture mapping

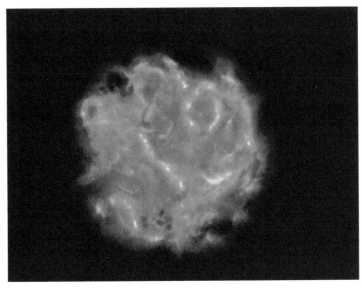

Figure 2.38 The material so far

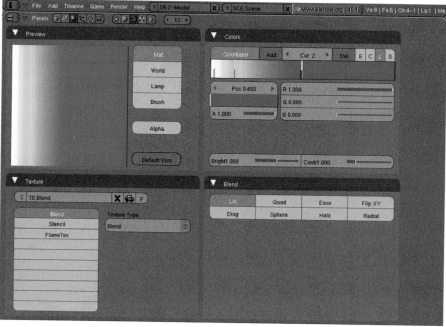

Figure 2.39 Stencil texture mapping

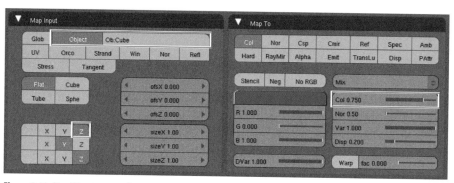

Figure 2.40 Stencil texture mapping

10. Now it's time to turn to the smoke. Add another particle system to the cube object by clicking the right-hand arrow of the system counter (which reads "1 Part 1") in order to set up a second particle system. A blank particle panel appears, displaying "2 Part 2" to indicate that you are working now with the second of two particle systems. Choose Add New from the Particle System drop-down menu. Set the new particle system's values as shown in Figure 2.41. This particle system is named Smoke_1 because it is the first of two smoke systems you will use. This system will represent the smoke that rises from the tips of the flames; this means that it will be set to emit directly from the flame particles as they die. Set the particles as Reactor particles with the Emit From value set to Particle. By default, Reactor particles are targeted to the first particle system on the same mesh, so you don't need to adjust this. On the Physics tab, give the particles a slight random initial velocity and a Z axis acceleration of about 4. On the Extras tab, set the size of the particles to 1.5 and the Rand factor to 0.5. On the Visualization tab, choose Billboard from the drop-down menu. The Render Material should be 2. In the next step, you will add the material that corresponds to this index.

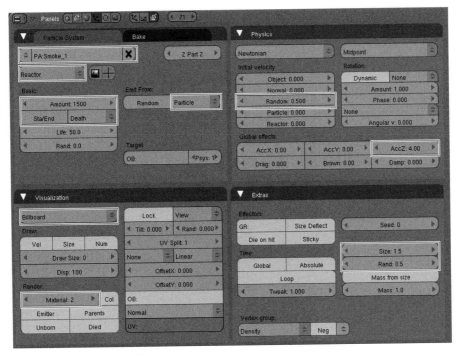

Figure 2.41 Reactor smoke particles

11. Add a new material index to the object in the Edit buttons. Set the Links and Pipeline values as shown in Figure 2.42. Like the Flame material, setting this material to be ray-traceable would be resource-intensive. Unlike flames, however, smoke does cast shadows, so buffer shadows are fine. In the Texture panel, put the Stencil texture that you created in step 8 in the top texture channel by selecting it from the drop-down menu on the Texture tab. Add a new texture beneath the Stencil texture and name it *Smoke*. You'll come back to this texture in a moment. The mapping for the Stencil texture should be done the same way as for the Flame material, except that instead of mapping to the Emit value, it should be mapped to the Alpha value. Also, set DVar to 0.3, as shown in Figure 2.43. This reduces the influence of the Texture value on the Map To value.

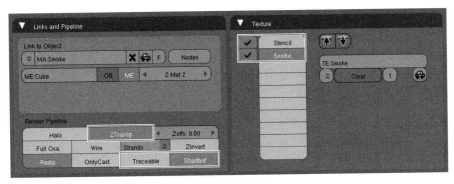

Figure 2.42 Smoke material index

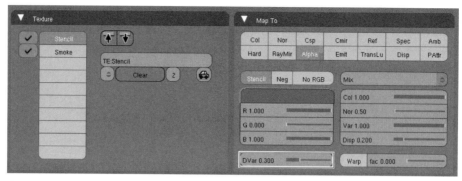

Figure 2.43 Mapping for the Stencil texture

12. The smoke texture is set up as shown in Figure 2.44. The cloud pattern is similar to the one used in the Flame texture: hard noise with maximal noise depth. The bright and dark ends of the colorband are reversed, and both the black color and white color should be set to alpha 1. The material settings are shown in Figure 2.45. Select Object on the Map Input tab and type the name of the empty, **Empty**, into the Ob field. The Map To value should be Col.

Figure 2.44 Cloud texture for smoke

13. Press Alt+A or the Play button on the Timeline to play the animation. At present, the animated particle flame looks something like Figure 2.46. The preview window shows what the flame and smoke looks like, and the actual 3D view shows how the billboard particle systems are being emitted. The effect is almost finished, but not quite. Although it's true that real smoke does rise from the top of a flame, the effect as it is currently set up has the transition as too abrupt. Some smoke should be mingled with the flame from the very beginning. To do this, add one more particle system to the cube, with the settings shown in Figure 2.47. The settings are similar to the original flame, although the initial outward velocity is not as high, so the smoke will not conceal the flame. The material for this particle system is the same as for the first smoke system.

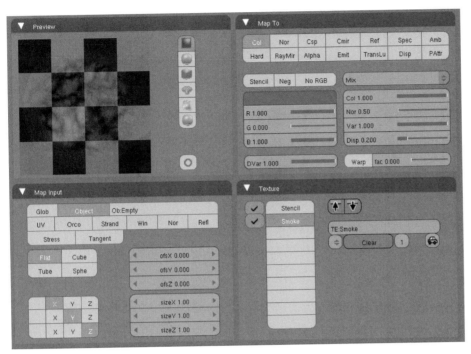

Figure 2.45 Smoke material settings

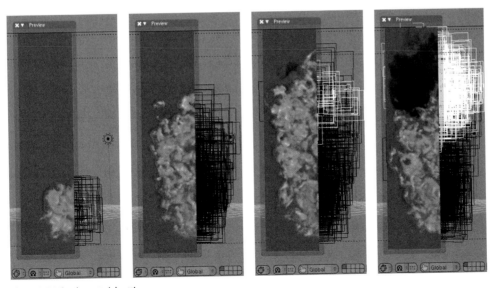

Figure 2.46 Smoke material settings

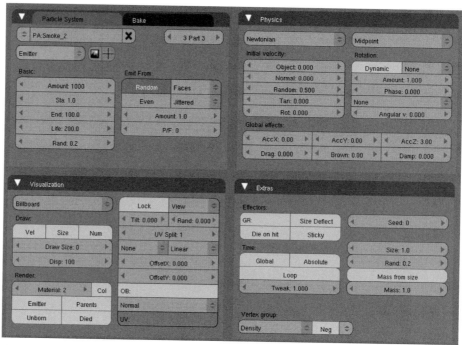

Figure 2.47 A second smoke particle system

14. If you render an animation now, you'll notice something slightly amiss with the flame and smoke. Although the particles move, the textures themselves remain static. This is easy to fix. You've already mapped the textures to the empty. To make the textures move, it is enough to simply animate the empty to move upward. Key the empty's location with the I key, advance a few frames, move the empty upward along the Z axis with the G key and the Z key, and key the location again. In the Ipo Editor, from the Curve menu choose Extend Mode > Extrapolation. You can adjust the angle of the LocZ curve easily by moving the curve control point around in Edit mode. You'll want the curve approximately as shown in Figure 2.48, although it's not necessary to be precise. Render your animation and adjust the speed of the empty as you think it looks best.

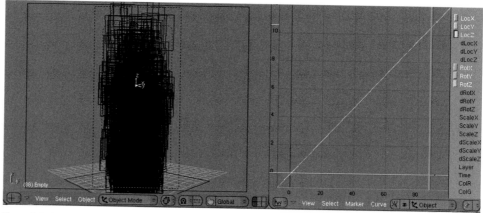

Figure 2.48 Keying the empty's location

15. The final results of this tutorial will render to look something like Figure 2.49. This should give you a general idea of how to make flames, but there are many ways you can continue to adjust and experiment with this effect. To make the appearance and disappearance of individual particles smoother, you can reduce the alpha values of the materials and textures. If you do this, you will probably want to increase the number of particles to maintain the vividness of the flames. Generally speaking, lower alpha values and higher particle counts will yield a smoother effect. Also, try applying forces to the flames. The flame particles will be responsive to wind and other forces upon them, and many interesting effects can be obtained in this way. If you want to control the motion of the flames more precisely (for example, to have flames billowing out of a house window), consider incorporating keyed particle systems with Newtonian systems as shown earlier in the chapter.

Figure 2.49 The rendered flame

As you can see, using textures is an important component of creating certain kinds of effects. In fact, you can use textures to control not only the material properties of particle simulations, but many of the particle attributes themselves, including the timing of their release, their size, and their life span. This is done by selecting the P Attr (particle attribute) option in the Map To panel for the texture. This method is discussed in more detail in Chapter 4.

The BB vs. the Crystal Ball: Using the Explode Modifier

Particles can be useful even when they are not visible. In this example, featuring a small metal ball smashing through a larger glass ball, you'll see that an interesting effect can be obtained with two particle systems, even though neither particle system is actually rendered. One particle system is used only as a trigger for a second Reactor system, and the second system is used as a basis for the Explode modifier, which causes a Mesh object to break apart according to the motion of the particle system. To set up this effect, follow these steps:

1. First add two Icospheres as shown in Figure 2.50. The materials, textures, and background are not important to this effect, so you can set them up however you like. Scale down the second sphere so that the spheres' relative sizes are approximately as shown in the image. The smaller sphere should be placed to the left of the larger sphere, directly along the X axis. Animate the smaller sphere as shown in the Ipo Editor in the figure, so that the small sphere flies through the center of the large sphere. The small sphere should take about 2 seconds to pass from one side of the frame to the other.

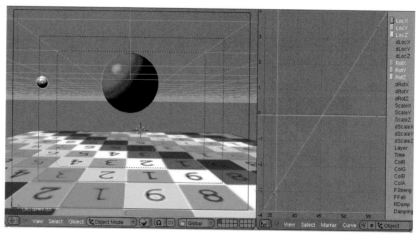

Figure 2.50 Two spheres

2. Set up an Emitter particle system on the small sphere as shown in Figure 2.51. This should have a small initial velocity in the Normal direction; in the example, the value is set at 2. The particles should be set to emit from random faces. I've set the visualization value to Cross only for illustration purposes, but it's not necessary for you to do this. After the particle system is set up, you should be able to run the animation and watch the particles trail out behind the flying ball, as shown in Figure 2.52.

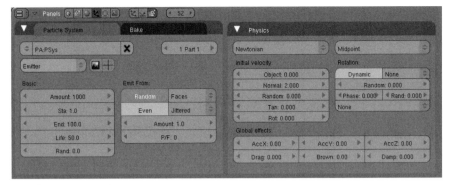

Figure 2.51 Emitter particles

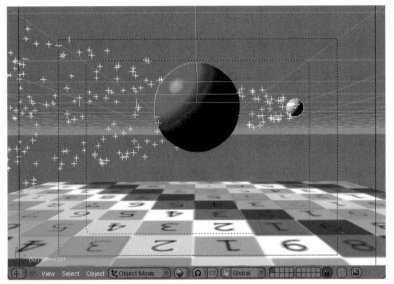

Figure 2.52 Particles trail behind the ball in motion

3. Set up a Reactor particle system on the large ball with the values as shown in Figure 2.53. This particle system will be triggered by proximity to the small ball's particle system, so set that particle system as the Target. Select the Near value from the drop-down menu in the Basic panel, so that the Reactor particles will be triggered when the target particles come near. The Reactor particles will be the basis of the Explode modifier, and their motion will determine the way that the glass ball shatters. They should have a downward (-Z) acceleration, and they should also have more Normal and Random initial velocity. In the example, the Normal and Random velocity values are set at 5, and the acceleration value on the Z axis is –5. If you run the animation now, you will see the Reactor particles emit from the large ball as shown in Figure 2.54. Notice how the Reactor particles (displayed as white circles) respond to the proximity of the Emitter particles (displayed as black crosses) by emitting from left to right across the large ball mesh. In the example, the textured plane beneath the balls is set to deflect particles, as you saw how to do previously in this chapter.

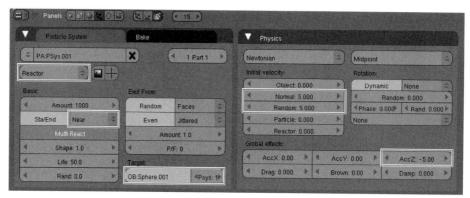

Figure 2.53 Reactor particles

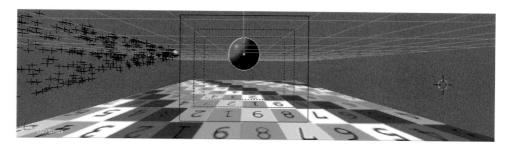

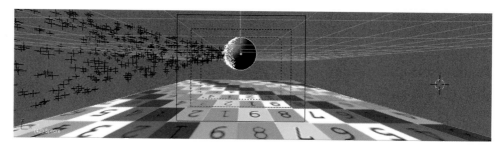

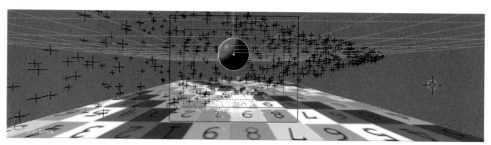

Figure 2.54 Reactor particles reacting

4. Finally, set up an Explode modifier on the large ball as shown in Figure 2.55. Note also that the Particle System modifier should be set not to render by clicking the button highlighted in the figure. This should also be set in the same way for the Emitter particle system on the small ball. (Another way to accomplish this is to set Visualization to None in the particle panels.) The Explode modifier causes the mesh to break apart and its pieces to follow the movement of the particles as they emit from the mesh, as you can see in Figure 2.56. With the particle set not to render, the resulting rendered animation will look something like Figure 2.57. Try experimenting with particle rotation here to make the smashing action even more dynamic.

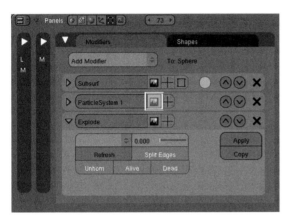

Figure 2.55 The Explode modifier

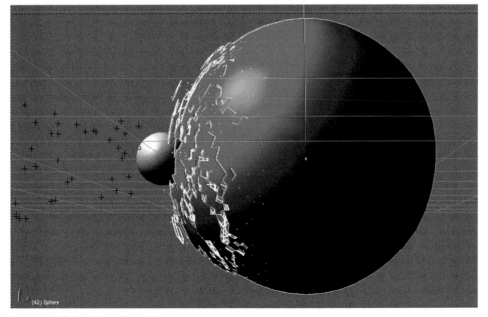

Figure 2.56 The Explode modifier's effect on the mesh

Figure 2.57 The full collision rendered

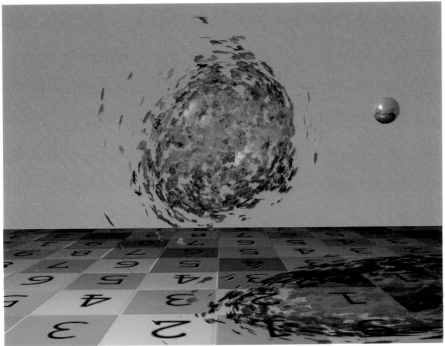

Figure 2.57 *(continued)*

Figure 2.57 The full collision rendered

Janne Karhu

The developer responsible for the most recent upgrade of the particle system is Janne Karhu (jahka), a 23-year-old student of physics at the University of Turku, Finland. Janne has been a Blender user since 1998, when he stumbled on the Blender website in a computer class in the eighth grade, but in the last two years he began to turn his attention to coding. Being a physics student, he was drawn to extending the existing particle system at first, but eventually realized that the functionality he was after would require a full recode. He writes, "I think the best thing in working with Blender both as an artist and a developer is the amazing community. Especially what kept me going during the rewrite were all the great ideas and positive comments that I got from the users and other developers."

Boids!

The third option for the physics of particles is boids. *Boids* are used to represent the movement of swarms of insects, schools of fish, flocks of birds, and other animals moving in groups. All have similar patterns of behavior that can be mimicked by using a fixed set of criteria to determine the direction and speed of each entity's movements at each point in time.

In a boids system, each particle is sensitive to certain local and global values: its own speed and direction; its neighbors' speed, direction, and proximity; the speed, direction, and proximity of other objects defined as predators, goals, or deflection objects; and the average velocity of the entire swarm. These values are the basis for calculating the constraints that guide the motion of the boids. You can think of these behavioral constraints as basic things that the boid wants to do or to avoid. The constraints are as follows:

Collision represents the boid's desire to avoid hitting deflection objects.

Avoid represents the boid's desire to escape from "predators." Predators are objects that have negative-strength force fields associated with them.

Crowd represents the boid's desire to avoid hitting other boids. High prioritization of this value results in flocks that are clustered less tightly.

Center represents the boid's desire to move toward the center of the flock. A high priority on this value tends to cluster the flock together more tightly.

AvVel represents the boid's desire to maintain the average speed of the entire flock.

Velocity represents the boid's desire to match the speed of nearby boids.

Goal represents the boid's desire to approach a goal object. A goal is an object that has a positive-strength force field associated with it.

Level causes the boids to tend toward the average Z value (distance from the camera) of the group.

These behavioral constraints each have a numerical value that determines their strength, and also an ordering, that can be changed by using the up- and down-arrow buttons to the left of each constraint's name. By adjusting the strength and priority of these constraints in the fields shown in Figure 2.58, you change the overall behavior of the boids system. By default, boids behavior occurs in 3D, as in the case of birds, fish, and flying insects. To simulate ants or other swarmlike behaviors that occur over a surface, you can select the 2D option in the Physics panel. Doing so will also present you with an optional Ob field that will enable you to enter the name of an object for the boids to crawl over.

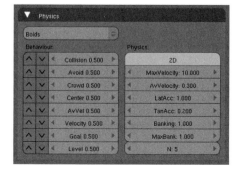

Figure 2.58
Boids constraints

Note: Boids have been around since Craig Reynolds first implemented a boids system in 1986 and coined the term. The idea behind boids was to use a minimal set of parameters and weighted constraints on the motion of entities in a group to simulate the way living things behave when moving in groups. When these simple rules are applied to individual boid entities' motion, a complex pattern emerges. Craig Reynolds' boids page is an excellent resource for learning more about boids and similar emergent behaviors. You can find that page at www.red3d.com/cwr/boids.

Setting Up the Boids System

Setting up a basic boids system is simple. As with other particle systems, it is necessary to create an emitter (boids themselves can be of either Emitter or Reactor particle types). Any mesh object can be an emitter. Set the Emit From value to Random and choose Boids from the drop-down menu on the Physics tab. That is all there is to it to create a simple swarm of particles. Figure 2.59 depicts a swarm of boids emitting from an Icosphere. All the values are defaults except for the visualization type, which I have set as crosses for illustration purposes.

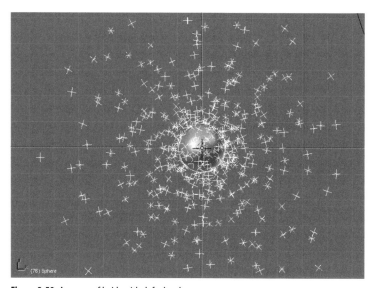

Figure 2.59 A swarm of boids with default values

As you can see if you press Alt+A with this setup, the boids emanate outward from the emitter object in indirect, wiggly trajectories. At each step, their velocity is recalculated to enable the boids to continue their current course, subject to the default constraints. Because the Crowd constraint makes it a priority for the boids to avoid colliding with each other, and there are no goals, predators, or deflection objects to influence their trajectories, they tend to move farther and farther away from each other.

Working with Goals and Predators

Goals and predators are created by placing an object on the same layer as the boids system with a Spherical force field. A positive value in the force field means the object is a goal, and a negative value in the force field means the object is a predator. There are three factors that determine how a boid behaves with respect to a goal or a predator: the priority of the Goal or Avoid constraint in the boid settings, the strength of the Goal or Avoid constraint in the boid settings, and the strength of the Spherical force field on the goal or predator object itself. Particularly when there are more than one goal or predator objects in the scene, or when there are multiple boids systems, these different values can be combined to create specific patterns and behaviors.

> **Note:** Spherical force field values have the opposite effect on boids as they do on particles with Newtonian physics. Positive Spherical force-field values repel Newtonian particles, and negative values attract them, whereas with boids, a positive value represents an attractive goal, and a negative value represents a predator to be avoided. Although this may seem counterintuitive at first, it does serve as a reminder of the difference between the concepts of *forces* for Newtonian particles and *goals and predators* for boids.

In Figure 2.60, you can see the effect of adding an empty with a Spherical force of strength 100, and setting the Goal value to top priority. The boids head straight toward the goal after being emitted from the emitter mesh. After they reach the goal, they circle back and pass through it again and again as long as they continue to be alive.

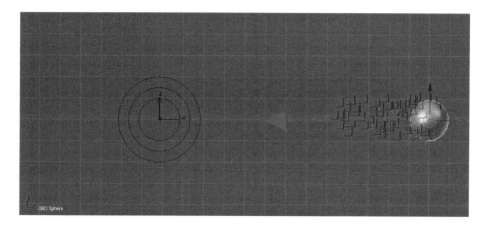

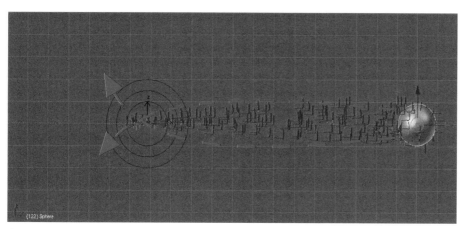

Figure 2.60 *(continued)*

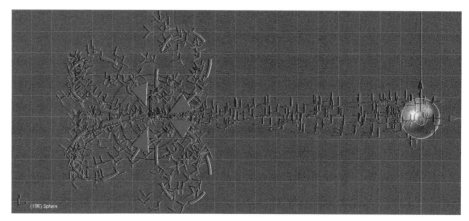

Figure 2.60 A boids system pursuing a goal

In Figure 2.61, a second empty is added, with a –10 strength Spherical force. This is a predator. I set Avoid to top priority in the boids constraints, and bumped Goal down to second. With these values, as you can see in the figure, the boids make a wide arc around the predator object and circle back to meet the goal object.

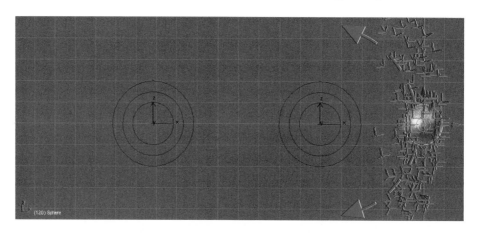

Figure 2.61 A boids system with a goal and a predator

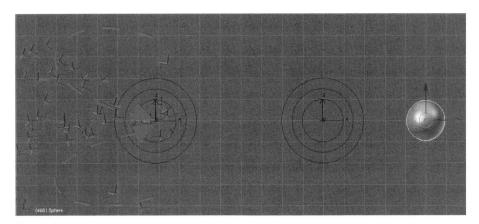

Figure 2.61 *(continued)*

Finally, in Figure 2.62, the same settings are used as in the previous example, except that the predator is animated to pass between the boids' origin and the goal. As you can see, the boids respond in real-time to this moving predator, making their way around one side and then the other as the predator passes. Both predators and goals can be animated, resulting in the expected boids' behavior. If you've ever been chased by a swarm of bees, you already know something about how boids behave when pursuing a moving goal.

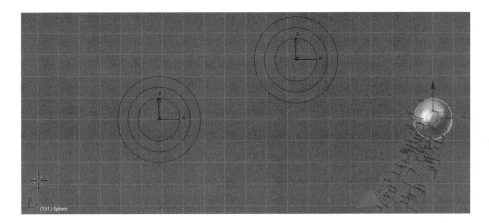

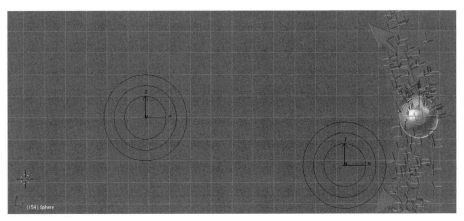

Figure 2.62 A boids system with a goal and a moving predator

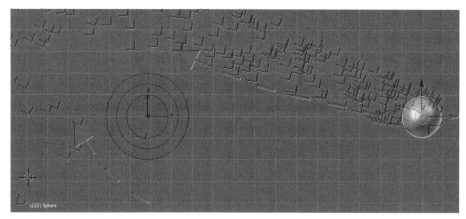

Figure 2.62 *(continued)*

Boids can be put to many uses, but because they are fundamentally intended to mimic the behavior of living creatures, one of the primary uses for them is to animate actual animals. In the next section, you'll see how to make a simple bird model that can be easily used with a boids simulation to create a convincing flock of birds.

Creating a Simple Flying Bird

An ideal example of the use of a boids system is a flock of birds. To create this effect, it's necessary to start by setting up the object that will exhibit the boids behavior. To set up a simple flying bird, follow these steps:

1. Model the bird along the lines of Figure 2.63. I started with a UV sphere with eight segments and eight rings, and I edited the nose and tail by using the proportional editing tool. The wings and the tail are separate divided planes. The object has a subsurface modifier, and Set Smooth is selected. The image on the left of the figure is seen from above, with NUM7. Make sure that the bird is facing this direction, pointing along the Y axis with its wings extending along the X axis. The scale of the bird is approximately 4 Blender Units (BUs) long and 8 BUs wide from wing tip to wing tip. In Object mode, press Ctrl+A to set the scale and rotation.

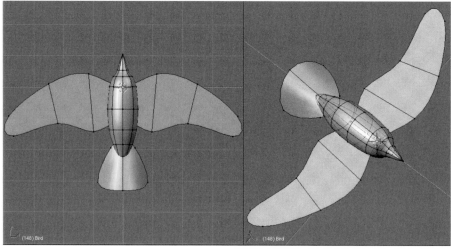

Figure 2.63 The bird model

2. Create a vertex group by clicking New under Vertex Groups and typing the name *Wings*. Assign vertices to this group as shown in Figure 2.64 by selecting those vertices and clicking Assign.

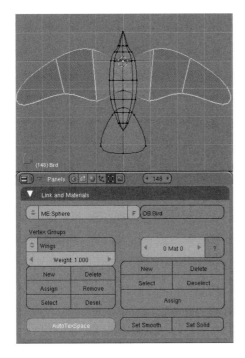

Figure 2.64
Wings vertex group

3. Tab into Object mode and add a Wave modifier with the settings as shown in Figure 2.65. By entering *Wings* in the VGroup field, you ensure that the modifier acts only on the vertices in that vertex group. Press Alt+A to test the motion of the wings. The wings should flap convincingly. If not, adjust the parameters of the Wave modifier until you are satisfied with the way the wings are moving. For truly realistic bird wing movements, it would be necessary to create a sophisticated rig and animate it. In this case, however, the birds are intended to be seen from a distance and in a large group, so the Wave modifier will be sufficient.

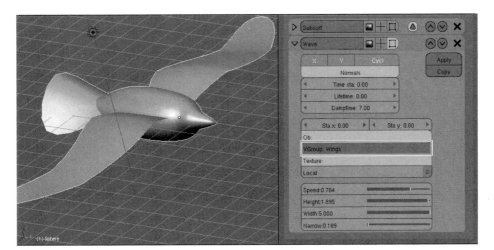

Figure 2.65 Wave modifier

After you have finished the model, you use it as a visualization object for a boids system like the one described earlier, as shown in Figure 2.66.

Figure 2.66 A flock of boids

As you can see, there are many possibilities for how to use dynamic particles. You can combine the methods described in this chapter in virtually unlimited ways. Use Reactor particles triggered by raindrops to create splashes on pavement, or trigger them with invisible Emitter particles to kick up dust devils. Target keyed strand particles on a boids system to create a writhing, lifelike bundle of tentacles. Use Group visualization and particle-emit Reactor particles to create a rocket that explodes in a shower of multicolored confetti.

As versatile and powerful as dynamic particles are, there is still more to learn about Blender's particle system. In Chapter 4, you'll see how to use this system to create realistic hair and other strandlike effects. But first, it's necessary to take a slight detour to look at how Blender deals with soft bodies.

Getting Flexible with Soft Bodies and Cloth

In nature, materials exhibit different properties of rigidity and structural responsiveness to the forces on them. Many materials are flexible, and deform when acted upon by forces such as gravity and friction. Blender's soft body simulation enables you to easily represent the behavior of a wide variety of flexible materials. Depending on the parameter settings you use, you can use soft body simulations to animate materials as varied as gelatin, sheet metal, and cloth.

3

Chapter Contents
Getting the hard facts on soft bodies
Getting jiggly with lattices
Creating cloth and clothing
Simulating demolition

Getting the Hard Facts on Soft Bodies

One of the basic aspects of animating with meshes is mesh deformation. In Blender, there are many ways to deform a mesh. You can use shape keys, hooks, and modifiers such as armatures, lattices, curves, displacement, waves, or others. Each of these methods enables different kinds of deformations, and the combination of them yields a considerable amount of control for animators. Nevertheless, some kinds of deformations are still difficult or impossible to achieve convincingly without a dedicated simulation. Soft body physics is a good example of this kind of deformation.

Soft body dynamics refers to the way that flexible materials deform in response to the forces on them. In real life, many things we deal with all the time exhibit soft body behavior: cloth, rubber, paper—even metal, when under the right kinds of stress. These objects bounce, crumple, and jiggle in ways that would often not be practical to try to animate by hand. By setting up a soft body simulator, you can get Blender to do the work for you.

Understanding Soft Body Basics

Soft body dynamics works by treating a mesh as a network of springs. In the default case, the edges of the mesh are given springlike behavior, as visualized in Figure 3.1.

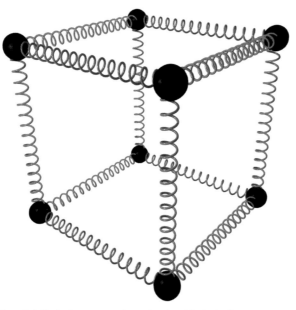

Figure 3.1 Mesh edges are treated as springs in soft body simulation.

You can set parameters to determine how these "springs" react to forces and how the soft body simulation itself interacts with the mesh. These parameters can be set in the Soft Body tab in the Physics Buttons area, after you have activated soft bodies for an object by clicking Soft Body. The parameters to determine forces are as follows:

Friction determines the degree to which the soft body simulation is affected by external forces.

Mass determines how much force is necessary to deform the soft body. Higher mass values lead to slower movement, less responsiveness to impacts, and greater momentum after the mesh is in motion.

Grav sets the value of gravity in meters per second per second. By default this is 9.8. This value should not be set to zero.

Speed determines how quickly the simulation moves. Unlike Mass, however, Speed does not affect how much force is needed to deform the object.

The Use Goal and Use Edges options restrict the freedom of the soft body simulation's movement. Use Goal restricts the simulation according to the weight values of a specific vertex group (the case is slightly different for lattices and curves, as you will see later in this chapter). Vertices with a value of 1 for the goal weight are not treated as soft bodies at all, and vertices with value of 0 are deformed completely by the soft body simulation. Vertices with a 0 goal value are not influenced by ordinary mesh deformers such as armatures. The degree to which vertices are held to their original position is determined by the parameter values in this section, as you'll see.

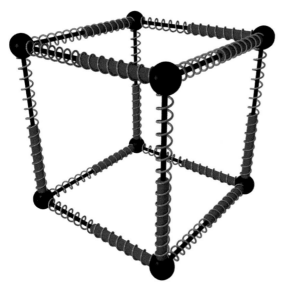

Figure 3.2 Edge damping works similarly to hydraulic shock absorbers.

The Use Edges option restricts the deformation of the soft body by affecting the spring properties of the edges. The stiffness of the edges is controlled by E Pull, which affects how far the springs can extend, and E Push, which affects how far the springs can compress. E Damp affects the force necessary to compress or extend the springs. You can visualize damping as being similar to the effect of hydraulic shock absorbers, as shown in Figure 3.2. The Bend value controls the degree to which vertices allow edges to move freely in relation to each other. When the Stiff Quads option (discussed in the next section) is selected, the diagonals across each quad face are also treated as springs, as shown in Figure 3.3. In this case, the Shear value controls how strong the diagonal strings are. The Aero value adds an effect that is similar to friction but results in a more-localized fluttering of the edges (the N to the left of Aero enables a newer implementation of the same basic functionality).

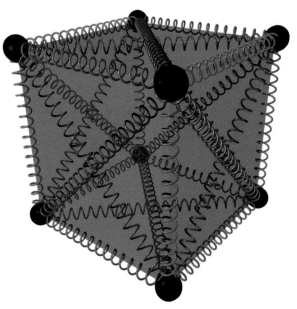

Figure 3.3 Diagonals are also treated as springs when Stiff Quads is selected.

Baking

As in the case of the particles system the results of soft body and cloth simulations can be baked to a cache for quicker access in subsequent plays of the animation. Baking for soft bodies and cloth is done on the Soft Body Collision and Cloth Collision tabs respectively, and works exactly the same as it does for particles; simply enter the values of the start and end frames for the time period you want to bake, and click the Bake button.

Animating a Spring with Soft Bodies

Because springlike behavior is so central to the way soft bodies work, this section demonstrates the simplest possible soft body setup, just a single edge, by using it to drive the motion of the posable spring from Chapter 1, "Re-creating the World: An Overview." If you made the spring in that tutorial, open the file you made now. Otherwise, you can find the file on the CD that accompanies this book. To create a soft body object that will control the movement of the spring, follow these steps:

1. The soft body object you'll be using will be composed simply of two vertices and an edge. I've created this by adding a cube (see Figure 3.4) and deleting the six vertices (see Figure 3.5). Any simple mesh object will do for this.

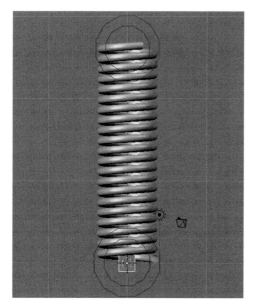

Figure 3.4 Add a mesh object.

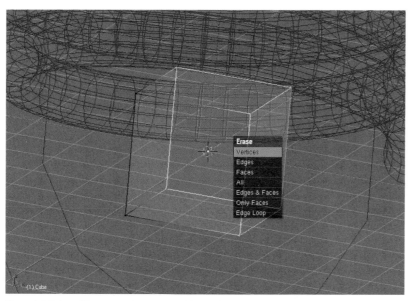

Figure 3.5 Delete all but two vertices, connected by an edge.

2. Select the armature and enter Pose mode. Select the lower control bone as shown in Figure 3.6 and snap the cursor to that bone, using Shift+S to access the Snap menu and choosing Cursor > Selection. Return to Object mode, select the Mesh object, enter Edit mode, and select one vertex. Snap the vertex to the cursor with Shift+S and then Selection > Cursor, as shown in Figure 3.7. Return again to Object mode, and add an empty to the same point, as shown in Figure 3.8. Because there is already an empty in the scene (the one controlling the Array modifier), this new empty will be automatically named Empty.001.

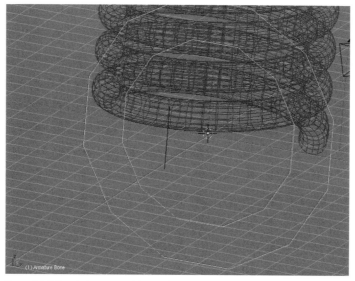

Figure 3.6 Select the lower control bone and snap the cursor to it.

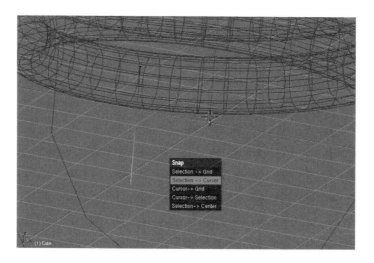

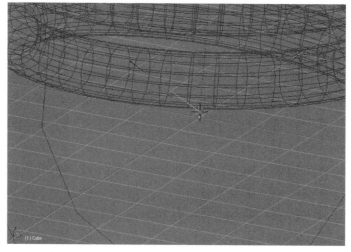

Figure 3.7 Snap one vertex to the cursor.

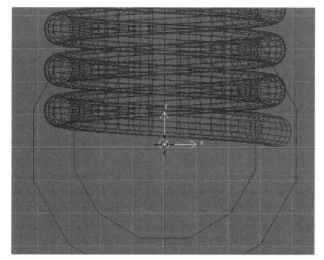

Figure 3.8 Add an empty.

3. Follow the same procedure as in step 2 for the top control bone. Using the cursor and Shift+S, snap the other vertex to the location of the bone, and add an empty. This empty will be named Empty.002.

4. In Object mode, select Empty.002, and then Shift-select the two-vertex Mesh object. Enter Edit mode and select the topmost vertex. Press Ctrl+P and select Make Vertex Parent, as shown in Figure 3.9. Follow the same procedure to vertex-parent Empty.001 to the bottom vertex.

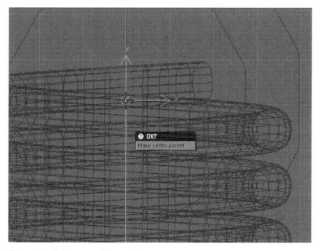

Figure 3.9 Vertex-parent the empty.

5. To make the empties' movement control the armature, set up Copy Location constraints for each of the bones. To do this, select the armature and enter Pose mode. Select each control bone and add a Copy Location constraint targeted to the appropriate empty, as shown in Figure 3.10. If you followed the steps in the same order as I did, the top bone will be constrained to Empty.002 and the bottom bone will be constrained to Empty.001.

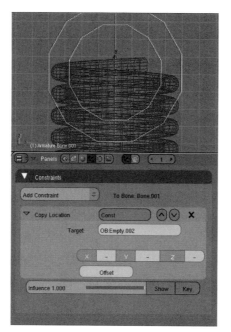
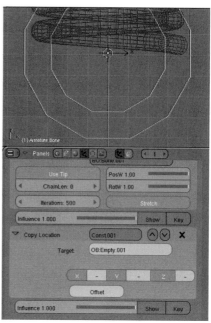

Figure 3.10 Copy Location constraints on the control bones

6. Now it's time to set up the soft body object. A common way to control soft bodies is by use of a vertex group and a *goal*. When this option is used, vertices that have a high weight for the group are fixed in place to the mesh's ordinary shape (including any non-soft-body deformations), and are not influenced by the soft body simulation. Vertices with a low goal weight are freer to move around in accordance with the soft body simulation. The mesh object in this example has only two vertices. You will use a goal vertex group to nail the top vertex in place, while allowing the bottom vertex to exhibit soft body behavior. To do this, select the mesh object and enter Edit mode. In the Links and Materials tab, under Vertex Groups, click New. Type **SoftGoal** in the name field of the new vertex group. Now select the top vertex of the mesh, as shown in Figure 3.11, and click Assign. The default weight assignment value is 1, so this will assign a 1 value to this vertex.

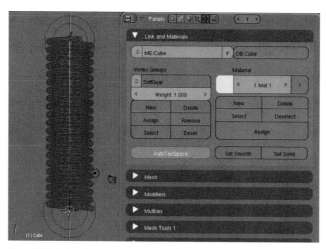

Figure 3.11 Assign the top vertex to the SoftGoal vertex group.

7. Finally, activate the soft body simulation. Return to Object mode and with the Mesh object still selected, click the Soft Body button on the Soft Body tab in the Physics Buttons area. To start, set the values as shown in Figure 3.12. Run the simulation by pressing Alt+A, and watch the spring deform as shown in Figure 3.13.

The point of this tutorial was to set up the simplest and most explicit possible example of what soft bodies actually do. You should experiment with this spring to find out how the different soft body parameters affect its behavior. Try changing the mass, stiffness, and speed values and see what happens. Try animating the location and rotation of the soft body mesh (remember, the armature is constrained to follow the empties, and the empties are vertex-parented to the mesh). If you bake the soft body and then animate the object, what happens? (Hint: To do this right, you'll need to free the bake by clicking Free Bake in Bake Settings.)

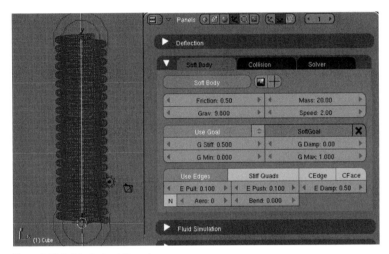

Figure 3.12 Soft body simulation values

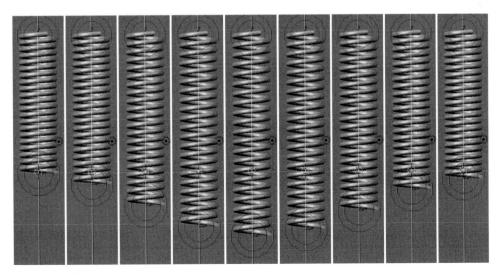

Figure 3.13 Soft body spring in action

Using Force Fields and Collision

Soft bodies can interact with other objects and forces in much the same way that particle systems can, as described in Chapter 2, "The Nitty-Gritty on Particles." Forces behave essentially the same for both particles and soft bodies. Soft body collision is slightly different from collision for particles. There is no permeability parameter, but there are two parameters, Inner and Outer, which create the effect of a thickening of the internal or external surface of the collision object. The optimal settings for these values varies depending on the situation, but a general rule is that increasing the value of one of these parameters should help diminish penetration from that side of the mesh. As you'll see, there are other ways to minimize penetration, if these parameters don't do the trick. The Damping value here has essentially the same function as the Damping value for particles collision: It reduces the amount of kinetic energy in the deflected object when it collides, resulting in a less-bouncy collision.

Figure 3.14 shows a still from an animation of drapes that uses both force fields and collision objects. For convincing, nonstretchy cloth, I set the Soft Body and Soft Body Collision tab settings as shown in Figure 3.15. Edge stiffness is high to reduce stretchiness, but goal stiffness is low to enable the cloth to deform freely. It is important to activate self-collision for cloth in order to avoid the object penetrating itself. The drapes themselves are simply subdivided planes. A goal vertex group is used to fix the drapes in place, and you can see the values of the vertices shown in Weight Paint mode in Figure 3.16.

Figure 3.14 Animated soft body drapes with forces and collision

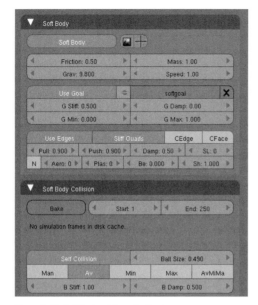

Figure 3.15 Soft body settings for the drapes

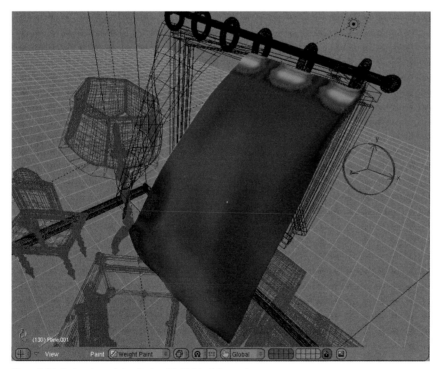

Figure 3.16 Goal vertex weights displayed in Weight Paint mode

For wind, I used two empties with Wind force fields activated. The empties are positioned outside the window, pointing inward. Their locations, rotations, and strengths are animated with keys as shown in Figure 3.17, to create a gently shifting wind.

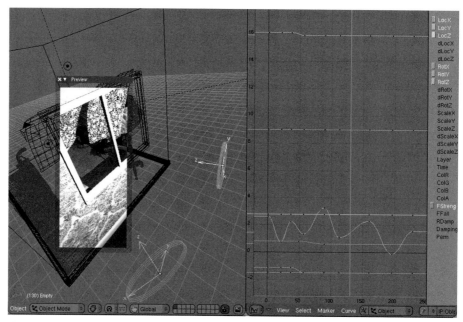

Figure 3.17 Forces animated with Ipo curves

Collision detection between soft body objects and collision objects is good, but not perfect. Even with Inner and Outer thickness parameters set to their optimal values, penetration can occur. In this example, when I set the lampshade as a collision object, I found that no matter what parameters I used, I had an unacceptable level of penetration with the drapes. It was very noticeable that parts of the lampshade were passing through the blinds at certain moments.

A useful solution for this is to create a separate, unrendered collision object to force the soft body to respect the original object's boundaries. I added a separate mesh, roughly the same shape as the original lampshade and slightly larger. This is the red object shown in Figure 3.18. As you can see by looking at this object's entry in the Outliner, it is set not to render. Normally when working, I set objects like this to Wireframe Draw mode so I can see where they are without them being obtrusive. I've set this one to Solid Draw mode only for illustration purposes. The collision values for this object are shown in Figure 3.19.

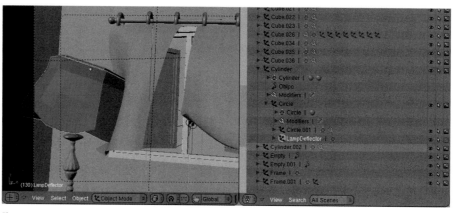

Figure 3.18 A special collision object for the lampshade

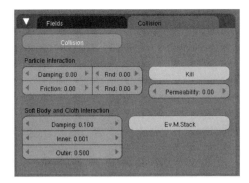

Figure 3.19
Collision values for
the lampshade deflector

Soft body objects also can be deflector objects and interact with other soft body objects, as in the case of the balls in Figure 3.20. The balls are initially set up as shown in Figure 3.21, with the plane beneath them set as a deflector object. The balls' own soft body settings are shown in Figure 3.22. Note especially the Bend value. The default is 0. To make the balls maintain their shape, Bend must be set to a higher value. A value of 1 will give the balls about the hardness of a well-inflated soccer ball. I've set the value to 0.8, which as you can see results in much softer-seeming balls.

Figure 3.20 Soft balls bouncing together

Working with Soft Bodies and Curves

Meshes are not the only objects that can be soft body objects. Curves and lattices can also have soft body simulations applied in a useful way. (Strictly speaking, Non-Uniform Rational B-Splines, or NURBS for short, surfaces also can take soft body simulations, but like most things about NURBS in Blender, the feature is only partially developed and is not really usable.) Later in this chapter, you'll see how lattices can be useful to create bouncy effects in objects. In this section, I'll show you an example of how a soft body curve can be used to control the movement of a mesh chain and pendant.

Figure 3.21 Ball setup

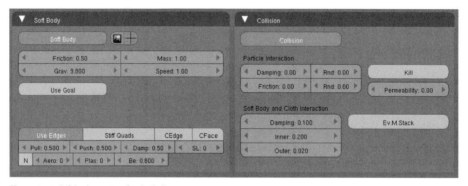

Figure 3.22 Soft body settings for the balls

Before you begin, check the CD for the file pendant.blend. Working with Curve modifiers can be tricky and sensitive to initial conditions, so if you get mixed up at any point along the way working on this tutorial, refer to that file to help get your bearings. In the file, you'll find the model of the cameo pendant shown in Figure 3.23. You can append the Pendant object from the file on the disc to your own new file by starting a new Blender session and choosing File > Append Or Link. When you do this, a file browser opens in Blender. Find the file pendant.blend in the file browser. Click on the filename and you will see that it behaves as a directory in the Blender file browser, and you will see a list of data types. Choose Object, and then finally select the object named Pendant. Click Load Library, and the pendant object loads into your current scene. (Note that by default, objects are appended to the same layer that they were in in the original file.)

If you prefer, you can make your own pendant. If you do use an alternate pendant, make sure the center of the Pendant object is at the point where the connecting link of the chain should be.

Figure 3.23 A pendant to start with

To create the soft body chain, follow these steps:

1. Select the pendant and snap the cursor to the object by using Shift+S to access the Snap menu and then choosing Cursor > Selected. Add a Torus object by pressing the spacebar and choosing Add > Mesh > Torus. Use the values shown in Figure 3.24 for the torus. The torus should look as shown in Figure 3.25. Tab into Object mode and add an empty in the same way, as shown in Figure 3.26.

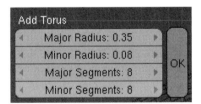

Figure 3.24 Values for the torus

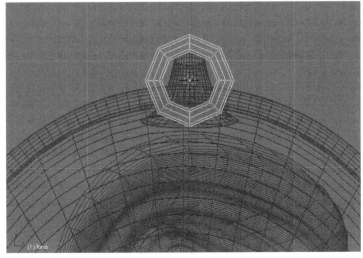

Figure 3.25 Adding a torus

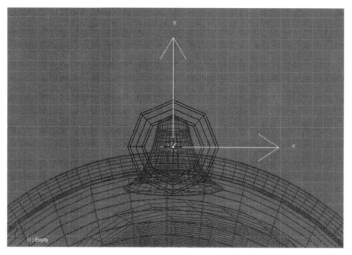

Figure 3.26 Adding an empty

2. Select the Torus object and click Add Modifier on the Modifiers tab of the Edit Buttons area. Select Array modifier from the drop-down list, and select Object Offset with an Ob value of Empty, as shown in Figure 3.27. You may recall a similar step in constructing the spring in Chapter 1. Move the empty upward along the Z axis to offset for the links of the chain, as shown in Figure 3.28. When the offset looks right, change the value of the Array modifier's Count from 2 to 51, as shown in Figure 3.29. After that, click Apply on the Array modifier to make the modified mesh real. With the gold material from the pendant applied and a Subsurf modifier added, the mesh modeling of the chain is finished.

3. For the purposes of this tutorial, it is better to have the Chain object's center nearer the top of the chain. To do this, select the loop around the topmost cross-section of the topmost link, by pressing Alt+Right Mouse Button (RMB), and snap the cursor to selection by pressing Shift+S, so that the cursor is positioned as shown in Figure 3.30. Tab into Object mode and click Center Cursor on the Mesh tab of the Edit Buttons area to place the cursor as shown in Figure 3.31. Next, apply scale and rotation to the object by pressing Ctrl+A.

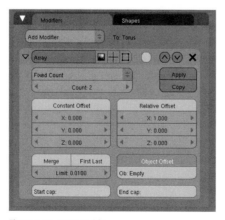

Figure 3.27 Array modifier

Figure 3.28 Object Offset with an empty

Figure 3.29
Change the Count value to 51

4. Snap the cursor to the chain's center, and add a Bezier curve by pressing the space-bar and then choosing Add > Curve > Bezier Curve as shown in Figure 3.32. In Object mode, rotate the curve 90 degrees on the X axis by pressing the R key, then the X key, and then entering **90**. Press the Tab key to enter Edit mode, and enable 3D curve editing by clicking the 3D button on the Curve and Surface tab of the Edit Buttons area. There are two control points by default on a Bezier curve, and each control point has two handles. Using the 3D cursor and snapping with Ctrl+S,

snap the leftmost control point of the curve to the location of the chain's center, and snap the rightmost control point of the curve to the pendant's center, at the bottom end of the chain. Note that it is a quirk of Blender curves that snapping a control point to a location will automatically snap both handles to the same location. This will cause problems later, so you should pull the handles away from the control point after snapping. Do this by right-clicking on the point where the control point and handles are. This selects a handle. Draw the handle upward by pressing the G key followed by the Z key. When you move one handle, the other will automatically move in the opposite direction. For this tutorial, it is enough to make sure that the handles are slightly offset from the control point itself. Finally, while still in Edit mode, select the entire curve by pressing the A key, and subdivide the curve twice by pressing the W key followed by Specials > Subdivide two times. The curve should now have five control points (including the two at the ends), as shown in Figure 3.33.

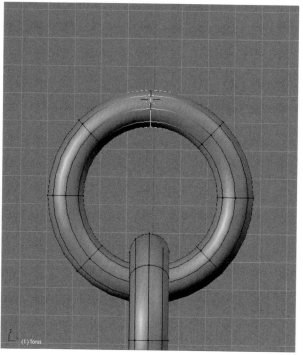

Figure 3.30 Positioning the cursor

5. Tab into Object mode and select the chain. On the Modifiers tab, add a Curve modifier, and set the values as shown in Figure 3.34. When you first add the modifier, don't worry if the object suddenly shoots out in a strange direction. The modifier needs to be set to operate along the correct axis, in this case –Y.

6. Double-check the position of the pendant in relation to the change and adjust the position if necessary because of deformation of the Curve modifier. When the pendant is in the right spot, vertex-parent it to the bottom link of the chain: Select the pendant, Shift-select the chain mesh, tab into Edit mode, select the three vertices shown in Figure 3.35, and press Ctrl+P.

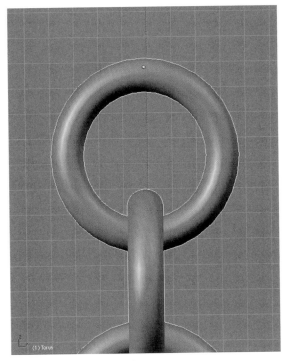

Figure 3.31 Repositioning the object center

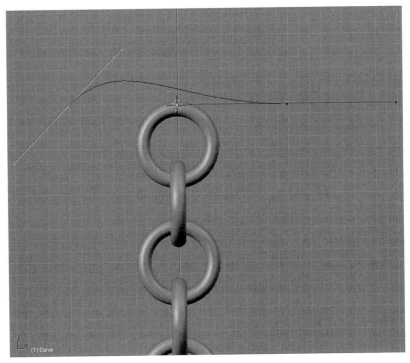

Figure 3.32 Add a curve.

Figure 3.33 Subdivide the curve twice.

Figure 3.34 Curve modifier

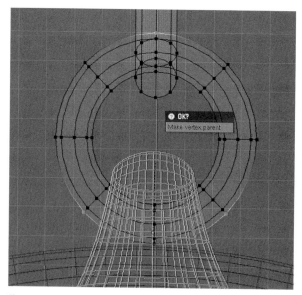

Figure 3.35 Vertex parent

7. You should now be able to pose the chain and pendant by moving control points of the curve, as shown in Figure 3.36. To return to the original position, press Ctrl+Z to undo the posing. Unlike the case of an armature, there is no concept of a "rest pose" for a curve. When you pose the curve like this, you will notice something else also: The curve deforms in only two dimensions. That is because you have not specified that the curve should be calculated in 3D. Change this by tabbing into Object mode and clicking 3D on the Curve And Surface tab, as shown in Figure 3.37.

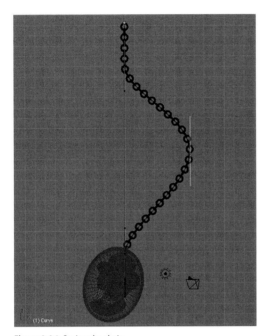

Figure 3.36 Posing the chain

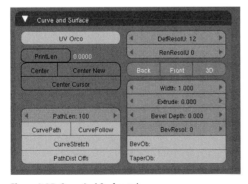

Figure 3.37 Curve And Surface tab

8. Curves do not support vertex groups, so a slightly different method is used to associate weights to control points. Similarly to the spring example in the previous section of this chapter, we'll fix one control point in place by associating it with a soft body goal later. To set up the weights, tab into Edit mode on the curve, select the topmost control point, and press the N key to open the Transform Properties window. Set the Weight value to 1, as shown in Figure 3.38.

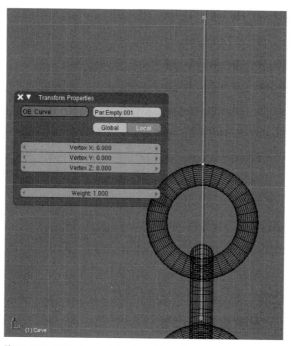

Figure 3.38 Setting the control point weight to 1

9. You'll add an empty to make it easier to control and animate the chain. Snap the cursor to the top control point, tab into Object mode, and add an empty by pressing the spacebar and choosing Add > Empty. Shift-select the curve, the chain object, and the empty (in that order), and parent the curve and chain to the empty by pressing Ctrl+P, as shown in Figure 3.39.

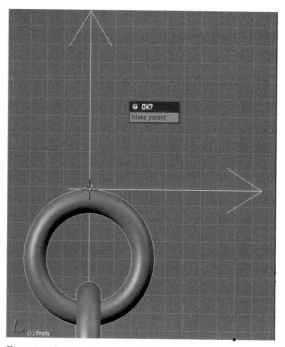

Figure 3.39 Parenting the curve and chain to an empty

10. Now you are ready to activate a soft body simulation on the Curve object. Do this in the same way that you did in the previous example: by clicking the Soft Body button on the Soft Body tab in the Physics Buttons area. Use the settings shown in Figure 3.40. Note the button highlighted in the figure. This option takes the place of soft-body goal vertex groups in the case of curves and lattices, and sets the goal weights based on the control point weights you set in step 8. This ensures that the topmost control point will stay fixed to its position and follow the movement of the parent object, the empty.

Figure 3.40 Soft body parameters

11. Animate the movement of the chain by keyframing the empty's movement. The empty will behave as a grip on the end of the chain that you can move or rotate however you like, and the soft body chain will react to the movement as shown in Figure 3.41. After keyframing the movement of the empty, click the Bake Settings button to select the bake options. Set the start and end frames appropriately and play the animation. When the animation has played through once, the simulation will have been completely cached, and you will be able to move forward and backward along the Timeline and see the deformation of the chain. The simulation is not completely natural, because it does not take into consideration factors such as the mass of the pendant on the end of the chain, but it is convincing enough for many shots.

You've probably noticed that this particular method results in a deformation of the actual chain mesh, which means that the links themselves are bending with the curve. For many purposes, this is not noticeable enough to be a problem. If you need more-realistic chain behavior, obviously the rigging will need to be more complex. For a more-realistic rigged chain, incorporating an armature might be the best solution. Empties can be vertex-parented to curve control points just as they can to mesh vertices, so techniques similar to those described in the spring tutorial earlier in this chapter can be extended to control more-sophisticated armatures. In Chapter 6, "Bullet Physics and the Blender Game Engine," you will also see how to simulate the behavior of rigid bodies interacting. You can draw on those techniques as well, and combine simulations in creative ways to get exactly the effect you are after.

Figure 3.41
Animating the motion of the empty results in soft body movement of the chain.

Using Stress-Mapped Textures for Rubbery Surfaces

Soft body simulations on simple surface meshes are a common way to get clothlike or rubbery effects. Later in this chapter, you'll see more on using soft bodies for clothing. This section demonstrates an interesting texture-mapping feature that can be useful for creating realistic stress effects on surfaces whose properties (such as transparency and color) change when stretched. Rubber is a typical example of this sort of thing. A deflated balloon is completely opaque, but when it is filled with air, it becomes transparent. If you stretch a balloon with your fingers, the spot where the balloon is most stretched has different properties from the rest of the balloon.

In Blender, the measure of how much an edge is deformed (by a shape key, armature, simulation, or modifier) from its base mesh length is called *stress*. A *stress-mapped texture* is a particular kind of Blend texture that maps the range of the Blend values onto the surface of the mesh based on the level of stress on the edges of the mesh. I took the following steps to set up an example of stress-mapping in a simple swatch of rubbery material:

1. First, I added a plane, pressed the W key, and selected Subdivide Multi with a value of 18. I added a Subsurf modifier and activated Set Smooth, and extruded the corner vertices without moving them to sharpen the corners. Do this by selecting the outermost edges of the plane, pressing Shift+E, and drawing the mouse away from the pivot point to crease the corners. I created a vertex group called SoftGoal and assigned the corner vertices to this vertex group with a value of 1. Then I entered Object mode and added a UV sphere with the default values for segments and rings. I added one more object, a torus, and modeled a hoop around the plane and parented the plane to the hoop. I translated the hoop upward along the Z axis. The full setup, including weight painting, is shown in Figure 3.42.

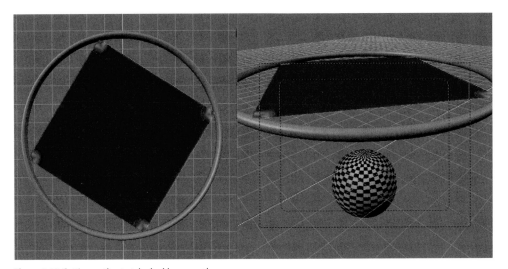

Figure 3.42 Setting up the stretched rubber example

2. I created a simple material for the Rubber object, just adjusting the default material to a reddish color and using a WardIso specular shader to give a shiny, rubbery look. I'll return to the material shortly.

3. The plane will be a soft body object, so turn on soft body simulation and set the soft body parameters as shown in Figure 3.43. Also, set up the ball as a collision object with the settings as shown in Figure 3.44.

Figure 3.43 Soft body settings for the rubber plane

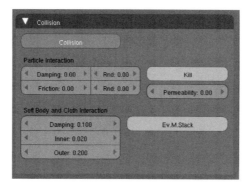

Figure 3.44 Collision settings for the ball

4. Animate the Hoop object as shown in Figure 3.45. If the shape of your Ipo curve (that is, the speed of the movement) or the sizes of your objects are different from mine, you might find that there is some penetration of the ball through the plane. This is not uncommon, unfortunately, and it can require some tweaking. In some cases, you might even need to use an invisible collision object as described in the drapes example earlier in this chapter.

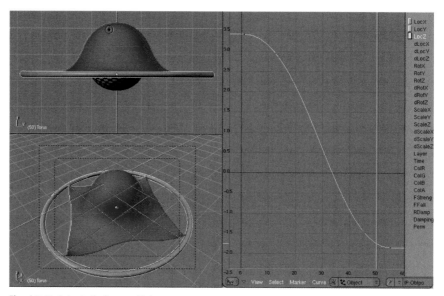

Figure 3.45 Animate the hoop and bake.

5. After you've run the animation and the soft body simulation has been cached, you can work with the stress values more easily. Set the current frame so that the rubber plane has been fully lowered and is maximally deformed by the shape of the ball. Figure 3.46 shows how the lengths of edges in the mesh have become stretched. The degree to which they differ from their original length is their stress. As you can see from the figure, the highest stress levels are in the area where the ball has pushed into the rubber.

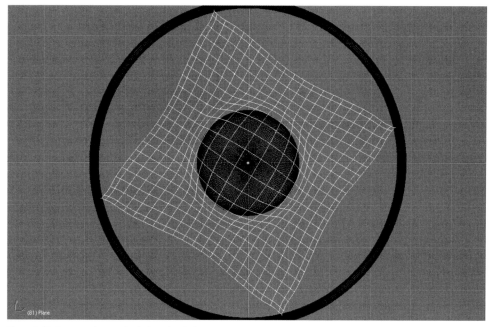

Figure 3.46 Stress can be seen in the lengths of edges.

6. Add a new texture to the rubber material. The texture should be a Blend texture, and the mapping should be as shown in Figure 3.47. Note that the Map Input value is Stress. For the Map To values, select Col and Alpha, and select Add from the drop-down menu highlighted in the figure. Also, set the material's Alpha value to 0.25 and turn on ray transparency by clicking the Ray Transp button.

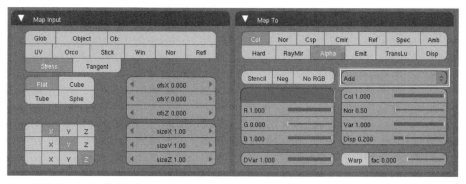

Figure 3.47 Mapping for the blend texture

7. Now you're ready to start experimenting with the blend texture values. In the Texture Buttons area, go to the Colors tab and click the Colorband button. Set the color index to 0 (to be fully black) and set the alpha value to 1. Click the right triangular arrow icon above the colorband to move the color index to 1 and set the color to solid white, and set the alpha value to about 0.33. Because the color is additive, the white portion of the colorband will lighten the mesh's color, while the black portion will leave the original color unchanged. The alpha values will also be additive, so at its most transparent, this setup will yield a material of about 0.5 alpha. As you can see from the images in Figure 3.48, the way the range of the colorband is set determines the range of values between high stress and low stress areas on the mesh. A wider, gentler fade on the colorband yields a gentle fade from low stress to high stress (in this case, too gentle). A narrow gap between the black and white values on the colorband yields an unrealistically sharp falloff in the material's opacity. The third example in the figure looks more natural.

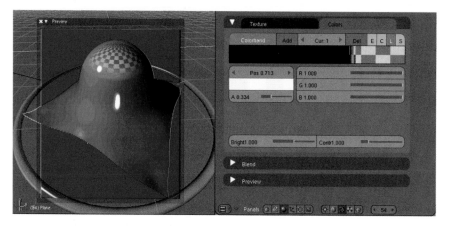

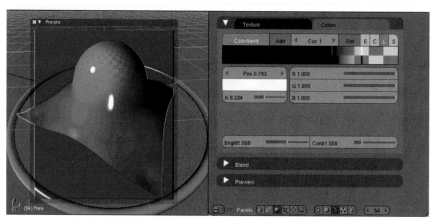

Figure 3.48 The effect of adjusting the color band

8. Rendering out an animation yields results along the lines of those you see in Figure 3.49.

Figure 3.49 *(continued)*

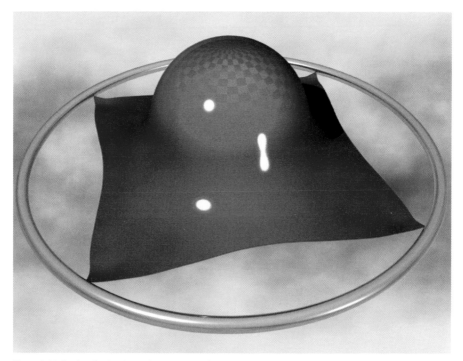

Figure 3.49 Rendered animation with stress-mapped texture

This was a fairly simple example of using stress-mapped textures. For more-general uses, it is a good idea to create a special stress map, with solid black and white alpha 1 values as shown in Figure 3.50. This can be incorporated into a node-based material setup to enable a variety of texture and material effects to be based on stress. As I mentioned, the stress can come from any kind of deformation, not just soft body simulations. You can use stress maps to control the appearance and disappearance of bump-mapped or normal-mapped wrinkles in a character's face when the face deforms in specific ways, for example.

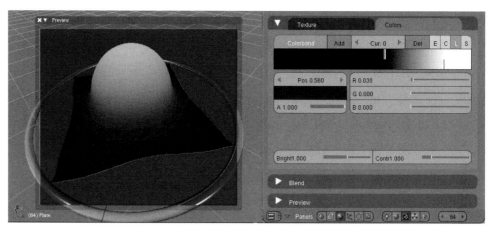

Figure 3.50 A general-purpose black-and-white stress map

Getting Jiggly with Lattices

One of the primary uses of soft bodies is to create bouncing, jiggling effects that would be difficult or impossible to key by hand. Readers of my book *Introducing Character Animation with Blender* (Sybex, 2007) will already be familiar with one important application of soft bodies in creating fatty areas on a character mesh that jiggle in response to the character's movements. If you are interested in applying soft bodies to an armature-rigged character, you should refer to that book for more information. In this example, I look at a more general case of jiggling behavior, a cube of gelatin.

If you think of how a cube of gelatin behaves, it's clear that the spring visualization of a cube shown previously in Figure 3.1 has a few problems. The main problem is that although gelatin does behave in a "springy" way, it does not simply behave like a hollow box made of springy edges. Figure 3.51 illustrates a cube with a soft body simulation applied directly, being struck by a spoon. Clearly, this is not right. When struck by a deflector object, the cube crumples up like some kind of rubber tent. Worse still, after it reaches a certain point of self-penetration, the simulation will quickly go completely haywire, losing all sense of where its vertices are in relation to each other. Later, you'll see how sophisticated cloth simulations can be accomplished with self-collision. But for a cube of gelatin, this isn't appropriate. Solid cubes of gelatin aren't supposed to collide with themselves to begin with.

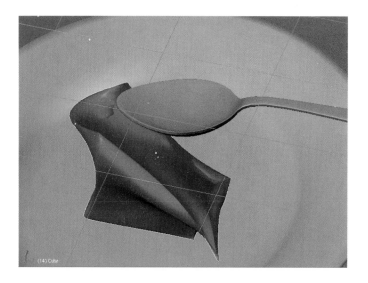

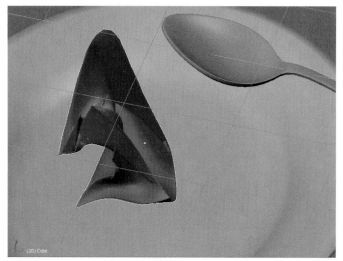

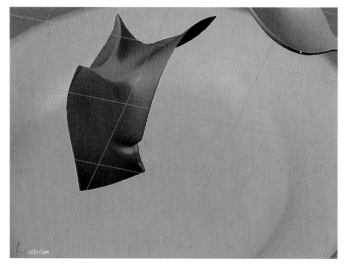

Figure 3.51 An example of how gelatin does *not* behave

As you can see, the thing missing in this example is internal structure. To represent the behavior of gelatin correctly, it is necessary to apply soft body springiness to the internal structure of the cube also. This cannot be done with meshes alone in Blender, because mesh geometry is used exclusively to represent surfaces. If you try to create internal structure for an object with internal vertices and edges, the outside surface will be affected. Subsurfacing is particularly problematic on a mesh with internal geometry. In the mesh modeling chapter of my book *Introducing Character Animation with Blender*, I illustrate the effect of internal faces on a subsurfaced object as an example of what to avoid in modeling.

One way to address this is to raise the Bend value, as in the case of the balls earlier in this chapter. In many cases, that will work fine. Nevertheless, even with the Bend value high enough to support the original shape, the internal structure is not being made springy. A useful method for adding bounce to the internal structure of an object, as you've probably already guessed by the title of this section, is to use lattices. Lattices have exactly what is needed for this: they have internal structure, they can deform meshes appropriately, and they are able to take soft body modifiers.

To illustrate how a jiggling effect can be achieved with lattices, I took the following steps:

1. I modeled a simple cube of gelatin by subdividing the default cube (see Figure 3.52). In Edit mode, press the W key and select Subdivide Multi and use a value of 2. I used the Loop Cut tool (K key) to cut loops around the edges of the cube in each direction, as a simple bevel to keep the cube shape after adding a Subsurf modifier. I added a Subsurf modifier, set Levels to 2 and Render Levels to 3, and clicked Set Smooth in the Edit Buttons area.

Figure 3.52 A simple cube of gelatin

2. At the same location as the cube (use the cursor and snapping with Shift+S to make sure the placement is right), add a Lattice object by pressing the spacebar

and choosing Add > Lattice. Scale the lattice in Object mode to be just slightly larger than the original cube. In the Lattice tab, shown in Figure 3.53, set the U, V, and W values to 3. This determines the number of subdivisions in each dimension of the lattice. As you can see in the wireframe shot in Figure 3.54, the lattice has the kind of internal structure that a mesh lacks.

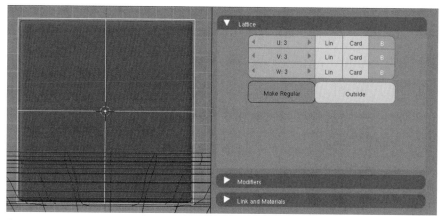

Figure 3.53 Scale and set the U, V, and W values for the lattice.

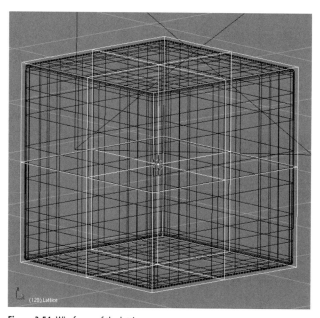

Figure 3.54 Wireframe of the lattice

3. Select the mesh again. Click Add Modifier on the Modifiers tab and add a Lattice modifier. Type **Lattice** (the default name for your lattice) into the Ob field. The mesh will now deform according to the lattice. However, it's possible to refine things a bit for this particular case. We know, after all, that gelatin typically tends to stick a bit to the plate it's on. Although it jiggles a lot *away* from

the plate, we wouldn't expect it to bounce and squirm *against* the plate at all. So it's not really necessary to have the bottom portion of the cube deform. As a rule, I try to keep soft body deformations as localized as I can, to minimize the chances of them going haywire. Do this by creating a vertex group called Lat-ticeGroup and weighting it as shown in Figure 3.55. The easiest way to weight these vertices is to select loops in the cube and enter the weights manually, but you can use weight painting if you prefer. Type the name of this group into the VGroup field on the lattice modifier.

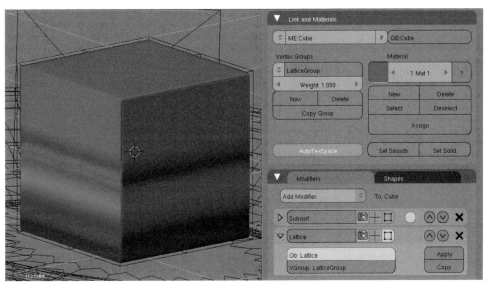

Figure 3.55 Lattice modifier and vertex group

4. Select the lattice and add a soft body simulation in the same way you did to other objects in the previous tutorials in this chapter. Soft bodies behave in the same way on lattices as they do on meshes, with the only difference being that the structure of the lattice contains internal edges. Set the values of the soft body simulation as shown in Figure 3.56.

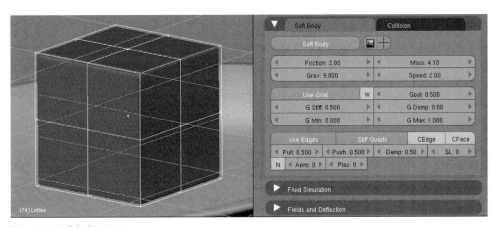

Figure 3.56 Soft body settings

5. In this example, there are two objects that interact with the gelatin. I downloaded the plate from the Kator Legaz model repository, where it and many other excellent models are freely available under the Creative Commons licenses. The spoon I modeled myself, but you can use any similar object to follow this tutorial. A simple cylinder would also do fine. In order for these objects to interact with the gelatin, it is necessary to set them as collision objects. The values I used in this example are shown in Figure 3.57.

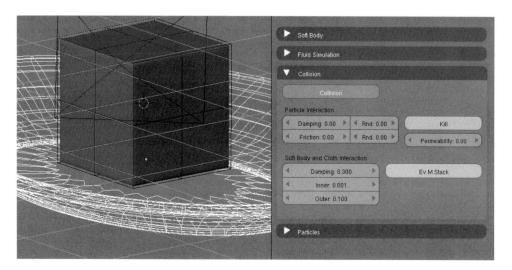

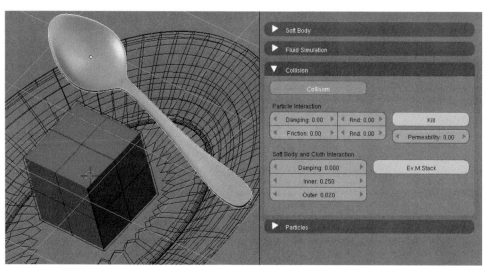

Figure 3.57 Collision values for the plate and spoon

6. The next step is to keyframe some movement. This part can be tricky and may take some trial and error. The important thing to realize is that although the keyframed collision object affects the soft body object, the soft body object does not affect the keyframed object. This obviously differs in real life: A real

cube of gelatin would exert an opposing force against the spoon, preventing the spoon from passing right through it. In this example, no such opposing force exists. If we keyframe the spoon to pass right through the gelatin, that's what it will do. Furthermore, if we do so, the soft body simulation will go haywire, because it is not intended to deal with the effects of squashing the gelatin, only with jiggling it. For this reason, it's necessary to keyframe in a "light touch" with the spoon. You can see in Figure 3.58 how I've keyframed the spoon to tap the gelatin, and stop just past the natural boundary of the gelatin's surface. If your spoon goes too far into the gelatin, you'll have problems. As it is, you can already see that in some cases, such as in the last frame shown in Figure 3.58, there is some penetration. If this penetration lasts only a frame or two, as it does in this example, you can probably live with it. If not, it may be necessary to adjust your keyframes to keep the spoon from going too deep into the gelatin.

7. When you're satisfied with your keyframes, select the lattice and run the animation. As you can see from the rendered stills in Figure 3.59, the soft body gelatin behaves as it should.

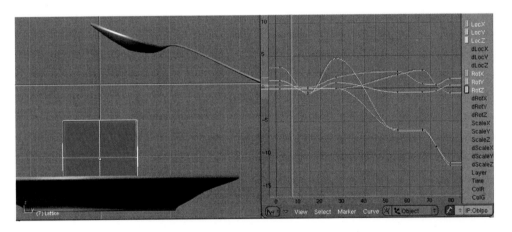

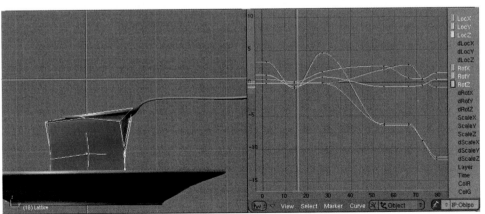

Figure 3.58 *(continued)*

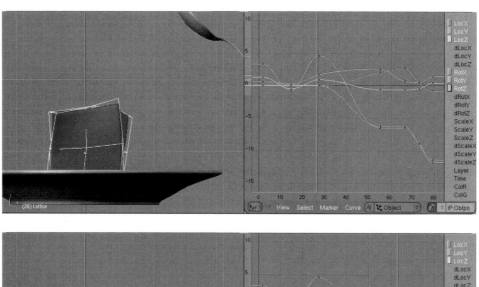

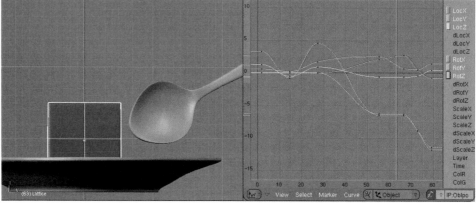

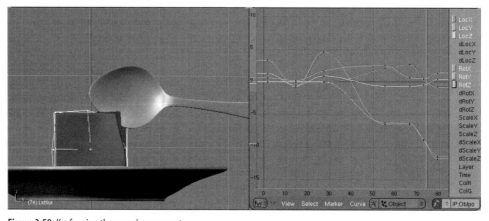

Figure 3.58 Keyframing the spoon's movement

Simulating Cloth and Clothing

As you saw in the preceding example of goal weight-painting, soft bodies can be used to obtain clothlike effects. Real cloth bunches together and influences its own motion by colliding with itself. As the curtain example demonstrated, Blender's soft bodies have self-collision capabilities, making them suitable for cloth simulation. Until recently, this was the best option for making cloth in Blender. However, now Blender has an even better solution: a fully functional, dedicated cloth simulator.

Figure 3.59 Final rendered animation of soft body gelatin

Putting Some Clothes on Mancandy

You've seen a brief example of clothlike behavior of soft bodies in the case of the curtains earlier in this chapter. However, although soft bodies can be used to create clothlike effects, they are primarily intended to simulate springy or bouncy objects, which behave quite differently from cloth in many cases. Blender's new cloth simulation, on the other hand, is designed specifically to simulate cloth and fabric, and is faster and more accurate than using soft bodies for this purpose. In many ways, working with cloth simulation in Blender is similar to working with soft body cloth. For clothing, appropriate weight assignment is important, as you'll see.

In this example, I'll use Bassam Kurdali's Mancandy to demonstrate how to put a cloth shirt on a rigged character. See the following sidebar for information about where you can download the latest version of the Mancandy character. When referring to specific bones and bone layers, I'll use the example of Mancandy. Of course, you can do the tutorial with any rigged character you like, as long as you know where the appropriate bones are located. To set up a cloth T-shirt for Mancandy, follow these steps:

1. Make a copy of the .blend file containing the Mancandy character and open it in Blender. If you aren't familiar already with how Mancandy is rigged and posed, spend some time studying the rig first. Plenty of resources are available for learning about Mancandy, and this tutorial assumes that you know the basics of the rig. The bones of interest to begin with are the deform bones of the torso and arms, which can be found on bone layer 14, shown highlighted in Figure 3.60.

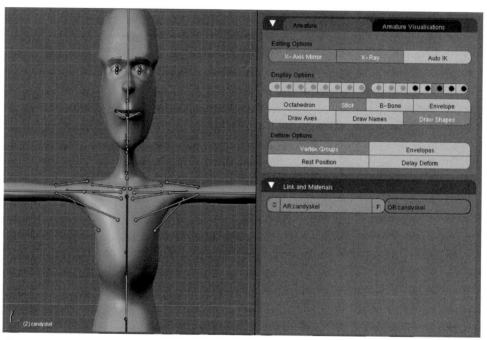

Figure 3.60 Mancandy with deform bones shown

2. Model the T-shirt to conform to Mancandy's body, as shown in Figure 3.61. The T-shirt mesh is a separate object. Be sure that there is a little bit of space between the shirt and the surface of the Mancandy mesh. I won't go through all the steps of modeling the shirt here, but if you've followed the Captain Blender modeling tutorial from *Introducing Character Animation with Blender*, your modeling skills should be up to the task. I used a Mirror modifier to do the modeling, and then applied it when I finished. The geometry of the shirt I'm using is shown in Figure 3.62. You can also find a copy of the T-shirt mesh on the CD that accompanies this book.

3. The next step is to rig the shirt. Although in theory the cloth might be expected to behave properly only with soft body/cloth collision activated on the body mesh, in practice it benefits a lot from a little bit of armature influence. Later,

you'll add a pinning vertex group to mitigate the influence of the armature. For now, add an Armature modifier to the shirt object, and type **candyskel** (the name of Mancandy's Armature object) into the Ob field. Again, if you are not familiar with how to add an Armature modifier to a mesh, you should refer to my previous book, *Introducing Character Animation with Blender*, or to one of the many online Blender rigging tutorials to get up to speed on basic rigging.

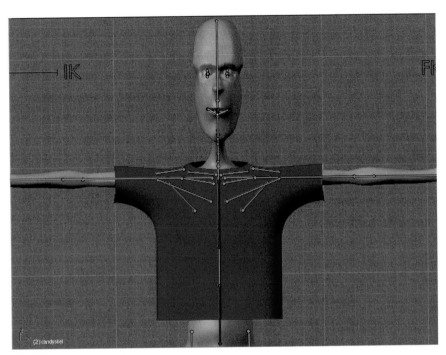

Figure 3.61 Mancandy with shirt

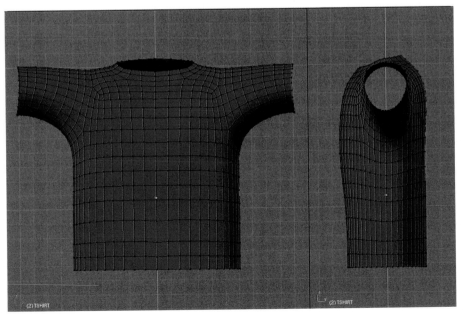

Figure 3.62 Shirt mesh

4. Select the armature and enter Pose mode. Select all bones by pressing the A key. Select the Shirt object and enter Weight Paint mode as shown in Figure 3.63. (I have hidden the layer that the Mancandy mesh is on). Press W and select Apply Bone Heat Weights To Vertex Groups to take advantage of the excellent new heat-based skinning feature, which yields considerably better results than the previous method of envelope weight-value assignment. You can see the weights assigned to each bone by selecting the bones one by one. The weights assigned to the left side and center bones are shown in Figure 3.64.

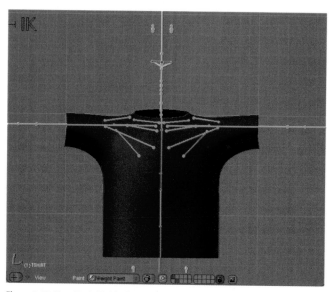

Figure 3.63 The shirt in Weight Paint mode

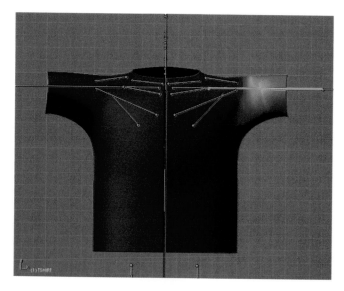

Figure 3.64
Heat-based weight assign-
ments for selected bones
(left side and center)

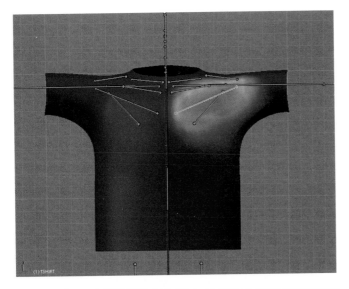

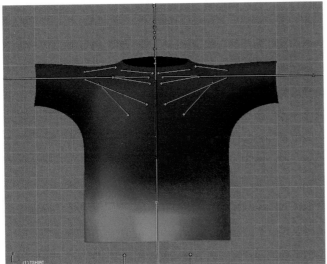

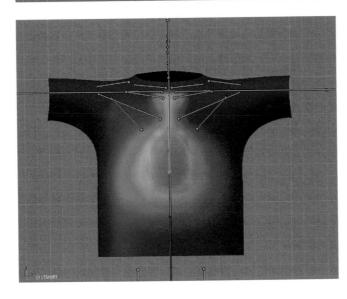

Figure 3.64
(continued)

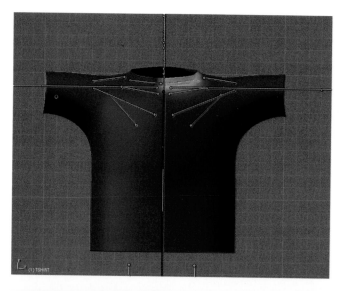

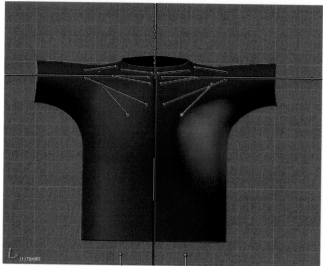

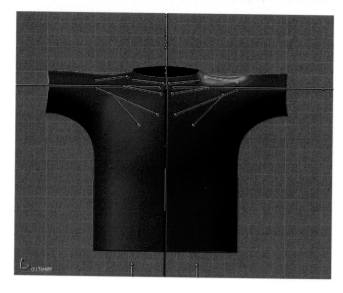

Figure 3.64

(continued)

5. Now add the pinning vertex group to the shirt mesh. Do this in Edit mode by clicking New under Vertex Groups. In this example, the pinning group is called Softgoal, in honor of it being essentially the same concept as a soft-body goal vertex group, but any name will do. As you've seen in previous examples, the soft-body goal vertex group weight values determine how fixed the vertices are to their positions as opposed to how freely they move in accordance with the soft body simulation. In cloth simulation, this is called *pinning*. The higher the weight, the less the simulation will affect the mesh and thus the more the mesh will be directly influenced by other deformers such as the armature in this case. Simply put, we want to paint the shirt mesh with high values around places that should not move freely, and with low or zero values in places where the cloth would be expected to move more freely. Tight, body-hugging areas should have high values, and loose flowing areas should have lower values. In the case of a T-shirt, the neck and shoulder area would be expected to stay relatively fixed in relation to the motion of the body. In nature, this is due to gravity and friction. In the simulation, this is helped along by weight painting. Paint the shirt similarly to how it is shown in Figure 3.65 to obtain this effect.

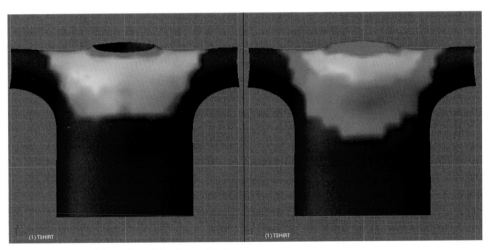

Figure 3.65 Painting cloth-pinning weights, front and back

6. With the shirt selected, activate the soft body simulation by clicking the Cloth button on the Cloth tab. Set the Cloth values as shown in Figure 3.66 to make sure that the cloth has the right degree of stretchiness. Click the Pinning Of Cloth button and select Softgoal as the vertex group for pinning. Next, select the body Mesh object of Mancandy. Activate Collision in the Collision tab, and set the values under Soft Body/Cloth as shown in Figure 3.67.

7. Mancandy is now clothed (at least on top) and ready to get active. But before you start posing, remember that it takes some time for the cloth simulation to settle into its place. Posing with cloth tends to work best if the posing starts in something close to the rest position, so it might be a good idea to key the rest position first, and then give the character a few frames' worth of a start to get into position before the actual shot you're trying to create begins. However, it is also possible to set any point in the simulation as the base form of the mesh, as you will see in the next section. I've added a Wind force field to add a little dynamism to the movement of the shirt in Figure 3.68.

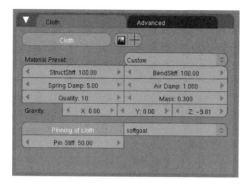

Figure 3.66
Cloth values

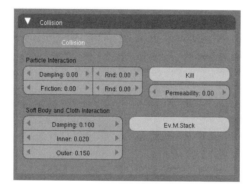

Figure 3.67
Collision values

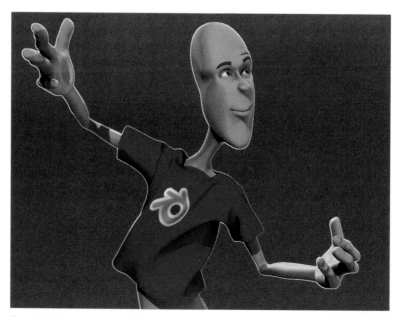

Figure 3.68 Mancandy shows off his Blender T-shirt

Note: When you activate Collision in the Physics Buttons area, a Collision modifier appears in the modifier stack that will interact with other modifiers. As in all cases when modifiers are used, it is important to be aware of the ordering of the modifiers in the modifier stack. Modifiers are evaluated from the top of the stack down. This means, for example, if the Collision modifier is positioned above the Subsurf modifier, collision will be calculated based on the *un-subsurfed* mesh, and if it is positioned above the Armature modifier, the collision will be calculated from the undeformed mesh shape. As you can imagine, this can result in wildly incorrect collision patterns, and it is an easy thing to overlook, because modifiers can be added in virtually any order. As a general rule of thumb, anytime you are getting unexpected results from modifiers, take a close look at the ordering of the modifier stack.

Mancandy

If any single character has come to be the face of Blender's character animation capabilities, it's Bassam Kurdali's Mancandy. Several versions of Mancandy have been released to correspond to different versions of Blender, and new features are incorporated into the development version of Mancandy almost as fast as they are coded. Mancandy is an extraordinarily flexible rig, incorporating numerous rigging techniques and advanced features. For anyone interested in rigging or technical direction with Blender, close study of the Mancandy rig is a must. For anyone interested in character animation, there is no better character rig available anywhere for practicing posing and animation.

The Mancandy rig is released as public domain content and is available completely free for all uses. You can download it at http://freefactory.org/posts/candy-for-everyone.

Bassam has also created *The Mancandy FAQ*, an outstanding training DVD full of tutorials and videos explaining Mancandy's construction and use as part of the Blender Institute's own Creative Commons–licensed training DVD series. *The Mancandy FAQ*, as well as other Blender Institute training materials, is available for sale exclusively at the Blender e-Shop at www.blender3d.org/e-shop, and like all purchases there directly helps to support the further development of Blender. And while you're there, you can also pick up a sexy Blender T-shirt just like the one Mancandy is wearing in this chapter!

Learning More about Cloth

Blender's cloth simulation system is remarkably powerful and is different from soft bodies in several important ways. One of the differences is that its collision accuracy does not depend on being highly subdivided, as is the case with soft bodies. Cloth collisions are calculated on the basis of cloth faces, not on vertices, so having a higher vertex count will not improve collisions (of course, it will enable more-detailed deformations in the cloth itself, just as in the case of soft bodies). To improve collision accuracy, use the Collision Quality value in the Cloth Cache/Collisions buttons. The higher this value, the better the interaction between cloth and collision objects. The Quality value on the Cloth tab is an overall quality value for the simulation, and it will also affect collision quality.

Cloth simulation uses the same caching system used by particles and soft bodies. As in those cases, changing values that affect the simulation will clear the cache. To prevent this from happening, you can set the cache to be protected on the Cloth Collision. Furthermore, you can set the option to Autoprotect the cache after a certain number of frames have been calculated. This setting is on the Cloth Advanced tab, and by default is 25, so that each time 25 frames are calculated, those frames' cloth deformations are automatically protected. Once again, this is a measure to prevent accidental deletion of computation-intensive cache data.

If the cache is unprotected, tabbing into and out of Edit mode will clear the cache. However, if the cache is protected, you can enter Edit mode and edit the cached cloth-deformed mesh directly, although you should not add or delete vertices in this state. As with other mesh-deforming modifiers, you can apply the modifier to make the base mesh assume the shape of the deformation at that frame.

The basic settings for cloth are found on the Cloth tab, as you've already seen. The parameters are as follows:

StructStiff determines the degree to which the cloth tends to hold its overall shape.

BendStiff determines the degree to which localized wrinkles occur. The higher this value is, the less the cloth will wrinkle and bunch up.

Quality indicates the overall quality and precision of the simulation.

Spring Damp inhibits the springiness of the cloth. If stiffness is set to a high value, the Spring Damp value will not have much effect. If the stiffness is set low, Spring Damp will affect how "loose" the cloth's springiness is.

Air Damp controls the effect that air friction has in slowing the movement of cloth.

The Gravity values are self-explanatory, and the default is –9.81 in the Z direction, representing natural gravity.

The Pinning Of Cloth option, as you saw in the Mancandy T-shirt tutorial, behaves very much like the soft-body goal vertex group option. In Figure 3.69, a single vertex is assigned to the pinning vertex group with a value of 1, and that vertex is hooked to an empty, which can then be used to drag the cloth by the corner.

Figure 3.69 Using a pinning vertex group to drag cloth by a corner.

Daniel Genrich

Daniel Genrich is the developer of Blender's cloth simulation functionality. He's currently a student of medical engineering with a background in mathematics and computer science. He began using Blender for video compositing and initially became involved in Blender development out of a simple desire to translate the interface into his native German. Puzzled by some of the more-cryptic button labels, he downloaded the source code to find out exactly what the buttons did. Before long, he was contributing his own patches. He became interested in the problem of collision detection and eventually embarked on the major project of the cloth simulator. His first priority as a developer is to create simple interfaces that can be understood without big manuals.

StructStiff and BendStiff values on a single mesh can also be made to range over the values of vertex groups. This is done by activating Enable Stiffness Scaling on the Cloth Advanced tab. With this activated, you can select vertex groups to control the range of values for both of these parameters.

Preset values for silk, cotton, rubber, denim, and leather can be accessed via the drop-down menu on the Cloth tab. For heavier cloth like cotton and denim, it is also a good idea to set the Friction value on the Collision tab to a higher value such as 20 (the default for that value is 5).

Demolition!

Blender's soft bodies and cloth simulations are good for creating objects with flexible physical structures. These simulators are designed to be robust and to minimize penetration and maintain their structures even when the mesh is under stress. However, at times you *don't* want the mesh to remain intact. Sometimes you want an object to tear, shatter, or smash. In Chapter 2, you saw one way to get an effect along these lines, with the Explode modifier and reactor particles, but as its name suggests, this method is really most appropriate for explosive shattering, and not very useful for effects such as crushing metal or ripping cloth.

The demolition.py script, created by Kai Kostack (and an alternate GUI version by BlenderArtists.org member Panzi) is a solution for these kinds of situations. As with the Cloth modifier, this script is not directly related to Blender's soft body system but has enough similarities to warrant mention in this chapter. The basic algorithm that demolition uses is similar to that used by the soft-body simulator in that edges are treated as springs. In demolition, however, the user can control how the edges break when under stress. Demolition enables you to set up convincing collisions between breakable objects and control a wide variety of parameters determining how the objects break when they collide. Demolition is very flexible; depending on the parameters you choose, you can create effects for tearing cloth, shattering glass, or collapsing steel girders. The demolition.py script is currently under active development, and you should refer to the thread at http://blenderartists.org/forum/showthread.php?t=101635 to find the latest released version and an extensive discussion on using the script.

As of this writing, the GUI version of the script is not fully integrated, so I have included only the non-GUI version on the CD accompanying this book. You must have a recent release of Python installed on your computer to use this script. To get started with using the Demolition script, follow these steps:

1. Place demolition.py and demolition_solidify.py in your Blender scripts folder. Place demolition_config.py in an accessible directory, such as your current project directory.

2. Set up two objects as shown in Figure 3.70. Do this by scaling the default cube in Object mode along the Y axis, and adding an Icosphere object in the ordinary way (use a subdivision value of 3). Translate the sphere upward along the Z axis. Before doing anything further, be sure to clear any rotation on the sphere by pressing Alt+R, and to apply the scale and rotation to the cube by pressing Ctrl+A. It is important to apply or clear all rotation and scaling prior to setting up the demolition simulation.

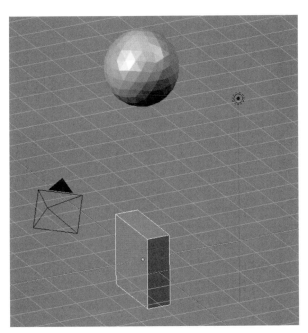

Figure 3.70 Setting up the objects for demolition

3. The demolition.py script determines the behavior of colliding objects based on their membership in groups. For objects to collide, it is necessary to set them as members in separate groups. The default group names in the script are Group and Group.001, which are also the default names for newly added groups in Blender. Select the sphere first, and in the Objects And Links tab of the Object Buttons area, click the Add To Group drop-down menu and select Add New. This will automatically create a group called Group and assign the sphere to this group. Do exactly the same thing with the cube, so that the cube is also assigned to a newly created group called Group.001. Figure 3.71 shows the group assignments for both objects.

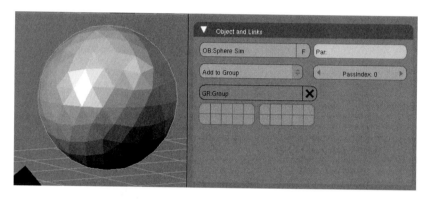

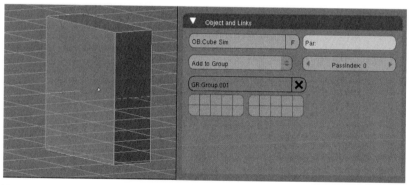

Figure 3.71 Group assignments for the sphere and cube

4. Open a Text Editor window in Blender. From the File menu, choose Open and find the demolition_config.py file in the file browser. This file will determine the parameters of the demolition simulation. The file is clearly annotated, and the best way to find out what all the different values do is to read the comments to the right of each value. To get started, edit the lines of the file highlighted in Figure 3.72. The first of these lines, the elast value, adds a slight elastic quality to the simulation, giving it some bounce on impact. Set this to 0.5. The gr1limit determines how much force is necessary to make the edges of the first group's mesh (in this case the sphere) break. Set this to 0.01 to make the sphere break

CHAPTER 3: GETTING FLEXIBLE WITH SOFT BODIES AND CLOTH

apart easily. The `gr1extrude` value sets an extrusion distance for broken pieces of the mesh. Without this, the pieces would be simply pieces of mesh surface without any depth. Set this to 0.05. The `gr1spd` value sets a velocity in the direction determined by the vector value. I've set this example to move straight down, with a velocity of –0.2 along the Z axis and no velocity on the other axes. The last two values, `gr2active` and `gr2rigid`, deal with the second group, Group.001, in this case representing the Cube object. The first of these values ensures that the group is calculated as part of the simulation, and the second makes the group rigid, preventing it from being deformed. This means that the cube will not break or deform on impact with the sphere. When `gr2rigid` is set as 1, the values controlling the way this group would break are ignored.

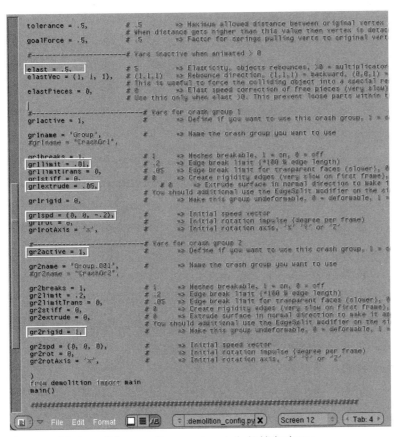

Figure 3.72 Edit `demolition_config.py` as shown in the highlighted areas.

5. By now you've probably seen several ways that Python scripts, commands, and definitions can be used in Blender. In this case, the method used is the Scriptlinks method. When you use script links, a Python script can be set to execute at certain points in an animation. The Scriptlinks Buttons area can be accessed by clicking the icon shown in Figure 3.73. On the Scriptlinks tab, click Enable

Script Links, and then the New button beside Scene Script Link. A list of currently loaded text files appears. Select demolition_config.py from the list, as shown in Figure 3.74.

Figure 3.73
The Scriptlinks Buttons icon

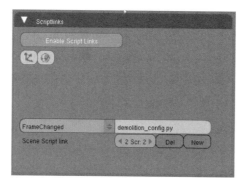

Figure 3.74
Enabling demolition_config.py
as a script link

6. After the script link is in place, you're all set to start the simulation. Start at frame 1 and press Alt+A in the 3D window to begin the simulation. The sphere should drop and collide with the cube, as shown in Figure 3.75. Play around with the settings to see what happens when you change them. Note that if you want the cube to demolish in an interesting way, you will probably want to subdivide it further.

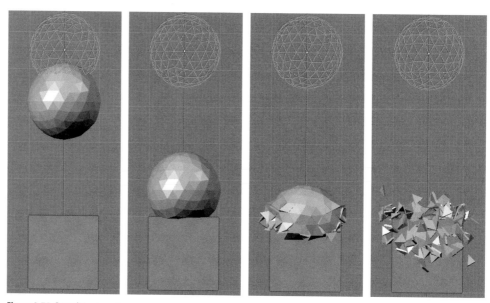

Figure 3.75 Demolition in action

The demolition.py script works by creating special simulation meshes that do the actual deforming. These meshes are all triangles, and their geometry is calculated based on the geometry of the base mesh. It helps to be aware of this, in cases where specific geometry is necessary to get certain effects. For example, the spiderwebbing effect of the breaking window in Figure 3.76 was made possible by manually creating the underlying geometry for the window, as shown in Figure 3.77.

Figure 3.76
Window breaking in a spiderweb pattern

The demolition.py script is powerful and flexible, but it has some serious limitations. For nontrivial vertex counts, it becomes very slow and at present cannot be easily baked, which means that it needs to calculate from scratch every time it goes through the animation, which can be a showstopper. The Psyco Python optimization can be used to speed up calculation times, but installation is not straightforward for all platforms. Nevertheless, it will be interesting to see how demolition continues to develop.

In the next chapter, you'll see how the particles system introduced in Chapter 2 can interact with the soft body simulations of this chapter to create convincing hair and fur effects.

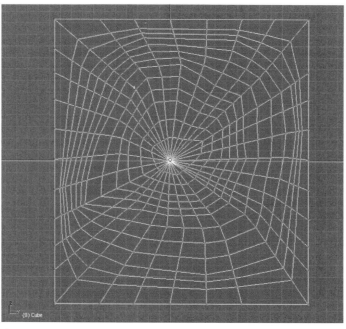

Figure 3.77 Geometry of a window for breaking

Hair Essentials: The Long and Short of Strand Particles

In the previous two chapters, you saw how to work with the Blender particle system to create dynamic particle effects and how to work with the soft body simulation functionality to enable objects to behave flexibly and respond to forces on them. This chapter draws on both of those chapters to introduce static particles, which are Blender's way to create the kind of dense, strandlike effects needed for hair, fur, and grass. The new particle system is powerful and much easier to work with than the previous method of creating these effects. When you finish reading this chapter, you should be comfortable using static particles to create everything from synthetic turf to the long, flowing tresses of a damsel in distress.

4

Chapter Contents

Introducing Blender hair
A trip to the beauty salon
Other uses for "hair" particles

Introducing Blender Hair

Although the Blender Foundation's open movie, *Elephants Dream*, was extremely successful as a demonstration of Blender's potential as a production tool, the movie itself provoked mixed responses as entertainment. Some people felt it was too dark, too arty, too difficult to comprehend, and too focused on grizzled, ugly old dudes. As visually stunning as the film was, the hairstyles you see in Figure 4.1 weren't exactly driving the ladies wild. Bald and scruffy had had its day, and a call rose up from the viewing public: *Give us cute! Give us fluffy!* And so the Blender Foundation, ever responsive to the wishes of the people—and noting that there happened to be a powerful new particle system already under development—took the call to heart. Thus the Peach project was born, with the mission to create a fun, irreverent comedy that would be, above all, *furry.* The resulting movie, *Big Buck Bunny*, was completed in March of 2008, and as you can see from the stills in Figure 4.2, it represented a major milestone in styling, animating, and rendering fur and strand particles with Blender.

Figure 4.1 Scruffy and bald in the days before new particles

As with all Blender Foundation creations, perhaps the best thing about *Big Buck Bunny* is that it is completely open content, available entirely under the Creative Commons license. You can download, copy, and distribute it freely, but there are some definite advantages to purchasing the DVD from the Blender.org online e-shop. For one thing, purchasing the DVD helps to support the development of Blender and the creation of future projects. For another thing, buying the DVD is a great way to get not only the movie, but all the production files in one convenient and accessible package.

This is a real treasure trove of material for people who want to learn Blender directly by studying the work of the most skilled Blender users around. If you're interested enough in Blender hair and fur to be reading this chapter, you will find this DVD to be an absolute must-have resource.

Figure 4.2 Fluffy, shiny Blender hair now

However, to get the most out of studying the *Big Buck Bunny* files, you will need to know the basics about how hair particles work in Blender, so let's get started taking a look at the functionality.

The Peach Team

Nobody has done more to help bring Blender's hair and fur functionality up to professional production standards than the Peach team of artists and developers. For six months, the team worked hard on both the open content movie and the open source tools to create it. The team is comprised of (back row, left to right) Brecht van Lommel, technical director; Enrico Valenza, lead artist; Campbell Barton, technical director; William Reynish, lead artist; Nathan Vegdahl, lead artist; and Andy Goralczyk, art director; (front row, left to right) Ton Roosendaal, chairman of the Blender Foundation and lead developer of Blender; Sacha Goedegebure, director; India, friend of the Institute; and Margreet Riphagen, Blender Institute producer.

Setting Up a Hair Simulation

This section walks you through the process of setting up a basic hair particle system on a sphere, in order to show you examples of some basic concepts in action. Throughout this process, I'll show you how the effect looks rendered out. Some of these renders are fairly time-consuming, so you might not want to do a full render at each stage. In the next section, you'll learn more about rendering hair particles efficiently and the features available that enable you to get good-looking hair rendered fast enough to be useful for animation. To set up the hair, follow these steps:

1. Begin with an ordinary UV sphere of eight segments and eight rings. The textured sphere can be found in the file hair_ball.blend on the CD that accompanies this book. I textured the sphere by using a simple colored pattern image that you will find packed in that file (you can unpack the images from .blend files by using the Unpack Data option in the File menu). To texture the sphere as in Figure 4.3, simply add an image texture to the base material (material index 1) and use Orco mapping with the Sphere option. I named this texture BaseColor. Don't worry yet about the other settings for this material. You'll be returning to this material

later. To light this scene, I used a simple three-point lighting setup with a key light slightly to the left of the camera, a fill light to the right side, and a backlight behind and above the sphere.

Figure 4.3 A simple UV-mapped sphere

2. Add a particle system to the mesh, as you learned to do in Chapter 2, "The Nitty-Gritty on Particles." In this case, however, select Hair from the particle Type drop-down menu shown in Figure 4.4. Select Random as the Emit From option. Set the initial velocity to 0.2 in the Normal direction. If you render now, you'll see something along the lines of Figure 4.5. Add a little downward acceleration in the form of a –0.25 value in the Z acceleration field so that the rendered particles look like Figure 4.6.

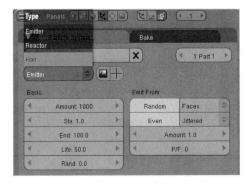

Figure 4.4 Select Hair from the particle Type drop-down menu.

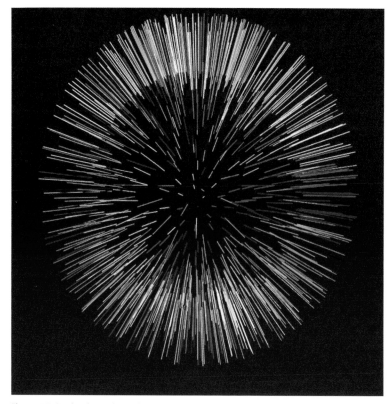

Figure 4.5 Rendered strand particles

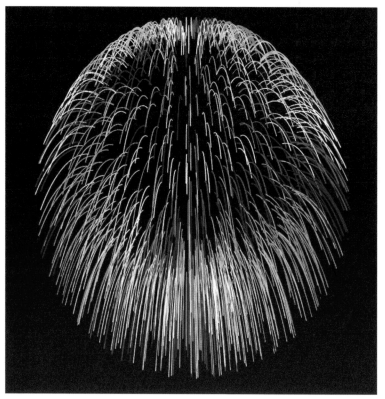

Figure 4.6 Strand particles with downward acceleration

3. As you can see, the ball itself is not being rendered. Furthermore, notice that the texture pattern you put on the ball is being expressed in the color of the strand particles themselves. By default, the particles use the material at material index 1, as you saw in Chapter 2. To give the ball a new material, add a material index in the Link And Materials tab of the Edit Buttons area. Tab into Edit mode in the 3D viewport and select the whole mesh by pressing the A key. Click Assign in the in the Materials buttons as indicated in Figure 4.7. When you access the Materials buttons, you'll see that the new material is a direct duplication of the original material, complete with the Orco-mapped texture. Remove this texture by clicking the Clear button on the Texture tab of the material. Set the new base material as you like it. I set the material to a slightly pinkish skin color. Finally, on the Visualization tab, set the Emitter to render. When you render now, you will see something like the image in Figure 4.8.

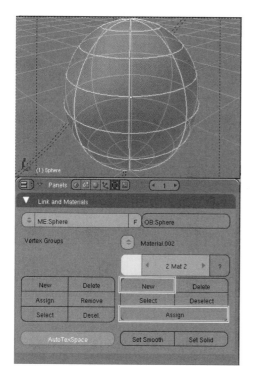

Figure 4.7
Assigning the mesh material

4. The strands here are far too sparse to make convincing hair. One solution might be to increase the number of strand particles. However, this would place great demands on memory and processing resources, because each particle's behavior would need to be calculated independently. In fact, we can get the effect we're after with *fewer* particles than the default by using the Children feature. To do this, first set the particle count to 500 instead of 1000; 500 hair strands will provide more than enough information to yield a convincing hair effect on a simple shape such as a ball. To add the required density, go to the Children tab and select Faces from the drop-down menu, as shown in Figure 4.9. Children particles follow the behavior of the real particles nearest them, and for this reason it is much more efficient to calculate their behavior in terms of physics, styling, and animation. As you can see in Figure 4.10, the children add a lot of extra density to the hair. Before you render, be sure to save your work. Later in this chapter, you'll see some options for rendering nicely without ray tracing, but you should be aware now that rendering hair with ray tracing turned on (as it is by default in Blender) can be demanding of time and memory. It's easy to exceed your system's RAM limits, which may result in Blender being unceremoniously terminated by your system. Blender's session-recovery files are generally not updated in this case, so you can lose work if you accidentally attempt to render a scene that's too heavy for your machine. If you start to render and find that it's taking an annoyingly long time, press the Esc key to quit the render.

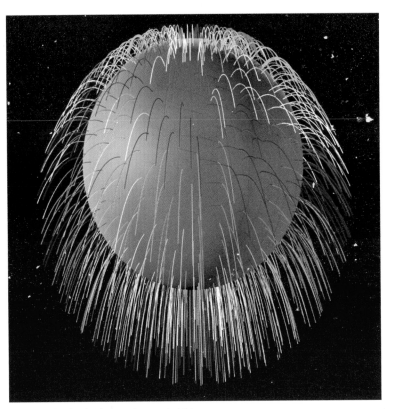

Figure 4.8 Rendered with the emitter mesh visible

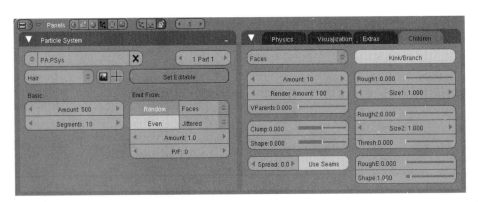

Figure 4.9 Setting up hair particle children

Figure 4.10 Rendered with children

5. What you have so far is sufficiently dense, but it does not look convincing, because each strand is too uniform in its appearance along its length. Real hair tends to become finer at the ends, and in some cases splits almost imperceptibly, creating the illusion of a smooth transition between hair tips and the background. In reality, individual hairs are much finer than the size of a pixel in most images. For this reason, it is necessary to simulate the wispy appearance of hair by tapering the alpha value along the length of the hair, so that the hair gradually disappears toward the tip. Do this by creating a second texture on the hair material as shown in Figure 4.11. I called this texture HairAlpha. In the Texture Buttons area, select Blend from the Texture Type drop-down menu. On the Colors tab, activate the colorband and add a third color to the colorband by clicking Add. Make two black colors with alpha 0 and one white color with alpha 1, and move the sliding colorband dividers so the colorband looks as shown in Figure 4.12. From left to right, this alpha gradation will represent the alpha gradation from the root to the tips of the hair. Notice that there is also an alpha gradation at the left side of the colorband, representing the root of the hair. This will help to minimize the abruptness of the hair root. Without any gradation here, visible roots are likely to look like doll hair or bad implants. With a brief taper of the alpha value at the roots, the hair will meet the scalp in a much more subtle way. It's not especially important in this sphere example, but in the next section's example, where a hairline is clearly visible, it will make a lot of difference. Map the texture to the Alpha value, using Strand mapping, as shown in Figure 4.13.

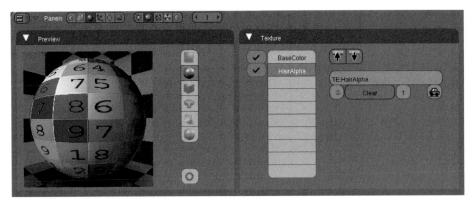

Figure 4.11 Add a texture to the hair material.

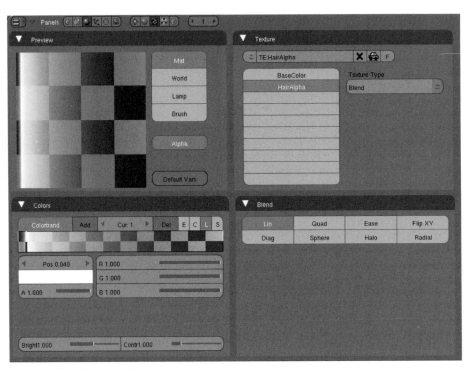

Figure 4.12 The alpha texture colorband

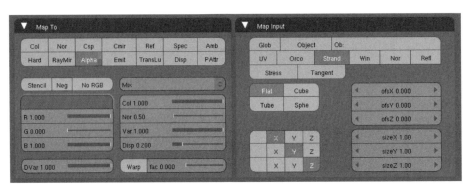

Figure 4.13 Mapping for the alpha texture

6. Finally, adjust the hair materials as shown in Figure 4.14. Set the material's alpha value to 0 on the Material tab, and select Ztransp in the Links And Pipeline tab to turn on Z transparency. I used an Oren-Nayar diffuse shader and a Phong specular shader with specularity set to 0.13 and hardness set to 17. Selecting the strand preview will give you an idea of how the material will look on your hair strands. Finally, set the Strands options on the Links And Pipeline tab as shown in Figure 4.15. This enables you to determine the thickness of the hairs at both ends and also the convex or concave shape of the taper from one end to the other. Set the hairs to start at 0.5 and end at 0.25 to make the hairs sufficiently fine. Click the circle icon button in the lower-right of the Preview tab to increase the preview render quality. If you render the image now, you should see something like the image in Figure 4.16.

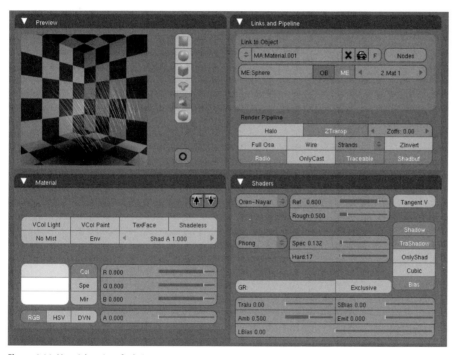

Figure 4.14 Material settings for hair

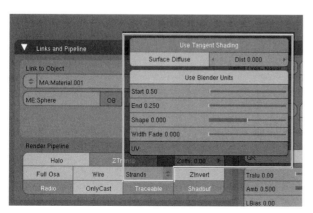

Figure 4.15 Strand values

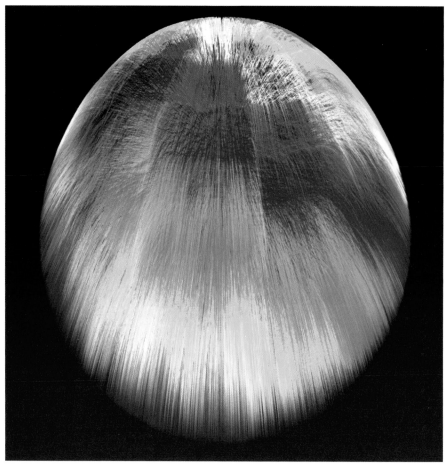

Figure 4.16 Rendered hair

Creating Clumping, Roughness, and Kink

When you've finished these steps, you'll have a reasonably convincing ball of hair you can start experimenting with. You'll notice right off the bat that the hair you've made so far is much too perfect. No animal or human hair is as unmussed and uniform as this. You can fix this by adjusting values in the Children tab.

A very useful parameter is the Clump value, which determines the degree to which the hairs cluster together in bunches around the parent hairs. Natural hair almost always clumps slightly, so adding a small clumping value often gives a more-realistic effect. A positive value makes the tips of the hairs meet, whereas a negative clumping value causes the roots to be bunched to close together and the tips to spread, as shown in the examples in Figure 4.17. The Shape value for clumping is analogous to the shape value for the particle strands themselves; a positive value causes the clumps' shape to be convex, bending outward, and a negative value causes the clumps' shape to be concave, as shown in Figure 4.18.

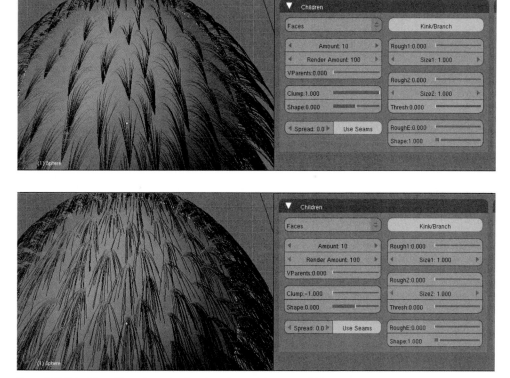

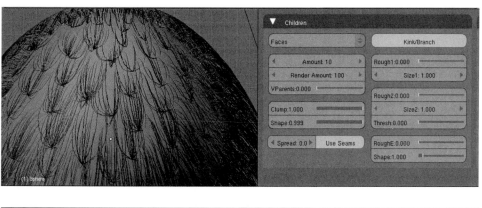

Figure 4.17 Hair with positive and negative clumping values and shape set to 0.00

Figure 4.18 Hair with positive and negative clumping values and shape set to 9.99

Roughness adds a random variation to the straightness of hair. The Rough1 value on the Children tab creates a location-dependent roughness. This means that the kinks of each hair will be similar to the kinks of that hair's neighbors. This is good for naturally kinky hair, as shown in Figure 4.19. Rough2 is random roughness, which affects each hair individually. For this value, you can set a threshold so that the roughness affects only a percentage of the hairs. This roughness creates a more-haphazard, disheveled look. The purpose of this rough value is to add realism by giving a little bit of looseness to an otherwise well-put-together hairstyle. It should usually be used with a very low percentage value. The RoughE value adds an uneven component to the edge of the hair, with the Shape value affecting the shape of the resulting jagged edges of the hair.

Figure 4.19 Location-dependent roughness

Selecting the Kink button displays a panel with a drop-down menu that has the default value of Nothing. Each drop-down option results in a different effect on the hair. All effects can be adjusted in terms of their Frequency along the strand, their Shape, and their Amplitude, or the amount of displacement from the strand's base path. The options in this drop-down menu are as follows:

Curl causes hair clumps to curl in a spiral, similarly to the way naturally curly hair behaves, as shown in Figure 4.20.

Radial causes hair children to twist around the length of the parent in a helix, as shown in Figure 4.21. The Amplitude value affects the radius that the child particles follow around the parent.

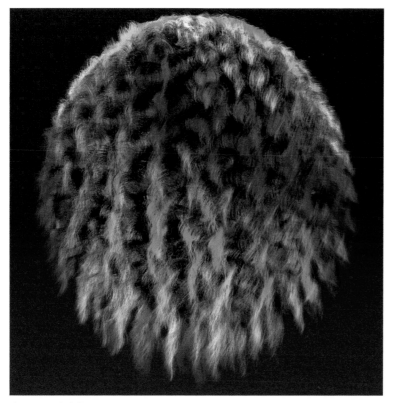

Figure 4.20 Curly hair

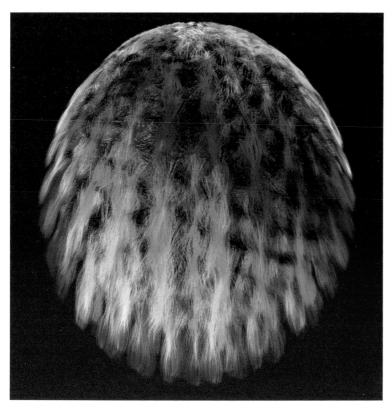

Figure 4.21 Radial kink type

Wave adds waviness to the hair, as shown in Figure 4.22.

Braid causes clumps of hair to weave together around the parent strand, as shown in Figure 4.23.

By using these effects in combination with the styling techniques discussed later in this chapter, you can create a wide variety of realistic hairstyles.

Texture Mapping

Hair color can be applied in several ways by using textures. As you saw in the previous example, the hair by default takes the color that the material would assign to that hair's root position on the emitter mesh. Alternately, by using Strand mapping, the texture is mapped directly to the length of the hair. I've used the colorband texture in Figure 4.24 to show clearly how the different mappings affect the way textures show up on hair strands in Figure 4.25. The image on the left is Strand-mapped, so the colorband runs along the length of each strand. The image in the middle is Orco-mapped, so the strands take their color from their point of origin on the emitter mesh. The image on the right shows how the mesh looks with the colorful hair material applied to it also. As you can see, the color of the mesh at the base of each strand determines the color of the emitted hair.

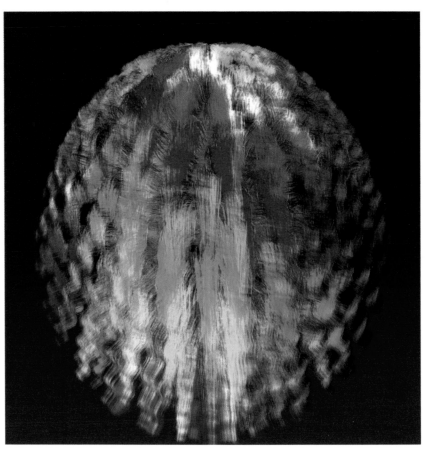

Figure 4.22 Wavy hair

Figure 4.23 Braided hair

Figure 4.24 A gratuitously colorful example blend texture

Figure 4.25 The effect of different mappings on hair

Lighting and Rendering

In general, most of the same principles apply to lighting particles as to lighting other things. Three-point lighting is effective if used sparingly. Shadows can be an important component to hair—it will be noticeable if an unshaded mesh can be seen under hair—so care should be taken that shadows are dealt with where necessary. This does not necessarily mean that ray tracing should be used. In fact, if you've tried to render any of the examples you've seen so far in this chapter, you should already have a sense of some of the issues with rendering hair. There is potentially a *lot* of geometry there for a ray-tracer to navigate. Fortunately, several new features enable scenes containing hair to be rendered more efficiently. It's notable that almost no ray tracing was used in the rendering of *Big Buck Bunny*, with the exception of a few shots in which flowing water figured heavily. This should be considered strong evidence for the kind of high-quality images that can be produced without resorting to ray tracing.

One new development that helps to make it possible to render large numbers of strands is the Strand Render option on the Visualization tab for hair particles. With Strand render, the polygons that make up the hair are created on the fly based on the strand's key points. Using Strand render is highly recommended for rendering large amounts of hair, because it is fast and memory efficient. However, when Strand rendering is used, ray tracing is not possible on the strands themselves. Instead, you can use buffered shadows. To use buffered shadows, make sure that your lights are of the Spot type and select Buf Shadow on the Shadow And Spot tab of the Edit Buttons area. On the Shader tab of the hair material, set Tralu (translucency) to an above-zero value to enable backlighting to shine through the hair.

When Strand rendering is used with child particles set to emit from faces (as is the norm in hair situations), the Simplification tab shown in Figure 4.26 becomes available. Activating Simplification on this tab will automatically remove child particles from portions of the scene that are distant from the camera. The Reference Size value refers to the true size of the object. When the object becomes smaller on the screen than this size (in pixels), child particles begin to be removed. The Rate value determines how quickly they disappear, and the Transition value determines how gradually individual child strands disappear, whether they blink out or fade out gradually. Selecting Viewport also removes strands that fall outside the borders of the viewport. The Simplification options can greatly speed up your renders, and in some cases make renders with a high strand count possible that wouldn't be otherwise.

Figure 4.26 Child simplification

There are several other new features that give you more options for lighting parti-cles. The Surface Diffuse option incorporates the mesh surface normals into the calcula-tion of the strand normals, leading to more-uniform shading. This can simplify lighting, because the particles will tend to respond to light less like many individual objects and more like a consistent single surface. It also can create a pleasing, somewhat impression-istic lighting effect.

Ambient occlusion (AO) is an attractive lighting effect when used appropriately, and as most users of Blender know, it traditionally depends on ray tracing and can therefore add a great deal of time to rendering. An approximated version of AO that can be rendered much more efficiently than ray-traced AO was developed for the Peach project. This is likely to be your best option for ambient occlusion. To activate this, turn on Ambient Occlusion on the Amb Occ tab in the World Buttons panel and select Approximate from the Gather Method drop-down menu, as shown in Figure 4.27.

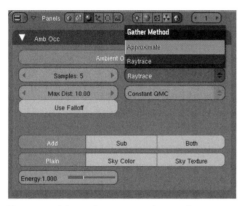

Figure 4.27 Selecting Approximate ambient occlusion

A Trip to the Beauty Salon

Perhaps the most exciting aspect of the new hair particles system is the relative ease with which you can control the hair to make convincing hair styles and animal fur. With previous Blender versions, hair was possible to control mainly through a combi-nation of vertex weighting, forces, and curve guides. These tools are all still available, and even enhanced, but the addition of the direct styling functionality of the new Parti-cle mode has revolutionized the way you will work with hair in Blender. In this section, you'll see how to use these tools to get the effects you want.

The model mannequin.blend, shown in Figure 4.28, can be found on the CD that accompanies this book. Of course, you can work with a model of your own instead.

Preparing the Mesh

For best results when working with hair in Blender, it's helpful to plan things in advance, and to decide how you want the hair to emit from and interact with the mesh. In my book *Introducing Character Animation with Blender*, I described a sim-ple approach to making a short hairstyle by using weight painting and curve guides. In that approach, I recommended creating a separate hair emitter mesh placed just beneath the mesh surface of the character's "scalp." This method is still perfectly valid and is a good method when you're working with simple, short hair that does not need to interact in any way with the character's head, neck, or body mesh. The advantage of creating a separate scalp mesh is that you can easily adjust the shape and geometry of the hair emitter without having to fool around with the mesh geometry of your model. If you want to learn more about that approach, please refer to that book. Although the example in that book uses the old particle system, the methods can all be employed in exactly the same way with the new system.

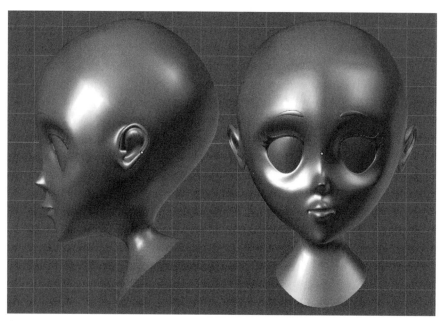

Figure 4.28 A practice head for hair

In this example, I'm taking advantage of new features that make it easier to work with hair emitted directly from the model mesh. Specifically, the new particle system is much better equipped to be deflected by the emitter mesh, making it possible to work with long hair that interacts with the head, neck, and shoulders. For obvious reasons, using a hair emitter mesh placed under the surface of the character mesh depends on *not* activating deflection, because the hair is intended to penetrate the scalp.

The geometry of the mesh has an effect on where the particles emerge from and on how weight painting and seams can be applied. Therefore, it's a good idea to organize your model's geometry to make the hairstyling job easier where possible. I planned the geometry of this model deliberately to give me an easy-to-work-with hairline, as shown in Figure 4.29.

The last thing to do to prepare the mesh is to decide where you want your particles to emerge from and to set up an appropriately weighted vertex group. I created a vertex group called Hair and assigned the scalp vertices to that vertex group with a value of 1. In Weight Paint mode, the weighted mesh looks like Figure 4.30. As you'll see, it is possible to add hair and to cut hair from the mesh later, as part of the particle-editing process, but using a vertex group is a simple and straightforward way to map out in advance where the hair will grow.

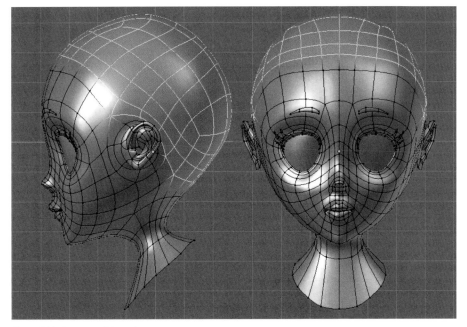

Figure 4.29 Geometry of the scalp

Figure 4.30 Weights for the Hair vertex group

Editing Hair Particles

Before you start styling, you need to give the model some hair to style. Do this by activating a Hair particle system with the values set as in Figure 4.31. Keep the default particle count (Amount) of 1000. Set the Emit From value to Random. Set Initial Velocity
to 0.1 in the Normal direction, which will cause the hair to stick straight out from the

scalp of the model. On the Visualization tab, set the Material to 2 and set the Emitter to render. Also on this tab, select B-Spline interpolation and Strand render. On the Extras tab, select the Density value from the Vertex Group drop-down menu, and in the field to the right, type **Hair**. This sets the hair density according to the weights of that vertex group, which as you saw were 1 for the scalp and 0 for the rest of the head. In this area, you can also set other values such as length to be controlled by separate vertex groups. For this example, we will use a vertex group to control only density.

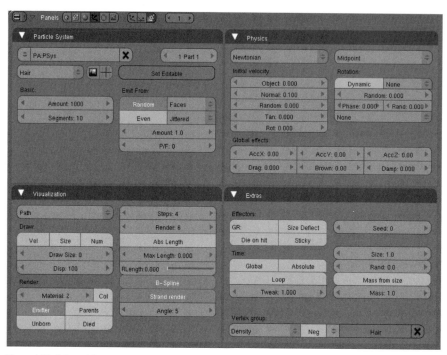

Figure 4.31 Hair particle system

A thousand hairs isn't nearly enough hairs to cover a human head, so it's necessary to add some thickness by using child particles. On the Children tab, set the child particles to emit from Faces by using the drop-down menu. Set the render Amount to 100 (or a bit more, if you find that your RAM can handle rendering more). The clumping and the roughness are completely arbitrary. Set these to a low value or leave them at zero for the time being and come back to them later. Because child particles themselves are not cached, you can change the values on the Children tab freely at any time, even after the hairstyle has been edited. Plan to experiment with these values a bit later.

On the Particle System tab, click Set Editable to enable the styling tools. However, as long as the particle system is editable, you will not be able to change many of the basic particle system values. Initial velocity, acceleration, basic (parent) particle count, Emit From, and other values are all inaccessible. If for any reason you want to go back and change these values, you will need to click Free Edit, [AU: Consider adding where this option is. SW]and doing so will discard all the changes you made in Particle Edit mode. There will of course be times when you will want to do this, but it is important to bear in mind that the main particle values should be set as you want them before you put a lot of effort into hairstyling.

After you have set the particles to be editable, enter Particle mode by selecting it from the Mode drop-down menu in the 3D viewport header, as shown in Figure 4.32. Particle mode is a new mode in Blender version 2.46, specifically for use in editing the behavior of hair particles. In Particle mode, you can control the behavior of particles directly by using paintbrush-style tools somewhat similar to the tools you might have used in Blender's Sculpt mode (this book does not cover sculpting in Blender, but you can find more information about the sculpting tools in the Blender Foundation's handbook, *Essential Blender*, which is available from the Blender e-Shop at www.blender.org/e-shop.)

Similar to the Sculpt tools, the hairstyling tools are designed to work directly on the particles in real time, and so the input device you use can make a big difference in how comfortable they are to use. Although you can do hairstyling just fine with a mouse or even a laptop touchpad, I highly recommend some form of a pen tablet if you plan to do a lot of this kind of work. An integrated tablet monitor such as the Wacom shown in Figure 4.33 is especially nice to work with, enabling very direct interaction with the particles and a much more ergonomic working position than is typical with a mouse. Such devices aren't particularly cheap, but then again, they *are* considerably less expensive than most major 3D software applications with functionality comparable to Blender. Another advantage of using open source software is the way it frees up your hardware budget!

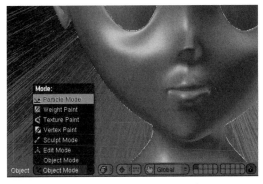

Figure 4.32 Enter Particle mode.

In Particle mode, the various tools are accessed via the Particle Edit Properties panel, which is toggled on and off by pressing the N key. Press the N key now to toggle the panel into view. It should look as shown in Figure 4.34.

By default, the None edit option is selected, which does nothing. The other edit options are as follows:

Comb As the name suggests, this behaves like a comb or brush through the hair, making the hair conform to the shape of the stroke you make. The size and strength of the tool can be adjusted. At full strength, the tool will fully influence all the hairs that it touches. At lower strengths, you have to do more brushing to get the particles to follow. Lower strengths are good for gentle tweaking of the hair without overly upsetting the overall hairstyle.

Figure 4.33 Wacom pen tablet monitor

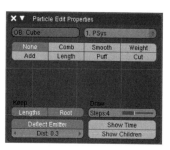

Figure 4.34 The Particle Edit Properties panel

Smooth This causes the hair to tend to straighten in the places that the brush touches. It can be adjusted for size and strength. Note that the Smooth effect on hair has a very different result from the Smooth effect on a mesh in Edit mode. Smooth is used here mostly to undo the effects of styling.

Weight This value sets a weight for each hair that determines how it behaves with a soft body modifier applied to it. The weight can range from 0 to 100, and influences the degree to which the hair moves under the influence of the soft body modifier. This is analogous to the soft body influence from the vertex/control point weighting you saw in Chapter 3, "Getting Flexible with Soft Bodies and Cloth." With hair, the strand will move according to the soft body settings depending on the weight of its points.

Add This adds hairs to the mesh. When you use the Add tool, actual (parent) particles are added to the system, so the particle count is increased. On this panel, you can set size, strength, number of keys, number of steps (which governs the precision of the hair display), and whether the position of new hairs is interpolated. You can add hairs anywhere on the mesh; you are not constrained by original settings such as vertex group density, although child hairs will still be restricted by any vertex group settings. In the same way that the Comb tool overrides the initial velocity and acceleration values, the Add tool overrides Amount and Density settings.

Length Obviously, this influences the length of the hair. Size and Strength may be adjusted, and you can choose between Grow and Shrink options. This tool works intuitively as the names suggest. Like other tools, the Length tool overrides any original particle settings determining length.

Puff With the Add option selected, this tool causes hair to angle away from the tangent of the mesh, and to tend toward a perpendicular angle from the mesh. When the hair is flat against the mesh or pulled under the surface of the mesh, this tool can be used to give the hair more body. With the Sub option selected, the tool tends to flatten the hair against the mesh.

Cut This is another straightforward tool. The Cut tool behaves like scissors, terminating the length of the hair at the point where the stroke of the tool intersects the hair. Size and strength can be adjusted.

For all the tools, you can easily resize the brush while you work by pressing the F key and adjusting the size of the circle with your mouse, and then pressing the left mouse button to set the new size. Brush strength is adjusted by pressing Shift+F. You can also quickly change between tool types by pressing Ctrl+Tab in the 3D viewport and picking the tool you want from the pop-up menu that appears.

Other options in the Particle Edit Properties panel include Keep Lengths, which ensures that the hair length does not change when the hair is combed, and Keep Root, which simply ensures that the root of the hairs remains anchored to the emitter. If this is unselected, your model will suffer massive hair loss when the hair is combed, as shown in Figure 4.35. You would use this option if you wanted to make something out of hair that was not connected to an emitter mesh.

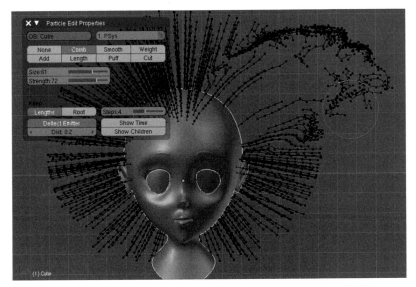

Figure 4.35 Going bald with the Keep Root option unselected

The Steps value determines the accuracy with which the hair paths are displayed in the 3D view. More steps equals greater accuracy at the expense of display speed. The Deflect Emitter option enables the emitter mesh itself to deflect hair. This is important to have activated, because it prevents hair from just dropping inside the head. With Deflect Emitter on, the hair tends to behave in a natural way and avoid penetrating the head. Sometimes stray hairs will penetrate the mesh and become stuck, so that the hair will not respond properly to combing. If this happens, temporarily disable the Deflect Emitter option and use the styling tools to fish the stray hair out of the mesh. Show Time displays the time steps from 0 to 100 along the length of the hair. Show Children toggles the display of child particles on and off. Seeing the child particles' location and behavior is helpful while styling, but because displaying child particles can slow down the display and sometimes interfere visually with the styling work, you will toggle this on and off a lot as you work.

There are three main selection modes in Particle mode, and you can switch from one to another by using the same buttons you would use to switch among Edge, Vertex, and Face select mode in Edit mode. The selection modes within Particle mode are called Path Edit mode, Point Select mode, and Tip Select mode. In Path Edit mode, the hair is displayed as shown in Figure 4.36. You can use the tools directly on the hair paths, and they will respond as you expect. It is not possible to select individual hairs in this mode; however, hairs that have been selected in other modes will be displayed white in this mode. You can select all hairs by pressing the A key. The main purpose for Path Edit mode is to provide a relatively uncluttered view of the hair. The other modes enable greater control by enabling you to select individual hairs and portions of hairs.

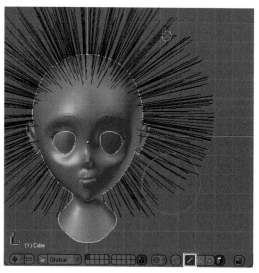

Figure 4.36 Path Edit mode

The Point Select mode is shown in Figure 4.37. When you are in this mode, you can select individual points on the hair in a way that is analogous to how you would select vertices on a mesh. In the figure, the orange points were selected by using the B key (Box Select tool). The double-B circle selection method can also be used in Point Select mode. To select full hairs in this mode, rather than just points, you can use the L key. It is possible to select multiple individual hairs by holding down L while moving your mouse over the points of the hairs. Note, however, that the L key selection method requires that the mouse pointer itself touch the hair points. It is not the same as circle select mode.

After you have selected the points you want to select, you can rotate, scale, and translate selected points similarly to the way you would with vertices in a mesh, by using the R key, S key, and G key respectively. The active hair-editing tool will work only on the selected points. In this way, you can comb, cut, lengthen, or otherwise edit specific hairs without affecting other hairs. By pressing the H key, you can hide selected hairs. Hidden hairs do not disappear, but rather are displayed as white. They are invisible to the edit tool, however, so you can use the hide function to mask off portions of the hair while editing others. You can also use Proportional Editing tools when editing hair, just as you would when editing a mesh.

Tip Select mode, shown in Figure 4.38, enables you to work with the tips of the hair only. In the figure, the tips displayed as orange were selected by using the Box Select tool. When you comb the hair in this mode, the effect of the combing is diminished along the length of the hair toward the root. This enables you to fine-tune the ends of the hair without disrupting the overall shape of the strand.

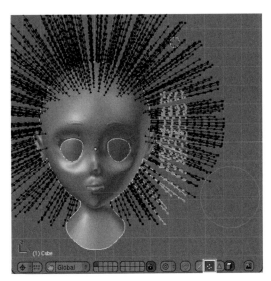

Figure 4.37 Point Select mode

By default, the Limit Selection To Visible option is selected. If you toggle this off as shown in Figure 4.39, you will be able to see and select hairs that would otherwise be concealed behind the mesh.

The W key opens up the Specials menu, as it does in Edit mode. The Specials menu in Particle mode enables you to choose to Rekey selected hairs and to Remove Doubles. Rekeying hairs means to change the number of key segments that compose the hair. If you need more (or fewer) key points to work with, you should rekey the hair. Removing doubles is analogous to the similarly named function in Edit mode. It removes unnecessarily duplicated hairs. If you are in Point Select mode, there are three other options in the Specials menu: Select First, which lets you select all the root points of the hairs; Select Last, which lets you select all the tips; and Subdivide, which adds extra key points in selected segments, analogously to the similarly named function for meshes and curves.

Figure 4.38 Tip Select mode

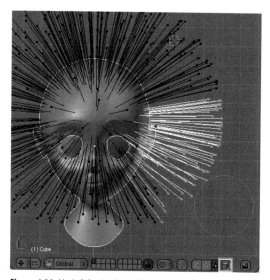

Figure 4.39 Limit Selection To Visible toggled off

Releasing Your Inner Hairdresser

After you have your hair set to be editable and have entered Particle Edit mode, you can begin to get down to the business of styling your model's hair. To start with, the model's hair is sticking out straight away from the head, if your settings are as I described them previously. Be sure that Keep Length and Keep Root are selected, and also that Deflect Emitter is selected.

Begin by combing the hair into a general shape. This is just an overall motion for all the hair, so set the view to wireframe by pressing the Z key so that the comb affects hairs on both sides of the mesh. View the model directly from the side by pressing the 3 keypad key, and make sure you are toggled into orthogonal view with the 5 keypad key. Because this is just general styling, go ahead and set your comb tool to full strength. You can get an idea of the motion of the strokes you should be using in Figure 4.40.

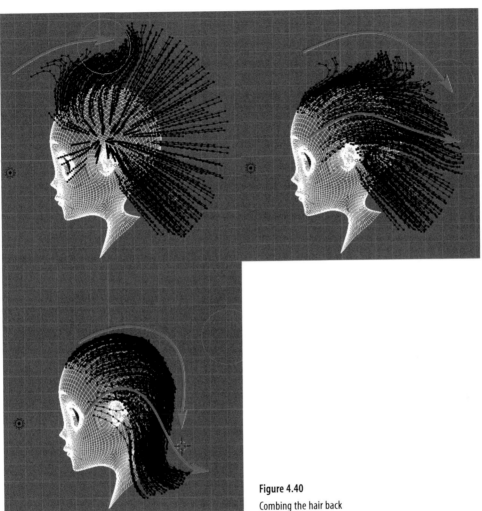

Figure 4.40
Combing the hair back

Switch to front view by pressing the 1 key on the keypad. If you haven't already entered Point Select mode, do so now. Using the Box Select tool (B key), select all the points on the left side of the model's head, as shown in Figure 4.41.

Switch back to side view with the 3 keypad key and comb the hair on the left side of the head behind the ear, using strokes something like the arrow in Figure 4.42. Now that you're working on more-detailed styling, you might find it easier to work if you reduce the strength of the Comb tool. At a lower strength, you will need to use more strokes to get the hair in the position you want it in, but it is easier to make subtle adjustments without upsetting other parts of the hair. Of course, adjust the size of the brush as necessary, by using the F key. Probably you will want the brush smaller for finer details than it was for the general combing. As you can see in the figure, Show Children is also selected. You will need to toggle Show Children on in order to make sure that child particles are not penetrating the ear. However, combing and selecting is easier to do without the child particles shown, so I find that I toggle this on and off fairly regularly. If you have the hair mostly as you want it but still find that a few stray children are penetrating the ear, try to narrow down which parent is responsible for those children and press the L key to select that parent strand only and comb it away from the ear. Remember that you can even select individual points and move them where you want them by pressing the G key if necessary.

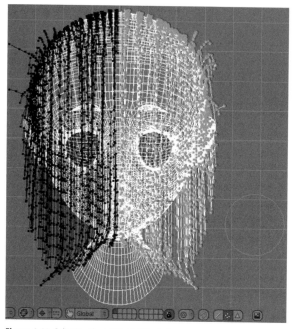

Figure 4.41 Selecting the left half of the hair

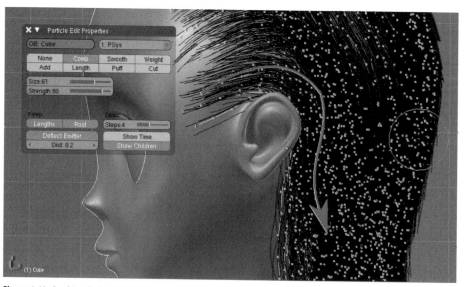

Figure 4.42 Combing the hair behind the ear

Now move the model around and view it from some different angles, combing the hair along the outline of the model to smooth it down, as shown in Figure 4.43. One useful way to ensure that the hair is behaving itself from all angles is to rotate the model incrementally by using the number pad keys 4 and 6. To do this, start in front view by pressing 1, and press 6 to rotate the model slightly. Comb the hair smooth along the outline of the model, and then press 6 again to rotate the model further. At each stage of the rotation, comb the hair smooth along the outline of the model as shown in Figure 4.44. For the other side of the head, do the same thing, but rotate in the opposite direction by pressing the 4 key.

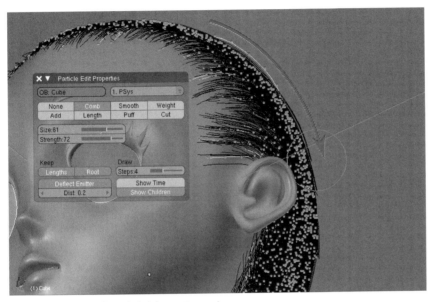

Figure 4.43 Smoothing down the hair from various angles

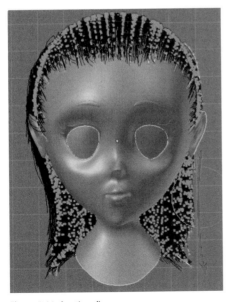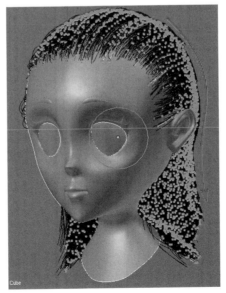

Figure 4.44 *(continued)*

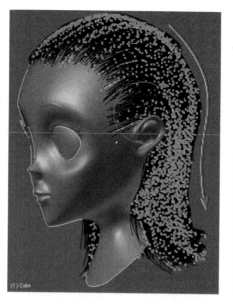
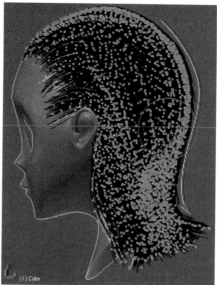
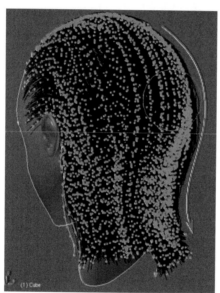

Figure 4.44
Combing the hair smooth while rotating incrementally

Note: In some of the figures in this section, I have selected all the hair points by using the A key, mainly to highlight them and make them more clearly visible. In fact, in hair editing mode, having *everything* selected is exactly the same as having *nothing* selected in terms of the hairstyling tools. In both cases, all hairs and points respond to the tool you're using. However, if *part* of the hair is selected, only that part will respond to the tool. If your hair is not responding for some reason, check to make sure that nothing is selected. Even a single selected point will prevent the other hairs from being editable. Unlike the styling tools, G key translation, R key rotation, and S key scaling will always affect only selected points.

At this point, the hair probably conforms pretty well to the shape of the head. However, this is only natural if the hair is wet or pulled tightly into a pony tail or bun of some kind. For more naturally flowing hair, there should be a little bit of body in the form of some space between the hairs as they lie on the head. To add this body, use the Puff tool. Like the Comb tool, the Puff tool is easiest to use by moving it along the edge of the model as shown in the viewport, so you can see the effect directly and control the direction of the effect. As you draw the tool along the curve of the scalp, the hair puffs up and rises away from the scalp, as shown in Figure 4.45. In most cases, simply puffing up the hair will not result in a very shapely hairstyle. You will want to go over this again with the Comb tool set at a lower strength (and probably a smaller size) to give this puffed-up hair a cleaner outline. If you want to clean up the tips of the hair only, comb it again in Tip Select mode so the roots stay puffed up and the tips respond to the comb.

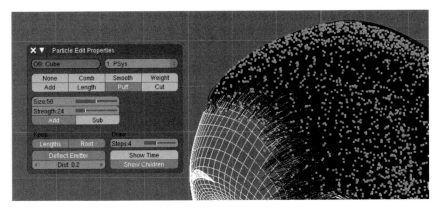

Figure 4.45 Puffing up the hair

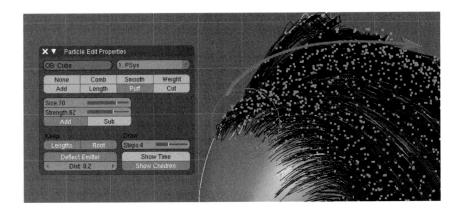

Following the steps I just described, I arrived at the hairstyle shown in Figure 4.46. The material settings are as described previously in this chapter, except for the colorband on the texture, which is shown in Figure 4.47.

There are several other important hair-editing features that you will often use. The Length tool adds length to or subtracts length from the hairs it touches. As with the other tools, I find it's easiest to use the Length tool by working along the contours of the model, as shown in Figure 4.48. The Cut tool works exactly as you would expect. Its effect is shown in Figure 4.49.

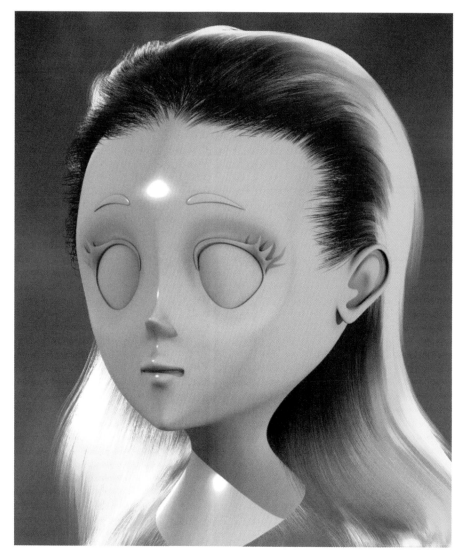

Figure 4.46 A simple long hairstyle

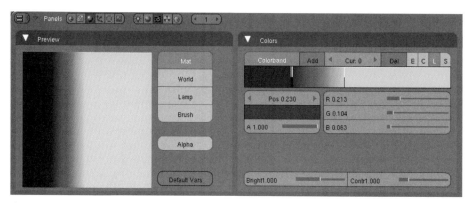

Figure 4.47 Colorband for the hair

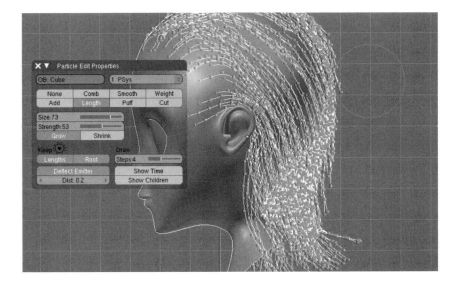

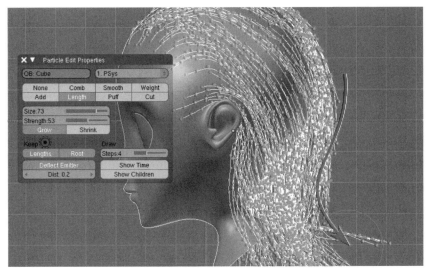

Figure 4.48 Length tool

More Tips and Tricks for Controlling Hair

By now, you should have a good sense of how to do some basic hairstyling. There are several other handy methods to get even finer control over how hair behaves.

Controlling Particle Attributes with Textures

As mentioned in Chapter 2, you can control particle attributes by using textures. By selecting a special Map To option called PAttr, you can set a variety of particle attributes to be controlled by a texture, as shown in Figure 4.50. The density, clumping, kink intensity, and roughness of the hair can all be controlled by a texture in this way. Use the DVar slider to control the strength of the texture's influence on these attributes.

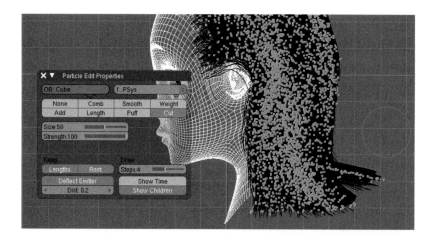

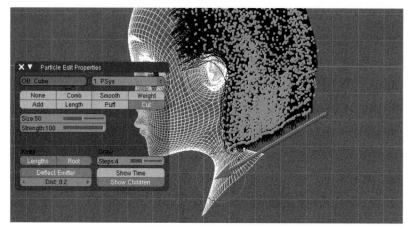

Figure 4.49 Cut tool

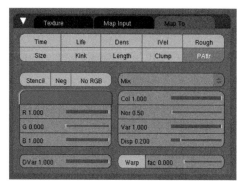

Figure 4.50 Particle attribute Map To settings

X-Axis Mirroring

You can do X-axis mirror editing of hair as well. To do this, you must first set the hair to be symmetrical on the X axis. If you haven't done any styling at all, you can select all the hairs by pressing the A key, and then press Ctrl+M to mirror all the particles on both sides of the head. This may result in doubled-up particles, so you should press the W key and select Remove Doubles if you do this.

If you have already styled one side of the hair and you want to mirror it, first select the other half of the hair with the Box Select tool and delete the unwanted hair with the X key (choose Particles from the Delete menu). After you've deleted the half of the hair you don't want, select the remaining hair by pressing the A key, and press Ctrl+M to mirror the half of the hair you had styled. When the hair has been mirrored, you can then use X-axis mirror editing, which can be selected from the Particles menu as shown in Figure 4.51.

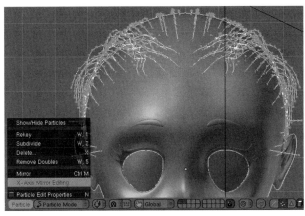

Figure 4.51 X-axis mirroring

Parting Hair with Mesh Seams

By default, the positions of child hairs are interpolated based on the positions of the parent hairs near them. Mostly, this is what you want; however, for parts, you will sometimes want to force child particles to follow one nearby parent rather than another, so that the child lies unambiguously in the direction it should.

You can control this by selecting the Use Seams option on the Children tab to restrict the child particles from parenting across seams. When this is selected, natural parts will occur on seams that you set on the mesh. In Figure 4.52, you can see the seam set on the mesh in Edit mode. Set a seam by selecting the edges you wish to make into a seam and press Ctrl+E to get the Edge Specials menu. Select Mark Seam from that menu, and the seam will be highlighted as shown. With this seam marked and Use Seams selected, it is easy to comb the hair to create the part shown in Figure 4.53.

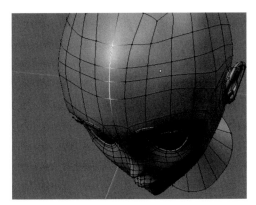

Figure 4.52 Marking a seam

Figure 4.53 Using the seam to part the hair

Once again, this method emphasizes the importance of the mesh structure when creating a hairstyle. If you want to use this approach to part hair in a specific way, it is necessary to consider this when modeling so that your mesh geometry allows the correct placement of a seam.

Taken together, these various tools form a powerful system for creating hair effects. Using combinations of the techniques and the various kink options described in this section, you can create a wide range of hairstyles. Figure 4.54 shows a small sample of some of the possibilities.

Figure 4.54 *(continued)*

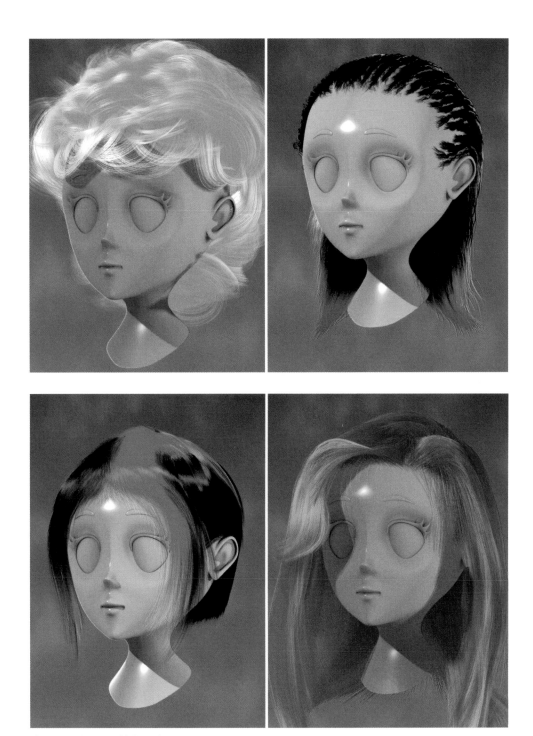

Figure 4.54 Some possible hairstyles

Soft Bodies and Hair

In Chapter 3, you saw how soft bodies work to create flexible objects that move with the forces on them. Obviously, hair—especially long hair—tends to behave in a similar way. You can obtain this effect easily in Blender by applying a soft body simulation directly to the hair particle system. This is done by first creating and styling the hair, and then selecting the appropriate particle system by name in the drop-down menu on the Soft Body tab. The default selection is Object, which will apply the soft body to the object itself. Select the particle system as shown in Figure 4.55.

Figure 4.55

Adding a soft body simulation to the particles

The soft body settings in Figure 4.56 are good for hair use. I turn stiffness as high as it will go in all fields, because there is very little actual stretchiness in hair. I also use a high Aero value to increase the amount of flutter on the ends of the hair.

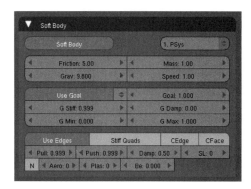

Figure 4.56

Soft body settings for hair

Simply setting up a soft body simulation on a hair particle system is not quite enough, unfortunately. The problem is that the soft body is not as sensitive to the deflection properties of the emitter mesh as the hair is, so when the soft body simulation kicks in, you can find your model's hair falling right into her head, as shown in Figure 4.57.

The solution to this is to use the Weight tool in Particle Edit mode. As mentioned previously, the Weight tool limits the degree to which the hair is influenced by the soft body simulation. You can paint weight values from 0 to 1 along the length of the hairs that correspond to the soft body goal values you learned about in Chapter 3. The root point of each hair particle remains at weight 1 regardless of how you paint the rest of the hair. Painting higher values around the crown of the head and near the roots of the hair, and leaving lower values at the end of the hairs, will result in naturally flowing hair that does not penetrate its own mesh.

The soft body hair will now respond naturally when the model moves. In Figure 4.58, the model is animated to simply rotate back and forth around the Z axis. You can get an idea from this sequence of how the hair moves in this situation.

Figure 4.57
A problem with soft body hair

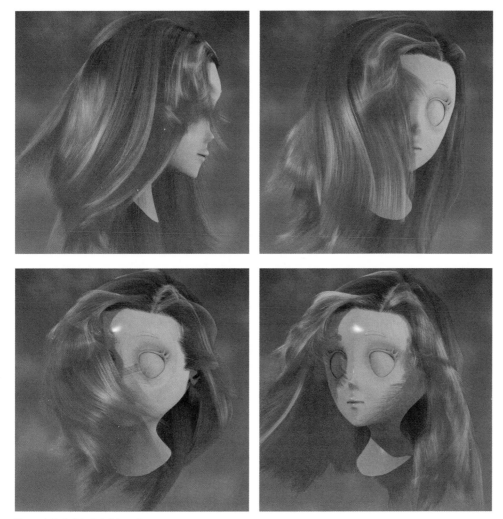

Figure 4.58 Soft body hair in action

Other Uses for "Hair" Particles

Although the drop-down menu option for strand particles is called Hair, these particles are useful for many things other than fur and hair. Fuzzy cloth such as cashmere, plush materials, shag carpets, and other hairlike surfaces are obvious uses. These particles are also useful for grass, moss, and similar natural effects. A variety of styles can be obtained with particle grass—from the bright, painterly atmosphere of *Big Buck Bunny*'s meadow, shown in Figure 4.59, to the somber, photorealistic mood of Enrico Cerica's *Le Chariot*, shown in Figure 4.60.

Figure 4.59 Particle grass in the meadow from *Big Buck Bunny*

Figure 4.60 Enrico Cerica's *Le Chariot* shows a realistic use of particle grass.

Creating grass is similar to creating hair; in fact, in most cases it's much simpler. To create a simple patch of grass, follow these steps:

1. Start with an ordinary plane. In Edit mode, in the 3D viewport, press the W key and select Subdivide Fractal. Set a factor of 7 for the number of subdivisions and 10 for the random factor. Add a Subsurf modifier and select Set Smooth to create the mesh in Figure 4.61.

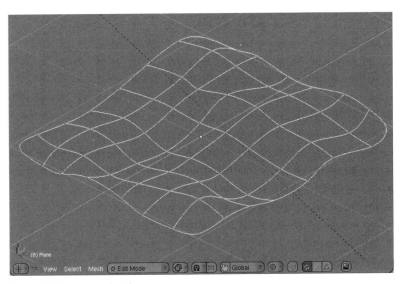

Figure 4.61 Simple ground mesh

2. Add a Hair particle system with the values shown in Figure 4.62. It's not necessary to have a lot of particles for this, because you don't need a great deal of control over their movement. A hundred particles is fine, and the rest of the density can be filled in with children. Also, the default 10 segments is far more than is necessary for grass, which needs to bend only slightly and doesn't need a lot of control over that, so set the segments to 3. The Emit From value should be Random, which is common for all kinds of naturalistic particle simulations. An Initial Velocity in the Normal direction of about 0.025 is enough to give the grass some length. On the Visualization tab, set the Emitter to Render, so you can see the ground, and set Strand render, to avoid a long wait for rendering. Set child particles to emit from Faces on the Children tab, and set the Render Amount to 375, to get sufficient density to cover the ground nicely. Finally, give the particles some roughness. The Rough1 value, as I mentioned previously, is location dependent. Grass roughness is not entirely random; wind, water, and objects that compress the grass operate on more than one blade of grass at a time, so much of the roughness is shared among blades that are near each other. I've set the Rough1 value to 0.10 with Size 4; the Rough2 value at 0.05 with Size 3 and Thresh 0.665; and the RoughE value at 0.5 with Shape 1.01.

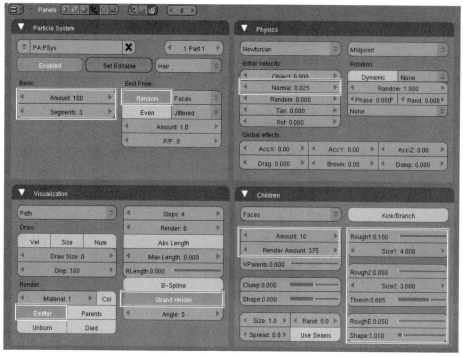

Figure 4.62 Grass particle settings

3. Add materials for the grass and the dirt. In the example, I've set the grass material index to 1 and the dirt material index to 2, which means it's necessary to reassign the base mesh material to ensure that the ground is made of dirt. The grass material is shown in Figure 4.63. The color values are R: 0.157, G: 0.725, and B: 0.170. It's not necessary to have any transparency set, so ZTransp is off and Alpha is 1. I used the Minnaert diffuse shader, which is good for making velvety surfaces that collect light from certain angles, with the Dark factor set at 1.262. The Specular shader is Phong with Spec at 0.4 and Hard at 36. The Strand settings are shown in Figure 4.64. The strands start at 3 pixel widths and taper to 1 pixel width. The shape is set to 0.56 to create a convex curve typical of a blade of grass. I used three separate cloud textures, shown in Figure 4.65, for coloring the grass. One is a midrange green, another is a darker green, and one is a light brown. The midrange green is mapped to Strand coordinates, and the other two are mapped to Orco coordinates.

4. The Dirt material is shown in Figure 4.66. To create its rough surface, I used a Voronoi texture, as shown in Figure 4.67 as a bump map, with a Map To option of Nor and a Normal value of 1. I also used a noise texture that mapped to both Nor and Spec. On this texture, the Nor value was set to 0.5 and the DVar set to 0.8.

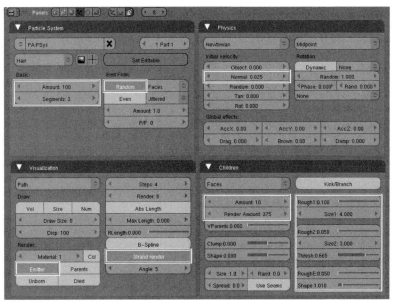

Figure 4.63 Grass material

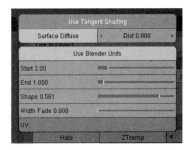

Figure 4.64 Strand settings

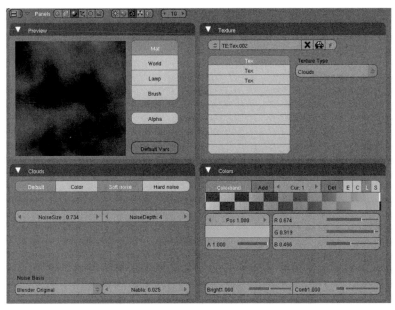

Figure 4.65 Grass textures

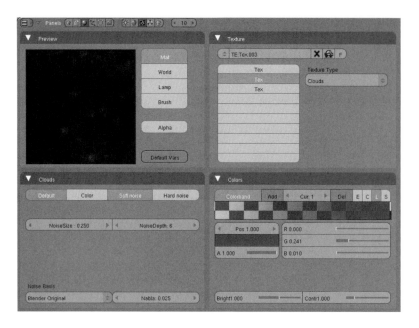

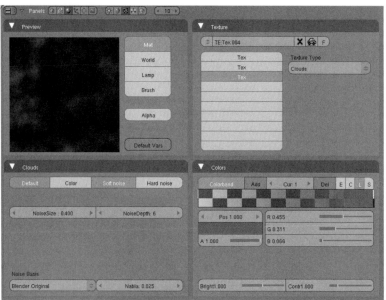

Figure 4.65 *(continued)*

5. Light the scene with Spot type lights and buffer shadows, and render the scene. You should have something like the patch of grass shown in Figure 4.68. Try experimenting with strand diffusion on the grass material. In Figure 4.69, you can see the more-uniform shading that results from using strand diffusion with a distance value of 10. There is also plenty of room to experiment with various clumping and roughness settings on the particles. Try introducing forces to get your grass to blow in the wind, or animating effects like tire tracks through the grass by using animated Particle Attribute textures.

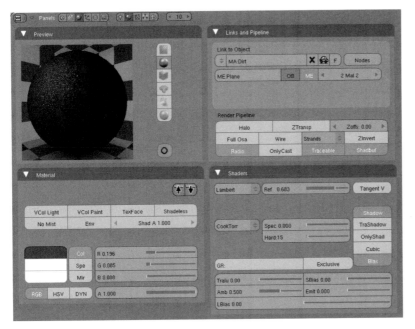

Figure 4.66 Dirt material

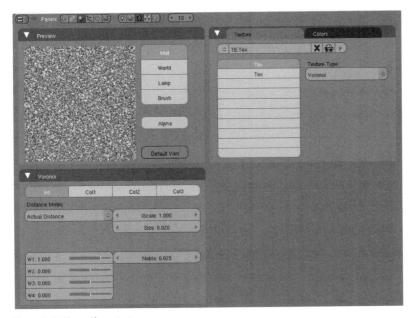

Figure 4.67 Voronoi bump texture

In the next chapter, you'll learn how to work with Blender's powerful fluid simulator. In one tutorial, you'll have an opportunity to exercise your particle grass skills to create grass on the banks of a flowing creek. Later, in Chapter 7, "Imitation of Life: Simulating Plants and Trees," we'll return to the topic of plants and foliage and you'll see various ways to create trees and bushes to go with the particle grass you've made here.

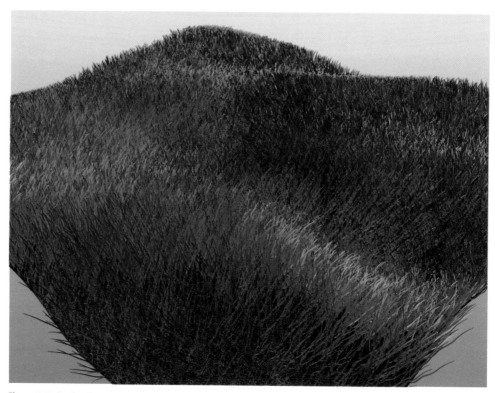

Figure 4.68 Rendered grass

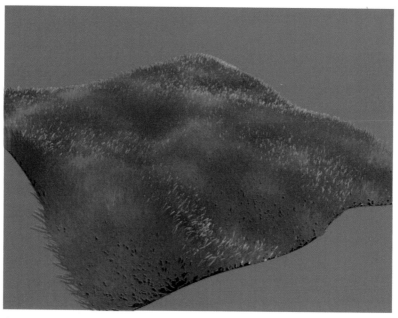

Figure 4.69 Grass with strand diffusion

Making a Splash with Fluids

One of the most important reasons to use simulations in 3D work is to obtain effects that would be extremely difficult or impossible by using only "traditional" methods of mesh modeling and keyframe animation. The case of free-flowing fluids is a good example of this. Earlier in the book, you saw how some simple liquid effects could be obtained by using various mesh modifiers and metaballs. However, these methods have their limitations for representing fluids. In this chapter, I talk about Blender's fluid simulator, a powerful system capable of animating a wide variety of free-flowing fluid situations much more realistically than could be done by hand.

5

Chapter Contents
Using the Blender fluid simulator
Getting the shot
Delving further into fluids

Using the Blender Fluid Simulator

Blender's fluid simulator was developed as a project sponsored by the Google Summer of Code 2005. The official name of the simulator is the El'Beem Fluid Simulator, a play on the name of the method it uses to calculate deformations, the Lattice-Boltzmann method.

The *Lattice-Boltzmann method (LBM)* is a state-of-the-art technique in computational fluid dynamics for calculating the movement of fluid surfaces. It operates by treating the fluid surface as a lattice of triangles over which a large number of particles travel and collide with each other. The transference of force from the collisions of the particles drives the movement of the fluid surface. This method is capable of producing convincing fluid movement and allowing a variety of parameter settings to influence the characteristics of the fluid. Furthermore, its calculations are local and so the algorithm can be parallelized. LBM is a good method for simulations in which detailed interaction between the fluid and solid objects is desirable, as in the case of CG animation. LBM also has the potential for considerably expanded functionality in the future. For now, there is more than enough interesting and useful functionality to keep Blender users busy exploring the potential of fluid simulation, so let's get to it.

Getting Started with Fluids

Every fluid simulation has two necessary components. The first is a defined area in which to carry out the simulation, and the second is a source for the fluid itself. The fluid simulation algorithm operates by dividing space into discrete units called *voxels*. You can think of voxels as being something like 3D pixels. In fact, the word *voxels* derives from the combination of the words *volumetric elements*, just as *pixels* derives from *picture elements*. In the same way that a single image or display must be limited to a finite number of pixels, an area of calculation for fluids is limited to a portion of space that can be divided into a finite number of voxels. This portion of space is called the domain, and its area is defined by the Domain object. Without defining a Domain object, it is not possible to initiate a fluid simulation.

One way to introduce fluid to the domain is via the *Fluid object*. This is a mesh positioned inside the domain that defines the volume of the fluid for the simulation. As you'll see later in the chapter, the name of this component is somewhat misleading. The properties of the fluid itself, and the mesh representing the simulated fluid in motion, are all dealt with by the Domain object. For example, when you want to assign a material or activate a Subsurf modifier on your fluid, you will do this on the Domain object mesh. The Fluid object is used to define the volume and to set some initial velocity parameters.

For your first fluid simulation, the Domain is already set up, if you're using a default Blender installation. The old familiar default cube will do fine. In fact, for your Domain object, you can always use the default cube and simply scale it to suit your needs. The Domain object never needs any special geometry, and although you can use another shape such as a sphere, a monkey, or even a plane for your domain, the domain will *always* be calculated as a 3D rectangular box.

Because the domain of your fluid simulation is going to be a 3D rectangle, you generally have an ideal domain mesh provided automatically in the form of Blender's trusty default cube. To get started on fluids now, I'll present a few examples that use the default cube entirely unmodified as the domain. Go ahead and fire up a session of Blender, and go into front view with NUM1. You should be looking at your cube in Orthogonal View mode. Press the Z key to enter Wireframe mode, as in Figure 5.1.

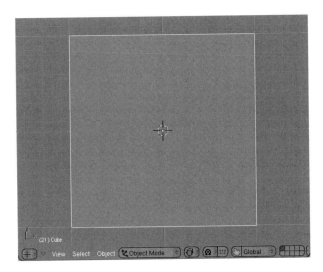

Figure 5.1
The default cube from the front view

Enabling the cube as a fluid domain is simple. The pertinent buttons can be found in the Physics Buttons subcontext of the Object buttons. You can get into this subcontext by pressing F7 twice. Make sure the default cube is selected. Then, in the Fluid Simulation panel, click Enable and select Domain, as shown in Figure 5.2. I've made one other change here, and that's to increase the preview resolution from 25 to 50, which is the same as the final resolution. I want to see a higher-quality representation of the mesh when I bake the fluid, and the added time for each frame does not make much difference, because the baking process does not happen in real time. If I want a quick and dirty real-time playback later, I may want to reduce the preview resolution.

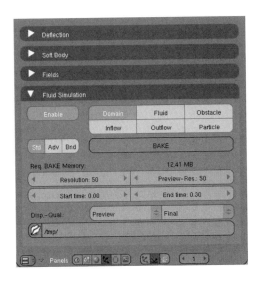

Figure 5.2
Enabling a fluid domain

That's all there is to setting up a fluid domain. This determines the area in which the fluid simulation will be carried out. There are several parameters to set, which I'll discuss shortly. For the time being, you can leave things as they are. There's still something important missing, and that's the Fluid object. Make sure that your cursor is snapped to the center of the cube (select the cube, press Shift+S, and select Cursor To Selected), and then press the spacebar to add an Icosphere mesh. Use the default parameters for the Icosphere so that you wind up with something like Figure 5.3.

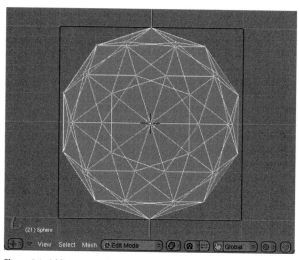

Figure 5.3 Adding an Icosphere

Any shape will do as a fluid. I've selected an Icosphere here mainly for visibility, although as you'll see shortly, the Boolean properties of Fluid objects mean that spheres can be especially easy to work with. The Fluid object mesh itself is used only to determine the initial shape and volume of the fluid. When the fluid simulation begins, a new mesh is created in that shape, so the geometry of the Fluid object mesh becomes irr elevant.

To enable the sphere as a Fluid object, once again go to the Fluid Simulation panel with the Icosphere selected and click Enable. Select Fluid.

You've now completely set up the fluid simulation and are ready to run the simulator, also called *baking* the fluid. When the simulator runs, it creates a new mesh for every frame of the animation, representing the shape of the fluid at that moment. These meshes are numbered and stored in your /tmp directory by default. For now, let's create a specific directory for each simulation example. Select the Domain object, and set the output directory on the Fluid Simulation tab to /tmp/ex1. Click Bake.

Depending on your hardware, the baking process may take a bit of time. The parameters are set low in this example, though, so it shouldn't be too much of a challenge for your computer. If it is, you might want to consider upgrading your hardware before going much further with fluids, because it gets only more resource-intensive from here. When you bake the fluid, the animated sequence is created frame by frame. Some illustrative sample frames can be seen in Figure 5.4. The bake will take a few minutes. If you get tired of waiting, you can press Esc at any time and you will be able to play back what you have baked so far. If you do stop in the middle but want to bake the whole simulation, you will have to go back and start baking from the beginning. If you want to go through these examples quickly and don't mind lower quality than what you see in the figures, try setting the Resolution value to 25 in the Fluid Simulation tab with the Domain object selected.

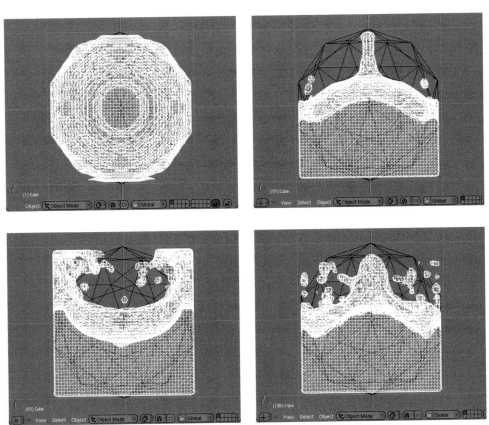

Figure 5.4 The fluid baking process

After the fluid is baked, take a look in /tmp/ex1. You'll find a lot of files with names such as fluidsurface_final_0000.bobj.gz. These files contain the actual meshes for each frame of the fluid simulation. For this reason, it's good to get into the habit of assigning a new output directory for each fluid project you create. If you do a lot of fluid simulations, these can begin to take up space, so be sure to clean out your fluid simulation output directories from time to time.

After you've baked your fluid, you can run the animation as you would run it ordinarily in Blender, using Alt+A or the animation playback button on the timeline. Of course, you can view the splashing fluid in Solid mode from a variety of angles to admire your handiwork. In Shaded mode, the Fluid object is still visible and will most likely occlude most of the simulation. Sending the Fluid object to a different layer will get it out of the way. Adding a Subsurf modifier and selecting Set Smooth will improve the overall look of curved surfaces but will greatly slow down the simulation. As you'll see later in this chapter, there are other, better ways to improve the look of fluid surfaces, which can make subsurfacing redundant, but in cases where the simulation looks choppy, subsurfacing can improve things considerably.

After a fluid is baked, the Domain object assumes the shape of the fluid simulation mesh and does not return to its original shape in Object mode, as long as the fluid sim meshes remain in the specified output directory. You can still see the Domain object's original shape in Edit mode. To return the domain to its original shape in Object mode, there are several possibilities. One is to clear the meshes from the output directory by hand, via your Windows, Mac, or Linux OS interface. Another is to select a new, empty output directory for your fluids.

Note: If you accidentally create Fluid and Domain objects that do not intersect in space, the volume of the resulting baked fluid will be zero. Because the Domain object assumes the shape of this fluid, the resulting Domain object is a null mesh, meaning it has no vertices and cannot be selected in the 3D viewport. You can still select the object in the Outliner, and you can see the object's original shape in Edit mode. To solve this problem, select the Domain object in the Outliner, make sure that the Fluid object properly intersects the domain, and rebake the fluid. Discarding previous baked meshes in the output directory also returns the Domain object to its original shape.

Multiple Fluid Objects

The fluid in the simulation takes its volume and initial shape from the Boolean intersection of the Domain object with the Boolean union of all enabled Fluid objects. To see this in action, let's return to the previous example. I selected a new output directory to clear the shape of the Domain object, so it's back to the original cube shape.

To see how multiple Fluid objects behave in a simulation, duplicate the Icosphere Fluid object from the previous example by pressing Shift+D and place both instances as shown in Figure 5.5.

When you make a duplicate of an object with Fluid Simulation enabled, the new copy has Fluid Simulation enabled to the same settings, so there's no need to touch that panel in this case. Right-click the Domain object and set the output directory to /tmp/ex2. Notice that when you select a new output directory, the shape of the Domain object pops back to the original cube shape. It's not necessary to do this—you can bake the new simulation to the same output directory as the old simulation, and the meshes are simply overwritten. However, if you want to see the Domain object in its original shape in Object mode, you need to have a fresh output directory selected.

Bake the fluid again. As you can see in Figure 5.6, the simulated fluid mesh begins in the shape of the union of the two Fluid object meshes, limited to the area that falls within the domain.

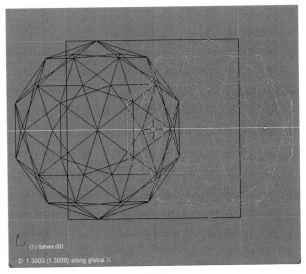

Figure 5.5 Placing the duplicate Fluid objects

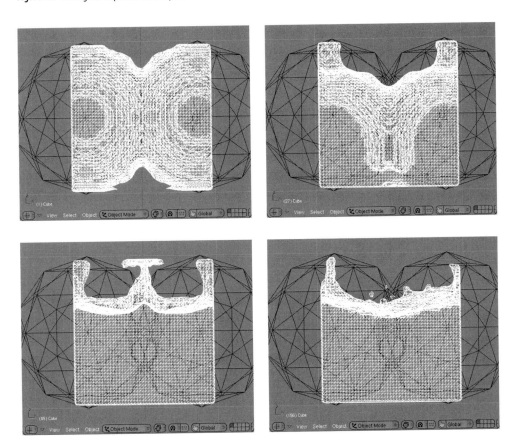

Figure 5.6 A simulation with intersecting Fluid objects

This behavior can be useful, because it enables you to work with fluids by manipulating simple shapes and doing very little modeling for the initial shape of the fluid. For example, when placing fluid in a container, it may be simpler to fill a container with overlapping balls rather than trying to accurately model the inside shape of the container. This is how I placed the fluid in two of the examples later in this chapter.

When multiple fluids do not overlap, they behave as you would expect. Try reducing the size of the Fluid object spheres in this example so that they don't overlap, and rebake the fluid. The result should look similar to Figure 5.7.

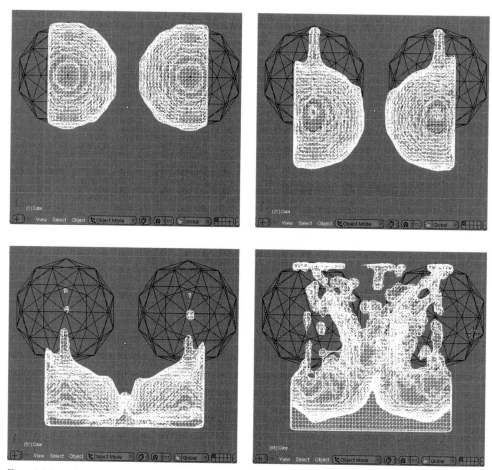

Figure 5.7 A simulation with nonintersecting Fluid objects

Init Volume, Init Shell, and Init Both

By default, the amount of fluid that is released from a Fluid object depends on the volume of the original Fluid object. This can be altered so that the amount of fluid depends on the surface area of the object's mesh. This makes it possible to use nonclosed meshes as Fluid objects. There are three options for initializing fluid volume from the Fluid object:

Init Volume initializes the fluid to the volume of the closed portion of the mesh.

Init Shell initializes the fluid to a volume calculated based on the surface area of the mesh.

Init Both initializes the fluid to the union of both of the previous volumes.

Init Volume produces fluid only if the mesh is closed. A nonclosed mesh (for example, an ordinary plane) does not have volume, so initializing the fluid by volume from a nonclosed mesh will not produce any fluid. If the mesh is a nonmanifold mesh with closed parts and open parts, only the closed parts produce fluid.

For an example of how these two initialization methods interact, consider the shape in Figure 5.8. You can create a similar shape by adding a UV sphere to a new session of Blender (I used eight rings and eight segments here), and then selecting the ring around the middle of the sphere by pressing Alt+right mouse button (RMB), and extruding by pressing the E key. Press the S key to scale the extruded edge outward. Enable a fluid simulation with the default cube as the domain and the sphere you just added as the fluid.

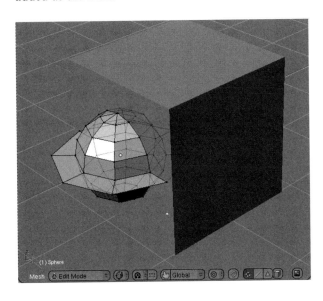

Figure 5.8

A nonmanifold mesh composed of a UV sphere with an extruded ring around the middle

For this example, I positioned the mesh to be bisected by the wall of the domain to show a cross section of the fluid that is produced. In Figure 5.9, you can see how the different Init options create different initial fluid states and amounts. The first image shows the Init Volume option. Note that the mesh ring around the middle of the sphere does not contribute any fluid, because Init Volume is concerned only with closed meshes. The second image shows the simulation with the Init Shell option selected. In this case, the fluid begins in a hollow state conforming to the surface of the mesh, with the nonmanifold ring producing fluid. In the third image, both methods are active. In the case of a simple closed mesh, this would result in a slightly larger amount of fluid than Init Volume. In this example, the nonmanifold portion of the mesh is taken into account.

Viscosity, Stickiness, and Compressibility

Every fluid has a particular *viscosity*, which determines the speed and ease with which it flows. Viscosity is a measure of the fluid's resistance to the forces that deform it. Fluids with high viscosity flow slowly and are perceived as "thick," whereas low-viscosity fluids, such as water, are "thin." For example, think of the difference between the way that fluids such as water, motor oil, honey, and magma flow—this mainly has to do with their viscosities.

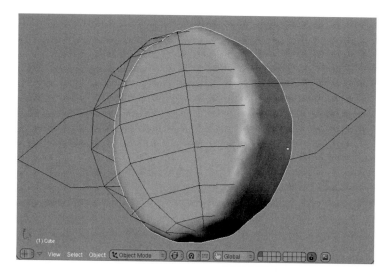

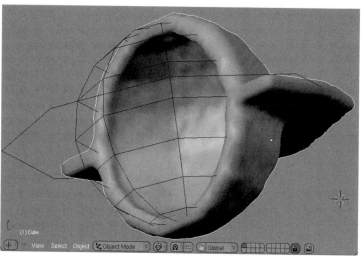

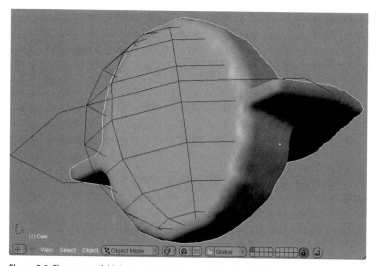

Figure 5.9 The nonmanifold shape with Init Volume, Init Shell, and Init Both selected

In Blender's fluid simulator, the fluid's viscosity can be entered by hand. More precisely, the value used in Blender is the *kinematic viscosity*. Preset viscosity values are available in the drop-down menu in the advanced (Adv) options in the Fluid Simulation tab, shown in Figure 5.10. The preset viscosities include Honey, Oil, and Water. The default is Water. If you select Manual, you can enter a viscosity value by hand. Remember, the viscosity setting is only one of several parameters that affect the *appearance* of viscosity in the simulation. Several other factors, notably the resolution of the simulation, have a great impact on how the fluid looks. The Manual setting can come in handy if you want to simulate a fluid with a significantly different viscosity than the presets, or if you are trying to fake the effect of a fluid simulation that occupies more than a 10-meter area, because that can "thin" the fluid out. Coupled with particle-based spray, this can contribute to an effect of larger-scale simulations.

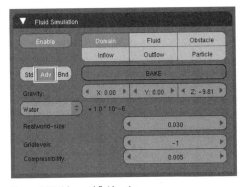

Figure 5.10 Advanced fluid options

Some fluids and their kinematic viscosities are as follows:

Fluid	Kinematic Viscosity
Water (20°)	1×10^{-6} (0.000001)
Oil SAE 50	5×10^{-5} (0.00005)
Honey (20°)	2×10^{-3} (0.002)
Chocolate syrup	3×10^{-3} (0.003)
Ketchup	1×10^{-1} (0.1)
Melting glass	1×10^{0} (1)

In addition to setting viscosity, you can set the degree to which the fluid sticks to a surface or slips off the surface in the boundary options (Bnd) of the Fluid tab. This is only an approximation to the behavior of real fluids. In reality, all fluid sticks to surfaces at the molecular level, but to the naked eye, fluids such as water appear to slide right off certain surfaces. Because the fluid simulator operates at resolutions much lower than molecular scale, it is unconvincing to have fluids such as water appear to stick to surfaces. For fluids that should not appear sticky or gluey, select Free for this option. Noslip will cause the fluid to stick to surfaces, and selecting Part will create a new field and enable you to input a PartSlip value to determine how much the fluid sticks to surfaces. You can set these options on individual obstacles as well.

Another quality of fluids that can be represented in Blender is *compressibility*. This is the degree to which the fluid shrinks in size or compresses under pressure. In nature, all fluids are very slightly compressible, but this is too slight to be noticeable at the scales that animators usually want to work with. In fact, the El'Beem simulator can work much faster if the fluid is considered to be slightly more compressible than it would be in nature, which is why this parameter exists. If you find that your fluid seems overly bouncy or elastic, you may want to consider lowering the compressibility.

Inflow and Outflow

When you use a Fluid object, the amount and initial location of the fluid introduced to the domain is determined by that object when the simulation begins. Animating the location or scale of a Fluid object will have no effect on the behavior of the fluid after the fluid has been generated. This is suitable for situations in which the amount of fluid you want to deal with is static, such as a sink full of water, but in cases where you want to introduce fluid to or remove fluid from the scene over time (such as an open tap or an unplugged drain), it is necessary to use Inflow and Outflow objects.

Using an Inflow object enables you to produce a steady stream of fluid into the simulation.

For a quick example, fire up a fresh session of Blender and do the following:

1. In the top view (NUM7), add a cylinder by pressing the spacebar and choosing Add > Mesh > Cylinder. Add a cylinder with the parameters shown in Figure 5.11. Make sure that Cap Ends is selected.

2. Scale the cylinder down by pressing the S key and holding down the Ctrl key while you scale down to 0.3, as shown in Figure 5.12. In a front view, select the bottom vertices as in Figure 5.13 and delete them, resulting in a disk.

Nils Thuerey

Nils Thuerey is a senior researcher in the Computer Graphics Laboratory at ETH Zurich, working on the development of new algorithms to enable real-time fluid simulation for games. While completing his PhD, Nils implemented the El'Beem Fluid Simulator for Blender as part of the Google Summer of Code 2005. Nils has published extensive research on use of the Lattice-Boltzmann method for fluid simulations (the method used in the El'Beem simulator) and continues to contribute to Blender as a developer. His *Magic Fluid Control* demo video was shown as a featured animation at SIGGRAPH 2007, showcasing several exciting new possibilities for Blender fluid animation. Nils' web page, which includes a list of his scholarly publications as well as an inspiring collection of fluid simulation animations and images, can be found at http://graphics.ethz.ch/~thuereyn. There you can see more of the potential of LBM for animated fluid effects and learn more about the fascinating field of computational fluid dynamics.

3. Tab into Object mode, rotate the disk –90 degrees, and place it in the upper portion of the default cube, as in Figure 5.14. For reference, turn on the Translate Manipulator (if it's not already on) and set it to indicate local axes.

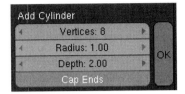

Figure 5.11 Add a cylinder.

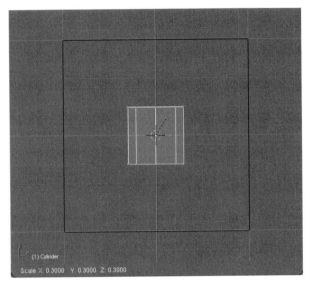

Figure 5.12 Scale the cylinder down.

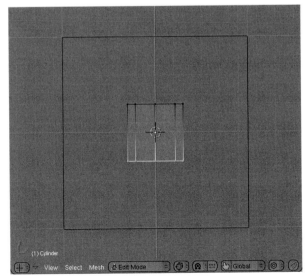

Figure 5.13 Select and delete the bottom vertices.

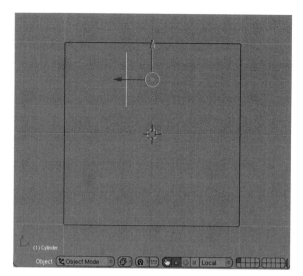

4. As in the previous examples, set the default cube to be the domain, and leave all the default parameters as they are, except for the display quality, which should be set to Final. Select the disk-shaped Cylinder object and enable the fluid simulation for the object, selecting Inflow and setting the options as in Figure 5.15. Because this object has no volume, it will produce fluid only by the Init Shell method, so this should be selected.

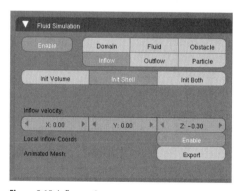

Figure 5.15 Inflow options

5. To give the in-flowing fluid some initial velocity out of the Inflow object, set Inflow Velocity to –0.30 on the Z axis. Select Enable for the Local Inflow Coords to make the Inflow Velocity direction local to the Inflow object. If this is not selected, the Inflow Velocity will be along the global Z axis, which is not what you want in this particular example. Increasing the velocity will increase the force with which the fluid hits walls and obstacles, resulting in more-violent splashing.

6. After you enter these options, select the Domain object and bake the fluid simulation. As you can see in Figure 5.16, the fluid enters the simulation through the Inflow object and fills up the domain. If you set the simulation to continue for enough frames, the domain will eventually fill up completely.

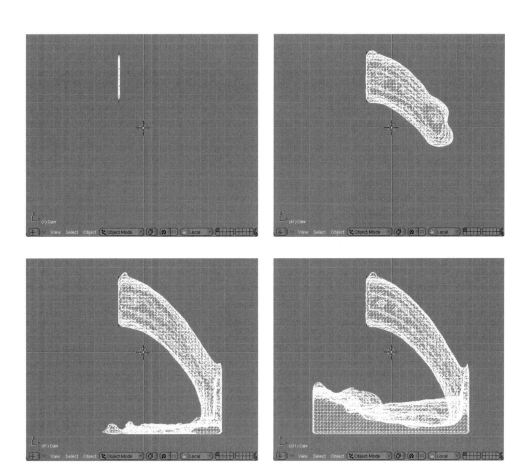

Figure 5.16 Fluid simulation with inflow

As you can probably imagine, the Outflow object is the exact opposite of the Inflow object, and it provides a way to get fluid out of the simulation domain. For an example of an outflow in action, set up a fluid simulation with the default cube and an Icosphere, as in the first example in this chapter, with the cube as the domain and the Icosphere as the Fluid object. Copy the default cube by pressing Shift+D and scale down to 0.2 along the X and Z axes. To do this, press the S key to scale, followed by Shift+Y to keep the Y axis constant, as seen from the front view in Figure 5.17. Place this new object in the lower corner of the default cube, as in Figure 5.18.

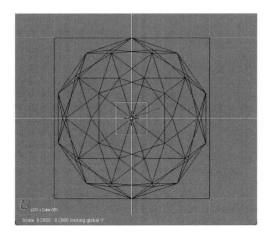

Figure 5.17
Scale the new cube along the X and Z axes by pressing S to scale, and Shift+Y to hold the Y axis constant.

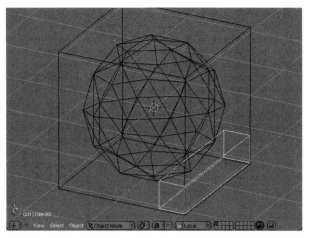

Figure 5.18 Place the object in the lower corner of the fluid domain.

Because this object was copied from the default cube, it already has Fluid Simulation enabled, but with Domain selected. Change this to Outflow. Otherwise, if Fluid Simulation is not enabled, enable it and select Outflow. As in the other examples, select the Domain object and click Bake. The resulting fluid simulation will look similar to the images in Figure 5.19. As you can see, the fluid is removed from the simulation when it comes in contact with the Outflow object.

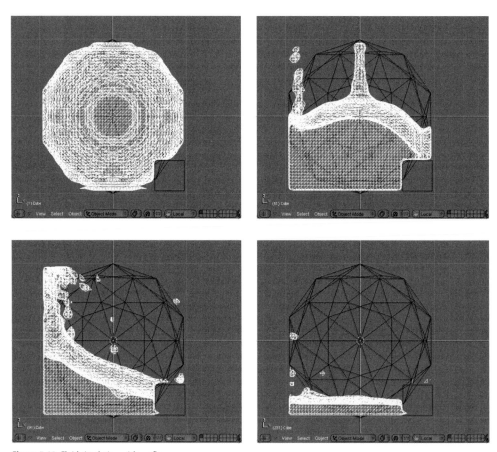

Figure 5.19 Fluid simulation with outflow

Time, Size, and Resolution

In running the previous examples, you probably noticed that this default simulation setup is moving in slow motion. This is because the fluid simulator's default time span does not coincide with the 10-second default animation length in Blender. The fluid simulator calculates time and space independently from what is going on in other parts of Blender, enabling you to set the parameters for the fluid simulation directly in real-world terms.

Starting and Ending

The time span for the fluid simulation is set in the Fluid Simulation panel of the Domain object, in the standard (Std) options. It is set in seconds. By default, the Start time of the fluid simulation is set to 0 and the End time is set to 0.30, meaning that the simulation covers a time span of 0.3 seconds. As I mentioned, this is totally independent of the actual animation length. The animation's length of time is the number of frames divided by the frame rate. By default, the number of frames is set to 250 and the frame rate is set to 25 frames per second, so the default length of a Blender animation is 10 seconds. If the fluid time span is shorter than the animation time span, the fluid simulation will "stretch" to fit the animation time, and so the fluid movement will be in slow motion when the animation is viewed at regular speed. If the time span set in the fluid simulation panel is longer in seconds than the actual length of the rendered animation, the motion will be sped up to fit into the time span of the animation. For realistic speeds, the time span of the animation in seconds should be equal to the number of frames divided by the frame rate of the animation.

The Start time and End time values refer to the time within the simulation. If you set the Start time as later than 0.0, the first frame of the animation will represent the state of the fluid at that time point. What if you want the entire fluid simulation to start later in the animation? To do this, you use a script to renumber the mesh files that the simulator outputs. The mesh files are numbered by frame number, and several scripts are available that will renumber them to start at a frame later than 1.

One such script is Claudio Dobniewski's reframe_sequence.py, which is included on the CD that accompanies this book. To use this script, open a Text Editor window in Blender and load the script as shown in Figure 5.20 by choosing Open from the File menu and finding the script in the file browser. Edit lines 40, 41, and 42 appropriately to suit the file path of your own fluid simulations. Line 41 deals with multiple simulations, so you can ignore it for now. Line 42 contains the offset value. In the illustration, the value is set to 50, meaning that the simulation will be shifted to begin at frame 51. After running this script, the Domain object will remain in its unbaked shape for the first 50 frames of the animation. You can simply key the Domain object onto an invisible layer until it needs to make an appearance.

```
23  # ***** END GPL LICENCE BLOCK *****
24  # -----------------------------------------
25
26  ''' reframe_sequence.py sirve para renombrar el numero de frame de ar
27  con el formato nombrearchivo0001.xxx donde 0001 representa los 4 digi
28  frame y xxx la terminacion que identifica el tipo de archivo (como no
29  importancia el tipo de archvio)
30
31  NOTA: No se verifica que los archivos pertenescan a la secuencia, el
32  de la carpeta
33
34  WARNING!!! this script renames ALL files on the specified paths, it d
35
36  import sys, os, os.path, string,shutil
37  from os.path import *
38  from string import *
39
40  path1 = "C:/tmp/fluidsim/" #path of fluid simulation files.
41  path2 = "" # for multiple simulation folders.
42  offset = 50 # how many frames to add to each frame file
43
44  archivos = os.listdir(path1+path2) # to get names of all files in pat
45
46  # fix: prevent a short offset overlap frames names (i.d., if first fr
47  # is 0001 in a range of 0001-0050, and add = 3, rename name0001 to na
48  # deleting name0004 file.
49  if offset < 0:
50      archivos.sort()
51  else:
52      archivos.sort()
53      archivos.reverse()
54
55  for a in archivos.__iter__ ():
56      _fullpath = path1+path2+a
57      print _fullpath
58      if isfile(_fullpath) == True:
```

File   Edit   Format   ☐ ⬚ AB   ◇ X:fluid_time_offset.py ✕   Screen 12

Figure 5.20
Edit lines 40, 41, and 42 with the appropriate information for your simulation.

Real-World Size

The real-world size of the simulation domain is set independently within the simulation itself and relates to how fast the fluid appears to move. The size is set in the RealworldSize field under Adv in the Fluid Simulation panel of the Domain object. The size is measured in meters, so the default size of 0.03 means that the fluid simulation is calculated within a 3-centimeter cube. If the shape of the Domain object is oblong, the size value represents the longest edge of the Domain's bounding box.

How you set the size value depends on the size of the area within your scene that needs to have fluid simulation enabled. Take into consideration the relative size of the props you are using, and also the area in which splashes and spills need to happen. The maximum real-world size for a fluid simulation is 10 meters.

Note: Obviously, with a real-world size limit of 10 meters, the fluid simulator is not designed to directly simulate large bodies of water. This is not a limitation of Blender's fluid simulation so much as a reflection of the astronomical computing resources required to do such a simulation at meaningful resolutions. In fact, the city-destroying tidal waves, raging oceans, and sinking ships you see in CG movies are usually not created directly with full-sized fluid simulations, which would be prohibitively resource-intensive and not offer sufficient control. Rather, these effects are accomplished by ingenious combinations of a variety of technical solutions. As you'll see in this chapter, there are ways to use particles to fake higher-resolution fluid simulations, but also remember that you have numerous tools at your disposal besides fluids: modifiers, animated textures, lattices, shapes, hooks, parenting, particles, compositing tools, and more. If you want to sink the Titanic or deluge New York, you will want to think in terms of solutions that bring these tools to bear.

Resolution

In terms of the time and memory needed for calculating the fluid simulation, and also in terms of the quality of the results, the most significant parameter to set is the resolution parameter. As I mentioned before, the fluid simulation domain is divided into discrete units called *voxels*. The density of voxels in the domain is the resolution of the fluid simulation. Resolution in this sense is directly analogous to image resolution; higher resolution yields clearer and more-detailed representations. The numerical resolution value you enter indicates the number of voxels that make up the longest edge of your domain. The amount of memory required to calculate a domain of a certain resolution does not depend in any way on the absolute size of the object or on the real-world size of the simulation, but it does depend on the volume of the domain with respect to the longest edge of the domain. This means that for any given resolution, a perfect cube-shaped domain will require the most memory.

In practice, the resolution you need is dependent on two factors: the precision or fineness of the interaction between the fluid and other objects, and the size of the area in which the fluid has to interact. Having a fluid that interacts in a convincing way with small objects but also involves a large area (and remember, splashing counts!) requires high resolutions. If your resolution is too low, your fluid will appear thick and gluey even if its viscosity is set correctly. In the bottle example shown in Figure 5.21, higher resolution (over 300) is needed because the fluid has to be fine enough to come out of the bottle smoothly, but the domain needs to be big enough to allow for a fairly spread-out splash. This example requires slightly more than 3 gigabytes of RAM. The amount of memory needed goes up with the cubed value of the resolution, meaning that slightly higher resolution can take considerably more memory. Blender's fluid simulator has a maximum resolution of 512, which requires almost 13 gigabytes to process. Hardware is not the only bottleneck here. Some operating systems also place limits on the amount of RAM that can be used at one time by a particular program.

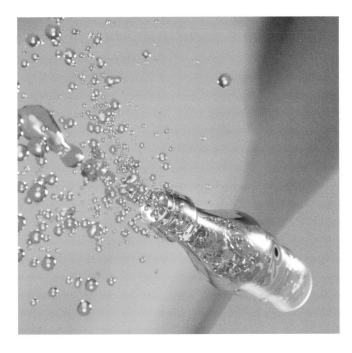

Figure 5.21

Splashing bottle of pop

Particles

Blender's fluid simulator has several options for using particles in conjunction with the simulation. Particles within the simulation are related to Blender's native particle systems, but are restricted in the degree to which they can be adjusted by hand. In this way, particles generated by the fluid simulator are analogous to meshes generated by the fluid simulator, which cannot be edited by hand, cannot take shape keys, and so forth.

There are two distinct ways to use the particles, although they are not entirely independent of each other. One use of particles is to enhance the appearance of the fluid sim meshes themselves. In this case, the particles are used to contribute actual geometry to the mesh, which can result in the appearance of higher-resolution simulations and greatly increase the "splashiness" of the simulation. The other option is to use the same particles in a more-traditional way, to add a halo-based haze to the fluid that follows the fluid's movement in a sensible way. This can be particularly good for simulating foam and spray from rushing water and can be useful when faking larger-scale fluid effects. Furthermore, there are three distinct types of particle systems created by the fluid simulator that are used in slightly different ways, as you will see in the next section.

Particle Splash

To see a good example of how particles can be used to get splashier fluids, set up a fluid simulation with an inflow along the lines of the example shown earlier in Figure 5.16.

The relevant fields for adding a particle-based effect can be found in the Fluid Simulation tab of the Domain object, in the Bnd (boundary) buttons area, accessed by clicking Bnd. The degree of splashiness (and the number of particles) is determined by the value in the Generate Particles field. The default value of 0 means no particles are generated. A value of 1.00 means a "normal" number of particles are generated, and a value of greater than 1 means more than a normal number are generated. The degree of splashiness that you actually see as a result of the particles depends also on the force with which the fluid strikes an obstacle or wall. This, in turn, depends on the initial velocity of the fluid, and on the impact factor of the obstacle, which I talk about in the next section.

In order for the particles to affect the mesh geometry, it is also necessary to set the Surface Subdiv to a value greater than 1. The values should be set as shown in Figure 5.22.

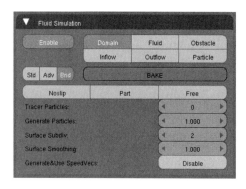

Figure 5.22

Generating particles to act on fluid meshes

Figure 5.23 shows several renders of the same frame in the same animation to illustrate the difference in using varying amounts of particles. As you can see, a greater value for particles increases the splashiness of the simulation. Increasing the fluid's velocity will also increase the violence of the splash.

Figure 5.23 Particles set at 0, 0.05, 1, and 5. All simulations are resolution 50 with Surface Subdiv set at 2.

Note: The Surface Subdiv field in the Fluid Simulation tab is analogous to the Subsurf modifier for meshes, but does a considerably better job on fluids. It is possible to apply an ordinary Subsurf modifier to fluid meshes, but if you have Surface Subdiv set to a value greater than 1, a Subsurf modifier is redundant and can lead to slow speeds and instability. If you experience a crash while rendering high-resolution fluid simulations with a Surface Subdiv value of greater than 1, it may be due to the presence of an unnecessary Subsurf modifier on the mesh.

Particle Haze

When you set a Generate Particles value of greater than 0, two particle systems are created: Drops and Floats. The two systems move differently and play complementary roles in augmenting the simulation. These same particles can also be used as halo particles, to obtain a haze or foam effect that follows the motion of the fluid simulation in a convincing way. An additional type, Tracer particles, can also be used in this way.

To access these three particle simulations individually, as objects in their own right, it is necessary to enable yet another type of object for the fluid simulation, namely a Particle object. You've probably noticed the Particle button on the Fluid Simulation panel by now. This is what you will select to enable the Particle object.

To see an example of this in action, set up a fresh fluid simulation with the default cube as the domain and a small Icosphere as the fluid, as shown in Figure 5.24. For the particle control objects, I've also added three Suzannes to the simulation by pressing the spacebar and selecting Add > Mesh > Monkey, and placed them in an accessible spot. These do not need to be inside the domain area, and any Mesh object will do. The entire setup should look something like Figure 5.24.

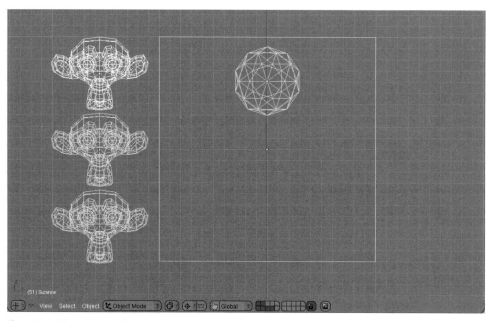

Figure 5.24 Cube, sphere, and three monkeys

You set up particle objects the same way you do fluid and domain objects—by enabling fluid simulations and selecting Particle. Each Particle object can be used to control one or more of the three types of particles available. The three types are as follows:

Drops are particles that break away from the main mesh in a splashing pattern. They represent droplets that result from impact with obstacles or domain boundaries. They affect the shape of the mesh and can also be used as a free-standing halo particle system.

Floats are particles that are produced within the shell of the fluid mesh. They add "bumpiness" to the fluid mesh, to give the impression of roiling and bubbling on the mesh surface. Like Drops, they affect the shape of the mesh and can be used as free-standing halo particles.

Tracers are particles that follow behind the fluid as it moves. They can be used to create trailing vapor, steam, or foam behind the fluid. Unlike Floats and Drops, Tracers do not affect the shape of the mesh; they are used only as free-standing halo particles. They are also activated separately on the domain by directly entering a number value in the Tracers field, rather than being created with Generate Particles.

Although it is possible to activate all three particle types on a single Particle object, I'm using three separate monkeys for visualization purposes. Enable fluids with the Particle options selected as in Figure 5.25.

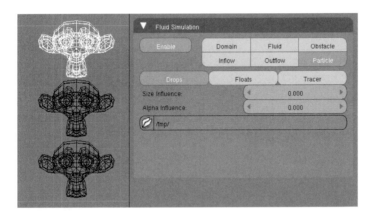

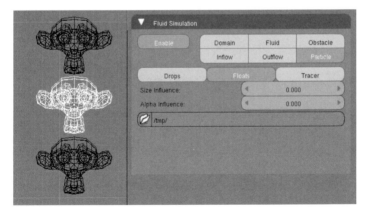

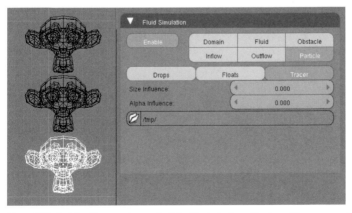

Figure 5.25 Enabling three monkeys as Particle objects for Drops, Floats, and Tracers, respectively

As for the fluid simulation itself, I've left all the values on the domain at the default, except of course the particle values. To create Drop and Float particles, you must enter a nonzero value into Generate Particles, and to create Tracers, you must enter the number of particles you want as Tracer particles. For presentation purposes in this example, I've set the particles at a very high level in order to make them as visible as possible in the screen shots. I set the Tracer particles at 10,000 and the Generate Particles value at 10.00. In practice, a Generate Particles value of 1.00 is considered "normal," and depending on the situation, even much less than this is often sufficient.

When you bake the fluid simulation, the three particle systems are generated. These particle systems now can be selected similarly to ordinary particle systems, by selecting their base mesh, which is the Particle object associated with the particle type. As you can see in Figure 5.26, when the monkey associated with Drops is selected, the float particle system shows up as a selected system, and likewise for Floats and Tracers. This figure should also give you an idea of the different roles that the Drops, Floats, and Tracer particles play. As you can see, Drops spread out from the center, whereas Floats tend to stay collected in a central area where fluid is. Tracers trail behind the falling fluid and lead back to the original sphere-shaped Fluid object mesh (over time, they will catch up to the fluid's current location).

You can add a material to a fluid simulation Particle object in the same way as you would with any other object. To edit the halo settings for the particle system, activate Halo on the particle material. Although the Particle object mesh is entirely separate from the particles, its relationship with the particles is similar to that of the emitter mesh with ordinary particle systems. You can parent another mesh to the Particle object and use Blender's dupliverts functionality to associate an instance of the mesh with each particle. You can manually edit some of the particle settings on the Particle object, such as the life span, but you are restricted from editing others, such as the number of particles, which are determined by the fluid simulator.

In the following examples, Tracer particles are turned off (set to 0) and Generate Particles is set at 0.05. Even with this light use of particles, you can already get an idea of the possibilities. Set the particle material values as in Figure 5.27, with a Clouds texture as shown in Figure 5.28 (mapped to alpha), to get a steam-like effect as in Figure 5.29. Changing the halo type as in Figure 5.30 and giving the particles a distinctive blue-green color will result in the eerie phosphorescent effect in Figure 5.31. Finally, by creating small spheres (I used Icospheres of subdivision 1, to minimize extraneous vertices) and dupliverting them onto the particles as discussed in Chapter 3 it is possible to create a reasonably convincing bubble effect, as shown in Figure 5.32. The material for the bubbles is a copy of the water material with Ray Mirroring increased slightly.

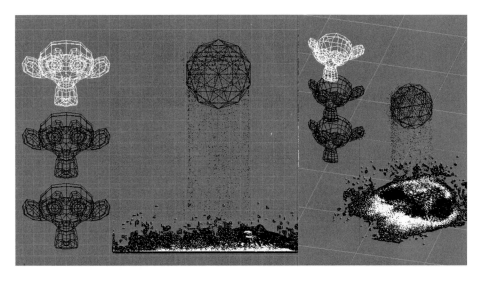

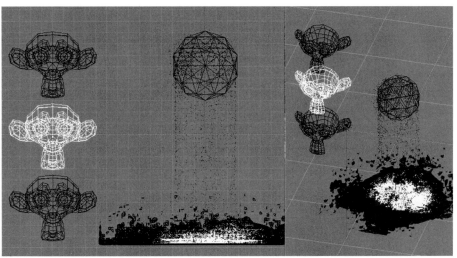

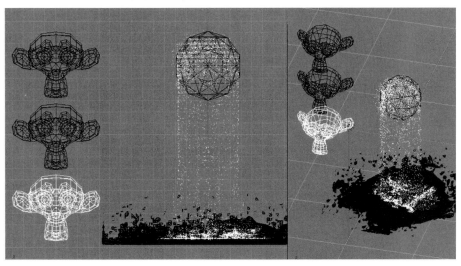

Figure 5.26 Selecting fluid sim particle objects

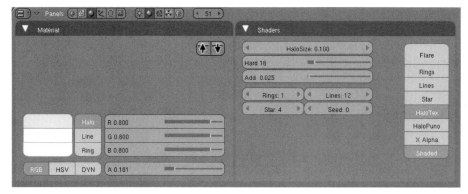

Figure 5.27 Material halo settings to create a steam effect

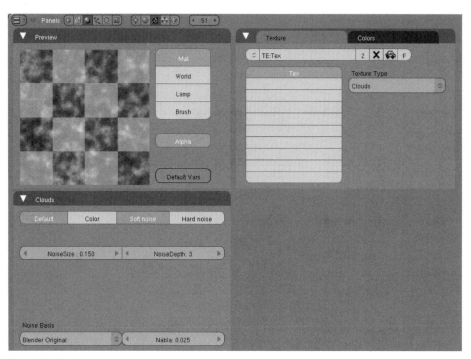

Figure 5.28 Clouds texture for steam

Figure 5.29 Steam effect with fluid particles

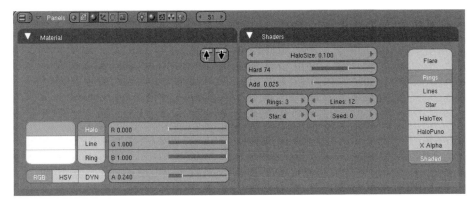

Figure 5.30 Material halo settings to create phosphorescent glow

Figure 5.31 Phosphorescent glow

Figure 5.32 Bubble effect with dupliverted spheres

Obstacles and Animation

Making fluid splash around in the shape of a cube is fun for a while, but the real use-
fulness of the fluid simulator only truly becomes clear when you introduce other objects
for the fluid to interact with. Such objects are called *obstacles* in Blender's fluid simulation. In this terminology, an obstacle is not just a dam or a wall, but any object that

interacts physically with the fluid. A cup is an obstacle for the coffee inside it, and your whole body is an obstacle when you scoop water up with your hands and splash it on your face—although in Blender these two cases are treated slightly differently, as you will see shortly.

In the simplest case of a nondeforming mesh obstacle, enabling the object as an obstacle for a fluid simulation is as simple as—you guessed it—enabling the fluid simulation for the object and selecting Obstacle.

To look at a simple example of this, start a new session of Blender and switch to front view by pressing NUM1. Set up a fluid simulation with the default cube as the domain and an Icosphere as the fluid. Scale the Icosphere vertically by pressing the S key and then the Z key and scaling down, and then move the Fluid object to the top of the domain area, as in Figure 5.33.

Place a second cube in the middle of the domain and scale it as in Figure 5.34.

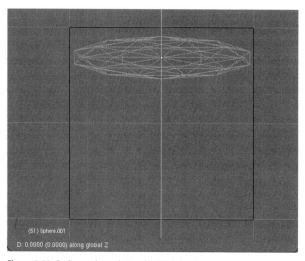

Figure 5.33 Scaling and translating the Fluid object

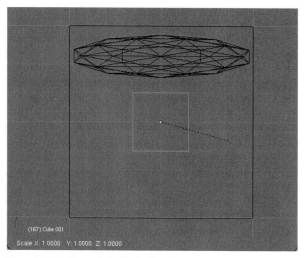

Figure 5.34 Placing a cube inside the domain

Enable fluid simulation for the new cube, with Obstacle selected. Because the cube is a solid mesh, use the default Init Volume to initialize the fluid. As with other elements of the fluid simulation, if your obstacle is a plane or nonmanifold mesh, you should use Init Shell. Bake the fluid. The simulation should occur along the lines of Figure 5.35.

If the obstacle and the fluid intersect at the beginning of the simulation, the place where they intersect is removed from the fluid. In Figure 5.36, the highlighted Obstacle object bisects the Fluid object completely, resulting in the simulation behavior shown in Figure 5.37.

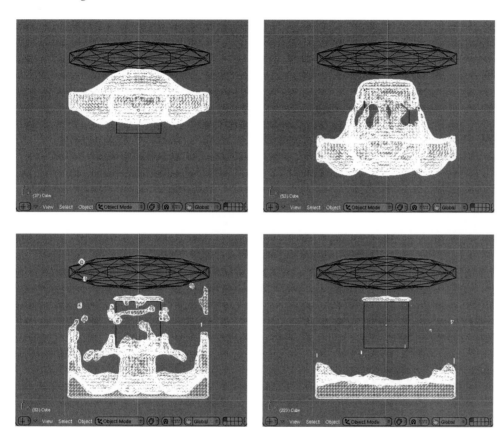

Figure 5.35 Fluid simulation with an obstacle

Figure 5.36
Fluid and Obstacle objects intersect

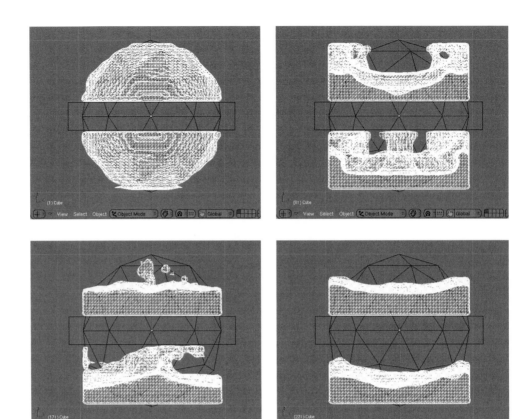

Figure 5.37 Fluid object bisected by an obstacle

Note: Leakage and poor obstacle interaction can be caused by inconsistent normals in the Obstacle mesh and by having obstacles that are too small. Be sure that your obstacle meshes are clean and that they are bigger than the size of a voxel in your simulation—that is, the length of the longest edge of the domain bounding box divided by the resolution.

Animated Obstacles

For a simple example of fluid interacting with an animated obstacle, set up a fluid simulation with a default cube as the domain and an Icosphere as the fluid. Copy the cube, scale it down along the Z axis to the shape of a thick board, and scale it slightly along the X axis, as shown in Figures 5.38 and 5.39. Set this to be an Obstacle object.

At frame 1, key the rotation of the Obstacle object by pressing the I key and selecting Rot, as in Figure 5.40.

Advance 20 frames and, in front view, rotate the object about 90 degrees counterclockwise. Key the new rotation at frame 21, as in Figure 5.41.

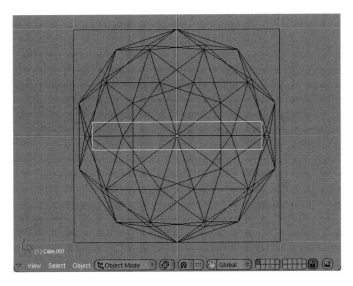

Figure 5.38
The Obstacle object from front view

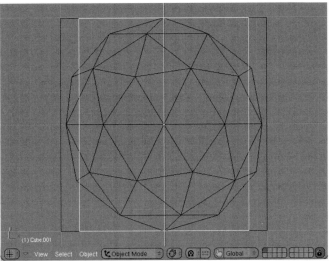

Figure 5.39
The Obstacle object from top view

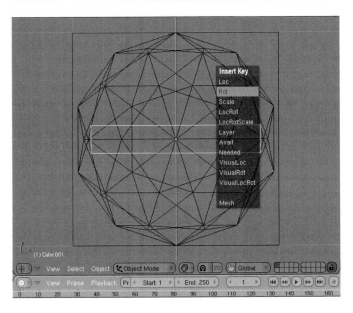

Figure 5.40
Keying rotation

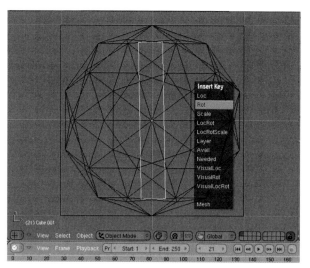

Figure 5.41 Keying the new rotation

Open an Ipo Editor window and Select the RotY Ipo. By default, the Ipo represents the Bezier interpolation between the two keyframes you set with a Constant extend. Choose Curve > Extend Mode > Extrapolation, as in Figure 5.42. The result is a straight Ipo as you see in Figure 5.43, representing continuous rotation of the object at a uniform speed.

This is it for setting up the animation. Now select your Domain object and bake. The resulting fluid simulation will animate along the lines of Figure 5.44.

If an object is deformed by an armature or some other way, it is necessary to click the Animated Mesh: Export button option when making the object an Obstacle, as in Figure 5.45. This takes extra computing time and should be used only when the actual shape of the obstacle mesh changes over time.

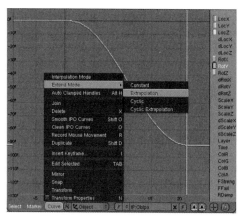

Figure 5.42 Extrapolating the Ipo curve

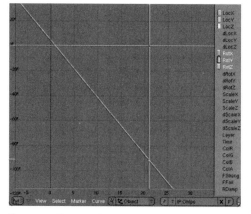

Figure 5.43 The extrapolated curve

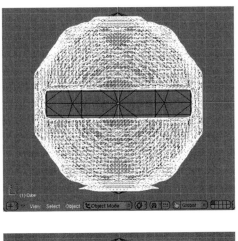
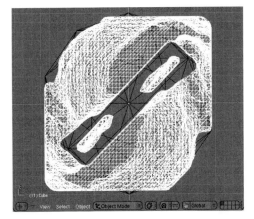
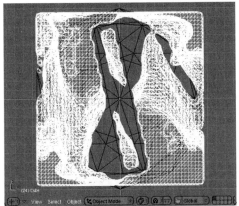
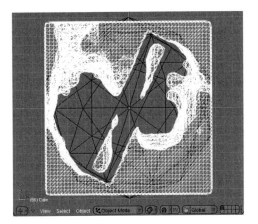

Figure 5.44 The fluid interacts with a rotating obstacle.

Figure 5.45 Animated Mesh: Export button

As an example of this, I set up a simple rigged arm obstacle and a fluid system that uses a rectangular fluid, placed at the bottom of the domain, as shown in Figure 5.46. In Figure 5.47, you can see the resulting fluid behavior when the armature is animated and the corresponding arm mesh splashes.

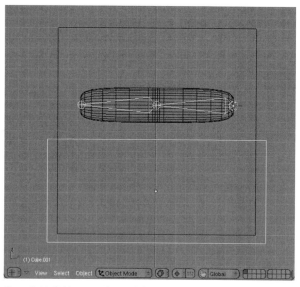

Figure 5.46 Fluid setup with rigged obstacle

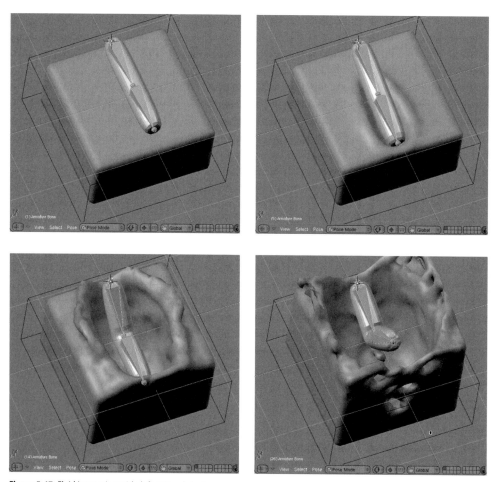

Figure 5.47 Fluid interacting with deforming obstacle

Getting the Shot

A CG fluid simulation needs to be set up in such a way that it looks right in the shot. When working in the highly controlled environment of CG, it's sometimes easy to forget the degree to which naturalistic phenomena can need time to get into position. Blender fluid systems often begin in unnatural states, and the transition into the correct state for the shot may involve unwanted movement or splashing. You may find it necessary to run a simulation for some time before your actual shot begins, in order to let the fluid find some equilibrium. You may need to apply off-camera "cheats" such as guiding or pushing your fluids in ways that do not show up in the shot itself. You'll have to be creative. The important thing is to get the shot you're after. Nobody sees what goes on before and after the shot, or outside the boundaries of the camera.

In this section, you will look at a few examples of fluid setups and see how to get the results shown. When dealing with fluids, there are few absolutes, and the settings you use will depend very much on the specifics of your own shot. These aren't step-by-step tutorials, but rather a broad look at how specific projects can be approached with the fluid simulator. The .blend files are available on the CD that accompanies this book so you can study the details more closely, and I have glossed over some steps that I assume intermediate Blender users can fill in for themselves. The intention of these examples is to get you on the right track to using fluids in your own projects, and to explain why certain choices are made so that when you do get down to fiddling with the parameters on your own work, you won't be fiddling blindly.

Strawberries and Milk

The image by Mike Pan shown in Figure 5.48 is a terrific example of how the appearance of fluids can be enhanced with well-chosen materials, lighting, and render effects. It is also a nice example of a simple and effective use of animated obstacles. You can find the .blend file for this image on the CD for this book.

Although the image is simple, there's quite a bit going on in the .blend file to get things just right. If you open the .blend and zoom around with layers 1 and 2 (counting from the left on the top row of layer buttons), you'll see the whole setup. Everything to be rendered is on layer 1, and the Fluid object mesh, shown selected in Figure 5.49, is on layer 2. As you can see, the Fluid object is a rectangular mesh taking up the entire lower portion of the domain. Because the only force active on the fluid to start off with will be gravity, this setup ensures that the fluid will be an undisturbed surface at the beginning of the simulation. At the start of the simulation, the strawberries are mostly outside of the domain altogether, but this doesn't matter. You can see the Ipos for one of the strawberries in Figure 5.50. To create these Ipos, Mike used the rigid body physics engine to record the fall of the strawberries, as you'll learn how to do in Chapter 7, "Plant Simulation." The resulting Ipos are just like any other Ipo curves in Blender. The strawberries' fall downward is shown in Figure 5.51. When they enter the domain, they will affect the fluid.

Figure 5.48 *Strawberries and Milk* by Mike Pan

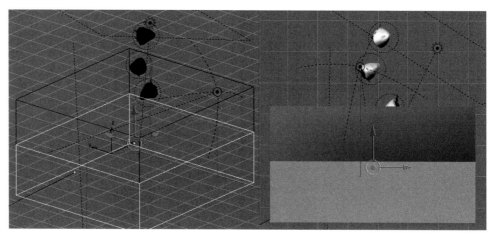

Figure 5.49 The full setup for *Strawberries and Milk*, with the Fluid object selected

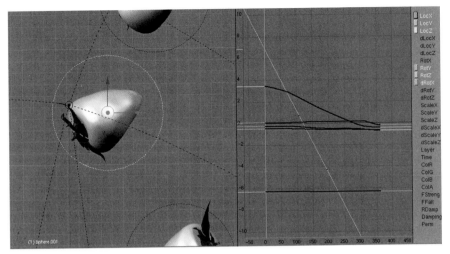

Figure 5.50 Ipos for one strawberry object

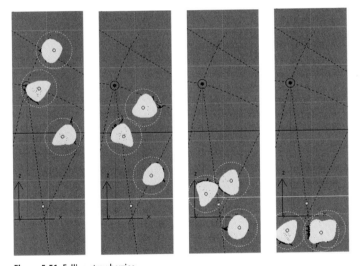

Figure 5.51 Falling strawberries

Each strawberry is two distinct objects: the strawberry itself, and the stem and leaves object, which is parented to the strawberry object. Although each of the three strawberries is a separate object, all three strawberries and all three stem/leaves objects share the same two meshes, shown in Figure 5.52.

Figure 5.52 Strawberry and stem meshes

Materials and Textures

The main material settings for the milk are shown in Figure 5.53. The color is almost white but with a slightly blue tint. Diffuse reflectivity is set low, which is common for specular materials such as water, but in this case specularity is considerably lower than it would be for a "shinier" fluid such as water. Hardness is set at 100 to give some definition to the specular highlights.

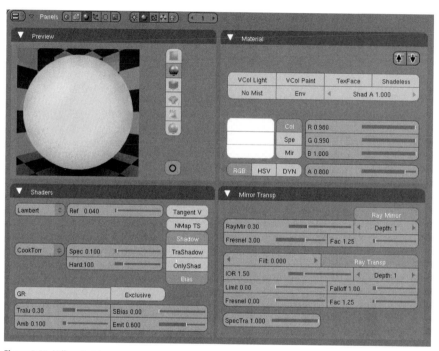

Figure 5.53 Milk material

The Ray Mirror settings enable the fluid to reflect the color of the strawberries in a way that winds up similar in appearance to radiosity. Because of the texturing of the milk's surface and the subsurface scattering effect, the reflections will be diffuse, as they should be, because milk does not reflect sharp mirror images in most viewing conditions. The Fresnel value ensures that the clarity of the mirroring depends on the angle of viewing the material.

To express the translucency of the milk, Ray Transp is activated, with the alpha value set to 0.8 on the Material panel. The index of refraction is set to 1.50, which is slightly higher than is normal for water. Because the material is almost opaque, the refraction effect will be subtle anyway.

Finally, a very fine cloud bump map texture, shown in Figure 5.54, is applied to the material, giving the effect of a coating of sugar on the milk.

The strawberry and leaves materials each have several textures associated with them, both procedural and image textures, including a noise bump texture that serves a similar purpose to the cloud texture on the milk. The image textures are shown in Figure 5.55.

Figure 5.54 Cloud texture for the milk

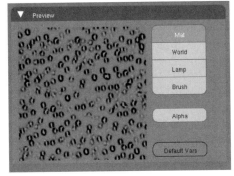

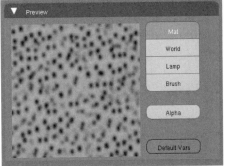

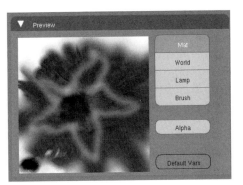

Figure 5.55 Image textures for the strawberries and the stems

The stem and leaves objects also have texture displacement modifiers placed on them, to add an extra level of realism, as shown in Figure 5.56.

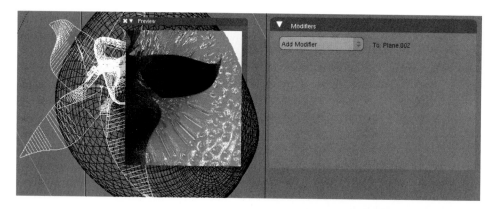

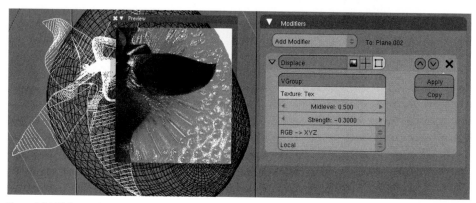

Figure 5.56 Without and with the displacement modifier

Fluid Settings

The fluid settings for the milk in this image are shown in Figure 5.57. In the standard (Std) options, the resolution is set to 250, which is reasonable for a good-looking image given a minimum of detailed interaction with obstacles. The only thing the milk has to do here is to splash when the strawberries hit it, so it's not necessary to have especially high resolution, although lower resolution would probably detract from the image quality. The start time and end time are 0.00 and 0.60, respectively, meaning that the real-world time of the fluid is 0.6 of a second. This animation is set up to span 500 frames, meaning that at 25 frames per second (fps), the resulting animation will be 20 seconds long. This is obviously very slow motion.

The advanced (Adv) options are left at the default values except for Gravity and Realworld-Size. Realworld-Size is set to 0.050, or 5 centimeters. This is slightly smaller than the actual size of real strawberries, but it is more or less the same scale. The Realworld-Size parameter is most important to get right when the animation is intended to be in real time, as it relates to how fast energy travels through the lattice. Slight variations are not noticeable, especially when dealing with slow motion or sped-up animations. The gravity of the fluid, likewise, is set here at –2 rather than the default (and natural) –9.8. This has been adjusted to give the most visually pleasing effect. Tweaking parameters such as gravity is one way that the animator can maintain control over a process that has many random aspects.

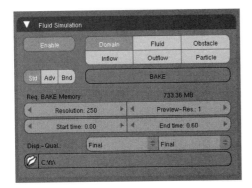
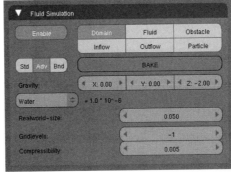

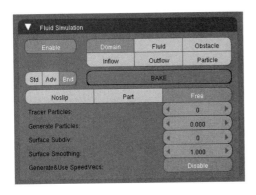

Figure 5.57

Settings in the Fluid Simulation tab for standard (Std), advanced (Adv), and boundary (Bnd) options

Mike Pan

The artist who created the *Strawberries and Milk* image is Mike Pan, an 18-year-old first-year student in engineering from Vancouver, B.C. Mike got started with Blender in 2001, when he was just 12 and Blender had not yet gone open source. Like many longtime Blender users, Mike is completely self-taught and relied almost entirely on online tutorials and resources to learn Blender. Mike's chief interests in Blender are texturing, lighting, and exploring the possibilities offered by Blender's physical simulation features. His website (http://mpan3.homeip .net/) has some excellent examples of fluid and rigid body animations, as well as a striking collection of still shots.

Bottle of Pop

The image you saw previously in Figure 5.21 required considerably higher resolution to accomplish than the *Strawberries and Milk* image, because of the very literal bottleneck preventing the fluid from flowing freely at lower resolutions. In this case, the minimal resolution enabling me to accomplish the effect was 335, which consumed 3 gigabytes of RAM. At lower resolutions, the voxels were simply too large to recognize the small opening.

The bottle's mesh is shown in Figure 5.58. It's a simple model, and the material is a standard glass material.

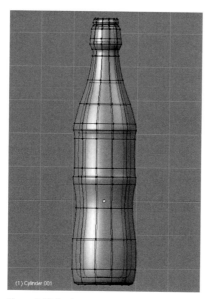

Figure 5.58 Bottle

Because I wanted to start the simulation with the bottle full of fluid, I needed Fluid objects that would fit nicely inside the bottle. Of course, it would be possible to model some kind of container fluid object to fit, but this may be more trouble than it's worth. Instead, I added a single Icosphere, enabled Fluid Simulation with Fluid set, and copied the sphere, resizing and moving the copies around as needed to fill up the inside of the bottle. The resulting collection of Fluid objects is shown in Figure 5.59. Remember, the fluid volume is calculated as the Boolean union of all these Icospheres. Alternately, in a simple case like this bottle, you could also create the Fluid object by selecting internal faces of the bottle object, duplicating them and separating them into another object, scaling down slightly, and then closing the mesh and recalculating the normals. I prefer the Icospheres approach because it requires no mesh editing at all and enables you to fill even complex spaces easily.

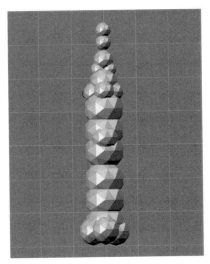

Figure 5.59 Fluid objects

The idea was to have the fluid splash out of the bottle as the bottle tumbled through the air. Obviously, there is a lot of randomness to this process, and controlling it precisely is not possible, so some trial and error is unavoidable. You can see one of my early experiments in Figure 5.60. The fluid movement in this attempt was fairly realistic, but I wanted a more-explosive, dynamic splash. To accomplish this, I turned particles on in the fluid settings and I added an invisible obstacle a small distance from the mouth of the bottle, parented to the bottle object, as shown in Figure 5.61.

Figure 5.60 An early attempt

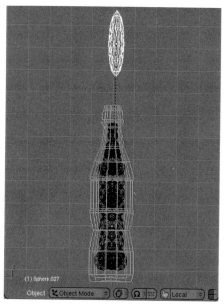

Figure 5.61 The bottle with Fluid objects inside and a parented obstacle to increase the splash

Because the splash had to take up a lot of space and I did not want the camera to see the splash hitting the walls of the domain, the domain needed to be fairly big in relation to the bottle, as you can see in Figure 5.62. This is why the resolution needed to be as high as it was.

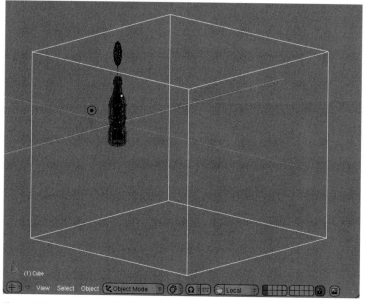

Figure 5.62 The bottle in the domain

Finally, I keyed the movement of the bottle by hand, as shown in Figure 5.63. Because I was mainly interested in using the frames as still illustrations, the actual movement of the bottle was not important to me; I wanted to produce only a variety of splash patterns that I could later render as stills. Note that although the bottle's movement is keyed, the Fluid objects stay in place, because the fluid has not been baked. After all the obstacles have been fully animated, the fluid simulation is run.

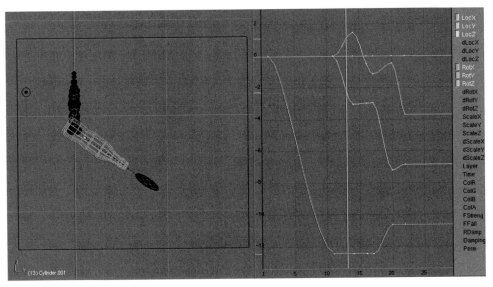

Figure 5.63 Ipos for the keyed motion of the bottle

The material for the orange soda is shown in Figure 5.64. Figure 5.65 shows the fluid settings, and Figure 5.66 shows some of the steps of the fluid as it baked. After you've baked the fluid, you can work on finding the best location for the camera, placing the background, and setting up the lights for the effect you want, as I've done in Figure 5.67.

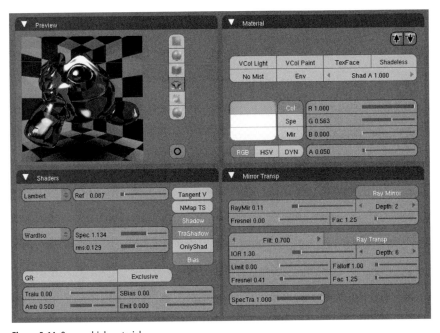

Figure 5.64 Orange drink material

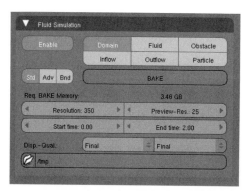

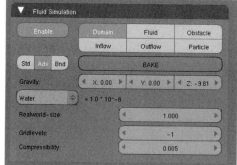

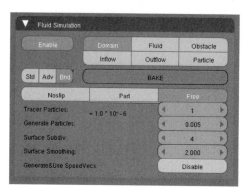

Figure 5.65
Fluid settings

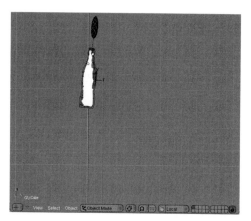

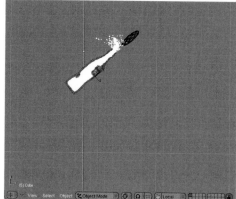

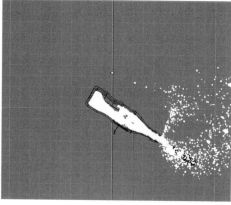

Figure 5.66 The baked fluid

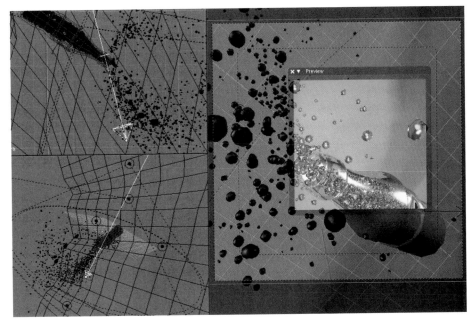

Figure 5.67 Light and camera setup

Rushing Creek

To create the image in Figure 5.68, I used a method of placing fluid similarly to what I did for the bottle of pop, except that in this case both inflows and outflows were also necessary, because the creek is flowing in and out of the frame.

Figure 5.68 A still frame from the rushing creek

To start, I created the simple creek bed shown in Figure 5.69. The object has Fluid Simulation enabled as an Obstacle object, with Init Shell, because it is a plane with no volume. For the rocks, I simply used subsurfaced cubes pulled in various oblong shapes to give them a bit of character, as in Figure 5.70, and I lined the creek bed with copies of the rocks, as in Figure 5.71. The rocks are all Obstacle objects with Init Volume, so it's easiest to set the Fluid Simulation settings before copying the objects. Otherwise, you would have to create fluid settings on each one later.

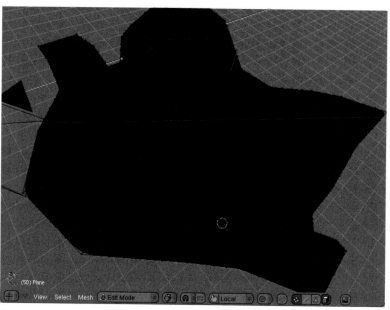

Figure 5.69 The creek bed mesh

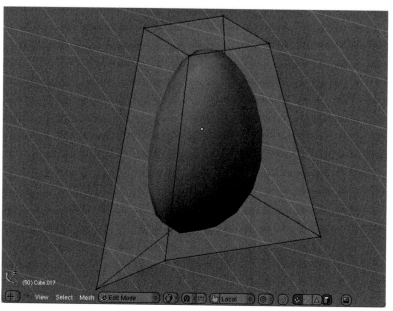

Figure 5.70 A rock

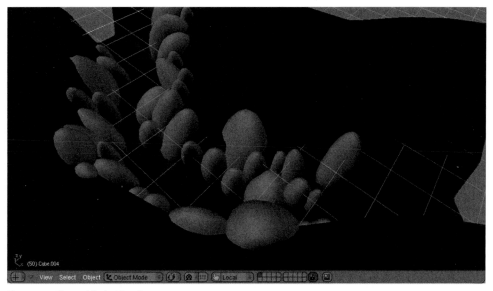

Figure 5.71 The creek bed with rocks

The fluid domain is shown in Figure 5.72. It covers the minimal area possible to ensure that splashes do not hit the domain wall in view of the camera.

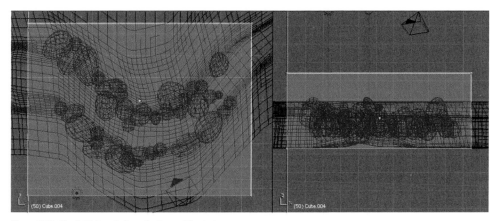

Figure 5.72 The fluid domain from the top and front views

Because I want the creek to flow in a specific direction, I know I will need inflow and outflow objects, but I also want to make sure that the creek starts out full, if only to save time so that I don't have to wait for it to fill up. I filled the creek in the same way I filled the bottle in the previous example, by using a number of Icospheres with Fluid Simulation enabled and Fluid selected for the type of object. The Fluid objects can be seen in Figure 5.73. For visualization purposes, I gave these objects a blue-tinted material. This isn't necessary for you to do, because the objects themselves will never be rendered. They are used only to give the fluid simulation its initial shape. I placed five Inflow objects among the Fluid objects. These are shown from below (Ctrl+NUM7), in Figure 5.74 in purple. I placed these Inflow objects slightly lower than the Fluid objects, so they are visible only from the underside of the riverbed mesh. Note that in both of these figures, the riverbed itself is seen in Wireframe view mode. The Inflow objects are all angled so that their local X axes point downstream, as you can see in the direction of the local axis manipulator for the selected sphere in the figure, and their initial velocity is set to be positive in the X axis. Each one was adjusted after several experimental bakes to keep the flow and level of the creek's water convincing.

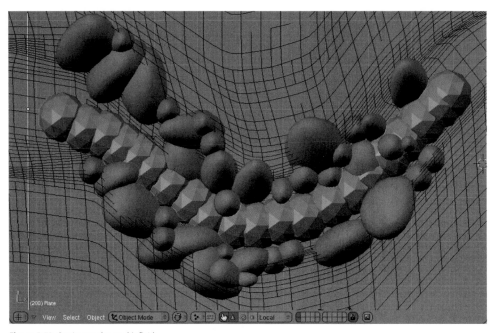

Figure 5.73 Setting up the creek's fluid

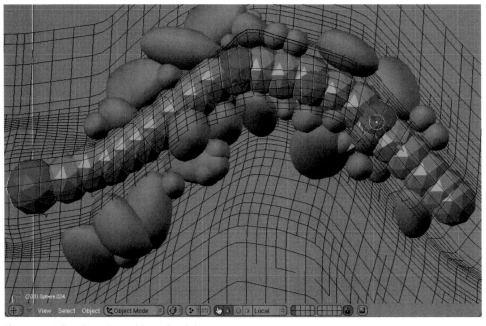

Figure 5.74 Inflow objects (in purple) seen from below

Finally, I placed three Outflow objects in the simulation domain, shown in red from the front view (NUM1) and at a slight angle in Figure 5.75. The main one occurs at the end of the creek simulation, just out of view of the camera. Another broad Outflow object was placed above the entire simulation to get rid of stray splashes that could cause unconvincing patterns, such as revealing the presence of the domain wall. Finally, a small Outflow object was placed above the first Inflow object, to control the flow and prevent the water from rising above the banks of the creek. You might also notice the unassuming monkey head off to the left of the simulation setup. This is of course the Particle object associated with Drops and Floats, set to a halo material.

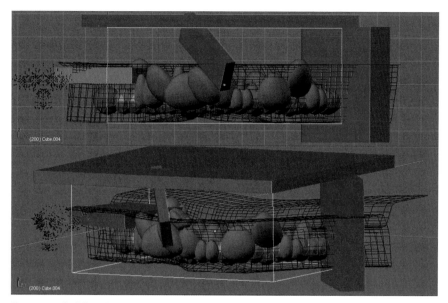

Figure 5.75 The full simulation setup

The banks of the creek should be grassy, so I add a grass particle system and weight-paint the banks as shown in Figure 5.76. Note that the weight-painting is done with this camera angle in mind. Grass that is farther away from the camera does not need to be as thick as grass that is closer to the camera. Even though the farther bank is less heavily weighted, it still appears denser than the close-up grass.

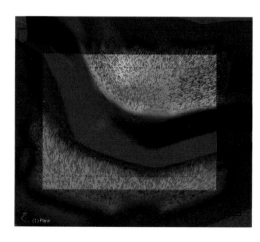

Figure 5.76
Weight-painting for grass

When the fluid is baked, it progresses as in Figure 5.77. The first frame is unnatural looking, because it still retains the shape of the series of spheres that provide the initial volume. Ten frames later, this shape is gone, but the creek has not begun to settle into its flow. About 60 frames into the simulation, the splashing is at its wildest, as the fluid has hit the banks and obstacles and the Inflow objects have begun to produce more fluid to push things downstream. The wild splashing subsides and the simulation settles into a normal flow at about frame 90, after which the motion remains fairly steady, and the simulation begins to most closely resemble the ordinary motion of a small river.

The simulation was baked with Generate & Use SpeedVecs enabled in the Bn buttons of the Fluid Simulation panel (it is enabled by default) and then rendered with Vec selected in the Render Layer tab, making it possible to use the vector blur composite node when compositing. Motion blur can greatly enhance the sense of rushing water in this kind of situation, and especially improves the appearance of the halo particles that follow the water's flow. The node setup for compositing is shown in Figure 5.78.

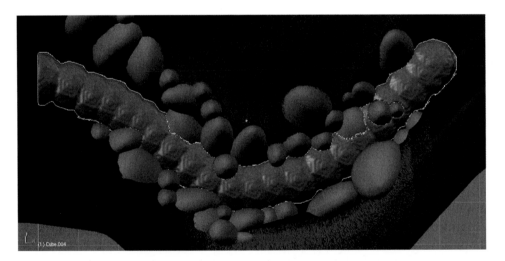

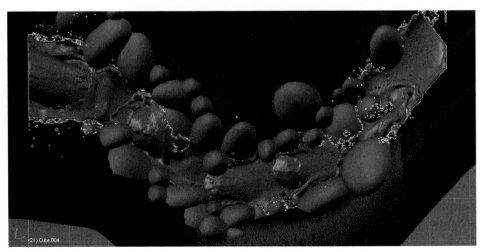

Figure 5.77 The baked simulation at frames 1, 11, 61, and 91

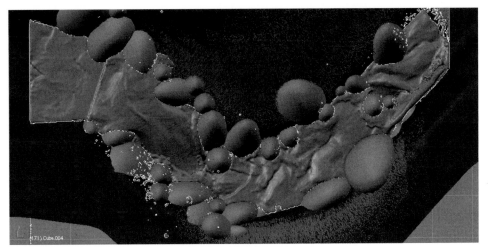

Figure 5.77 *(continued)*

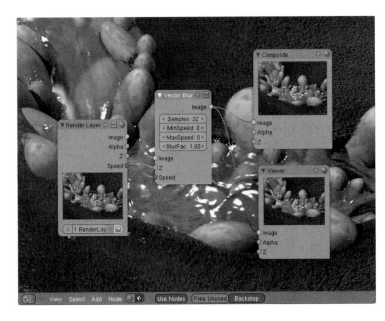

Figure 5.78
A rendered still with the
vector motion blur node

Delving Further into Fluids

There's quite a bit more to know about fluids, and as you work with them more you will surely discover potential uses that I have not covered here. In this section, I touch on a few more notable features of the fluid simulator.

Ipo Animation

Many of the fluid simulation parameters can be animated. By selecting the Fluidsim Ipo option from the drop-down in the Ipo Curve Editor, shown in Figure 5.79, you can set Ipo curves for various fluid sim values:

- Viscosity (Fac-Visc)
- Time (Fac-Time)
- X gravity (GravX)
- Y gravity (GravY)
- Z gravity (GravZ)
- X velocity (VelX)
- Y velocity (VelY)
- Z velocity (VelZ)
- Active

Figure 5.79
Fluidsim Ipo option

The Active Ipo is used to turn inflows on and off throughout an animation. By keying this curve, you can make an uneven inflow. Be sure that the Ipos are associated with the correct objects. The Active Ipo will not have any effect if it's associated with the Domain object; it must be associated with the Inflow object it is intended to control. Obviously, because the fluid simulation itself depends on the value of these Ipos, it is necessary to set the keys prior to baking.

Scripts and Exporting

In addition to the .blend files and animations of the examples in this chapter, you'll also find several useful scripts on the CD of this book. One is reframe_sequence.py, which was mentioned earlier in this chapter, for offsetting the start time of the simulation. Another useful script is bobj_import.py, which enables you to import fluid simulation meshes as ordinary editable meshes, such as you see in Figure 5.80. To do this, simply open the script in a Blender Text Editor window and run the script. The file browser will open, and you can select one of the .bobj files produced by the fluid simulator, with a filename such as fluidsurface_final_0075.bobj.gz (where the number indicates the corresponding frame in the animation). The mesh will be imported directly into the 3D viewport, and you can work with it in Edit mode just as you would with any other mesh object, as you can see in Figure 5.80.

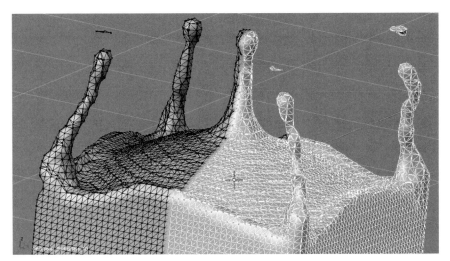

Figure 5.80 A mesh object derived from the fluid simulation with vertices selected in Edit mode

To export your fluid simulation for use in a different software package, select the baked fluid (the Domain object) and use the Export script in the File menu to export the mesh to an .obj file, as shown in Figure 5.81. After you've indicated in the file browser where you want to export the meshes, a dialog box will appear, like the one shown in Figure 5.82. Click the Animation button as indicated to export a separate .obj file for each frame in the animation.

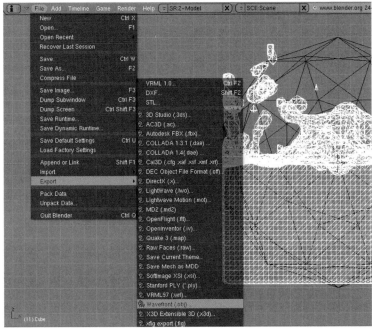

Figure 5.81 Exporting a fluid in .obj format

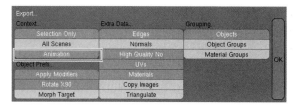

Figure 5.82 Select animation context

Exploring Further Resources

After reading this chapter, you've gotten your feet wet with the Blender fluid simulator. As you can imagine, there are a lot more things you can do with fluids that I haven't been able to touch on here. Making creative use of materials, compositing, particles, and the fluid settings themselves can open up a lot of possibilities. With the right materials and blurring effects, for example, you can use fluid effects to create convincing volumetric smoke by reversing the influence of "gravity" so that the fluid flows upward rather than downward. An excellent resource for further inspiration and tips is Jason van Gumster's *Advanced Fluid Dynamics In Blender* DVD. The DVD includes three hours of tutorials and goes into detail about achieving several interesting fluid effects not touched on in this chapter, including a paintball splash effect, a waterfall, a rotating mill wheel, and others. The DVD also includes an in-depth tutorial for creating the volumetric smoke I just mentioned.

For more in-depth technical information about the Lattice-Boltzmann method used in the Blender fluid simulator, a technical report by Nils Thuerey and Ulrich Ruede is available online at www10.informatik.uni-erlangen.de/Publications/TechnicalReports/TechRep05-7.pdf.

Currently, the implementation of the LBM in Blender is an excellent, straightforward fluid simulator that allows the simulation of fluids of whatever viscosity you like. Still, one of the advantages of the LBM is that it has the potential for considerably expanded functionality. Using LBM-based simulation, it will be possible to extend Blender's fluid simulator to combine fluids of multiple viscosities, and to exploit the underlying particle structure of the fluid simulation to control fluids in a way analogous to the way particles can currently be controlled. This is sure to lead to many exciting developments in Blender fluid simulation. Keep an eye on the Blender release notes to see what improvements future releases bring.

Like everything in Blender, fluid simulations are best used in conjunction with a selection of appropriate tools. Keep in mind how you can use other Blender functionality to enhance your effects. For example, the fluid simulator and the dense meshes it creates are demanding of computer resources. You can get much more mileage out of your hardware if you make good use of Blender's compositing functionality to break up complex scenes. For the same reason, never use a fluid simulation when a wave-modified plane will do!

In this chapter, you saw how to make fluids interact with solid objects and containers, including objects that were animated in various ways. The fluid simulation distinguishes between meshes that deform and objects that do not deform. However, aside from this, from the standpoint of the fluid simulation, an Ipo is an Ipo; it's not important whether it was hand-keyed or derived in another way. In the *Strawberries and Milk* example, the Ipos were derived from another physical simulation, namely the Bullet physics functionality of Blender's game engine. This enables you to simulate the motion of solid objects affected by friction, gravity, and collisions, and to bake that motion into Ipos for general animation use. In the next chapter, you'll find out how to use these powerful features to make your animations even more dynamic.

Bullet Physics and the Blender Game Engine

Blender is a unique 3D animation suite in that it contains a full-featured game engine for the creation of games and other free-standing interactive content. Nevertheless, in spite of its core of devoted fans, the game engine is an all-too-often overlooked feature of Blender.

In this chapter, you'll learn the basics of working with BGE and Bullet Physics to the point that you can easily create dynamic rigid body animations, which can then be used in the Blender animation environment you're accustomed to. If you are new to BGE, you will be surprised by how much amazing functionality it will open up for you. If not, this chapter should provide some interesting ideas for how to integrate real-time generated physics simulations with rendered animations.

Chapter Contents
The Blender Game Engine
Rigid body simulation and Ipos
Constraints, ragdolls, and robots

The Blender Game Engine

It goes without saying that for people who are mainly interested in creating games, the game engine is one of Blender's major attractions. The BGE is widely used by hobbyist game creators, and lately its appeal has begun to broaden to larger game projects. Luma Studios used BGE to create their prototype racing game ClubSilo, shown in Figure 6.1. The Blender Institute, the creative production extension of the Blender Foundation, is currently planning "Project Apricot," which will use BGE in conjunction with the Crystal Space game development kit and other open source tools in producing an open game of professional quality to be released under the Creative Commons license.

Figure 6.1 ClubSilo

As everybody who's ever played a game knows, game worlds can be pretty rough-and-tumble places. Cars crash, walls crumble, and bad guys go flying across rooms. This is all made possible by physics simulation, and any quality game-creation tool these days needs a good real-time Newtonian physics library. For Blender, this is the open source Bullet Physics Library. Indeed, Blender is not alone in this; the Bullet Physics Library, authored by Erwin Coumans, simulation lead at Sony Computer Entertainment America, is being used by professional game developers with parallel optimizations for PlayStation 3 and Xbox 360. The companies that use Bullet contribute back to Bullet under the zlib license.

Recently Bullet was showcased in an entertaining way in the Bullet Physics Contest 2007, in which contestants competed to create the most impressive Rube Goldberg machine in BGE. Some stills from Christopher Plush's winning machine can be seen in Figure 6.2.

This chapter shows you how to access the features of this powerful library for use in your own animation work.

Figure 6.2 Stills from Christopher Plush's winning Bullet Rube Goldberg machine

Figure 6.2 *(continued)*

Figure 6.2 *(continued)*

Getting Started with BGE

This book is written primarily with animators in mind, so I'm going to assume that you've never touched BGE. For a lot of animators and illustrators, the little Pac-Manesque Logic Buttons icon in the corner of the Buttons area is ignored and slightly intimidating, and pressing P by accident can be a nasty surprise. If that sounds like you, then it's time to change that. If you do have experience with BGE, you might want to skim this section. The goal here is to get comfortable enough with BGE to make full use of its physics simulation functionality. I'm not going to tell you much about making actual games, although after you get accustomed to using BGE, you'll probably find that doing so quickly becomes intuitive.

In this chapter, I will also discuss an excellent new method of getting game physics into your animation environment: By using the Ctrl+Alt+Shift+P key combination, you can bypass many of the inconveniences of using BGE directly. However, in order to get the most out of that method, it is necessary to have some idea of what is going on in BGE.

To get started, fire up a session of Blender. In the top view (NUM7), do the following:

1. Add a plane and scale up as shown in Figure 6.3.

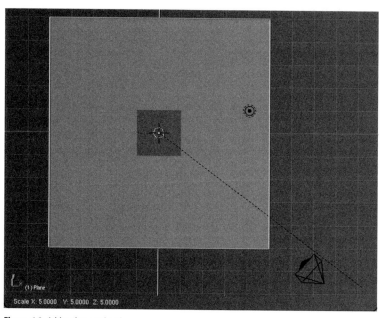

Figure 6.3 Add a plane and scale up.

2. Translate the plane downward along the Z axis, as shown in Figure 6.4.

3. With the cube selected, press F4 to enter the Logic Buttons context, or press the Logic Buttons icon in the Buttons window header.

4. In the Buttons area, click Actor, as shown in Figure 6.5. Set the parameters of that panel as shown in Figure 6.6. Select Dynamic and Rigid Body, and select Box from the Bounds drop-down menu. You have now activated the cube as a physical object in BGE.

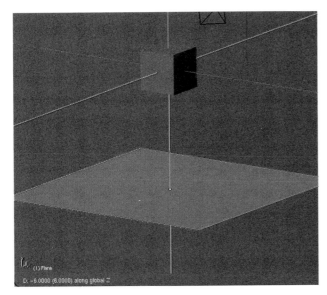

Figure 6.4
Translate downward.

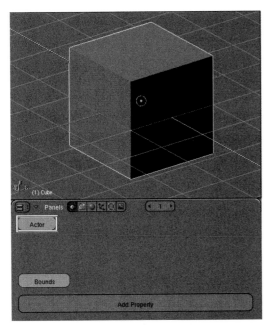

Figure 6.5
Enabling the cube as an
actor in BGE

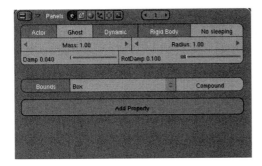

Figure 6.6
Actor parameters

5. Before entering Game Play mode, switch to Shaded view mode from the drop-down menu in the 3D viewport header, as shown in Figure 6.7. This isn't strictly necessary, but things will look much better in the game-play environment if you do this. After you've set this, press the P key to begin Game Play mode. You should see the cube fall and bounce against the plane, following a trajectory similar to what's shown in Figure 6.8. The angle you view this from will depend on the angle you're viewing the scene from when you press P. After the cube has come to rest, press Esc to leave Game Play mode.

Figure 6.7 Switch to Shaded view mode.

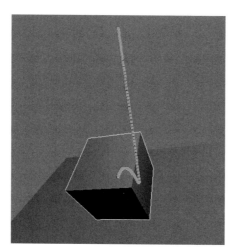

Figure 6.8 The cube bounces against the plane.

6. You can now begin setting up some basic game logic by using the buttons shown in Figure 6.9. Game logic is the main way to define what events or actions lead to others inside the game environment. Interactive controls are set up here. To set up the game logic, begin by adding a sensor. Click Add, and then select Keyboard, as shown in Figure 6.10.

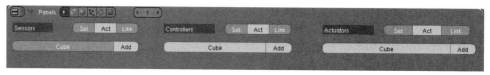

Figure 6.9 The Game Logic area

7. The game action you're setting up will be triggered by pressing the spacebar. To determine this, click the button indicated in Figure 6.11. When prompted to press a key, press the spacebar.

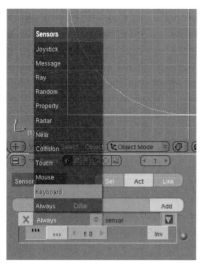

Figure 6.10 Setting a keyboard action sensor

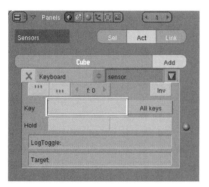

Figure 6.11 Press the button indicated, and then press the spacebar when prompted.

8. A sensor registers the event that will trigger an action. An actuator defines the resultant action. In order to connect these two things, you need to create a controller. Do this by clicking Add under the Controllers (middle) column. Link the sensor to the controller by clicking the LMB and dragging the mouse between the two logic connectors, as indicated in Figure 6.12.

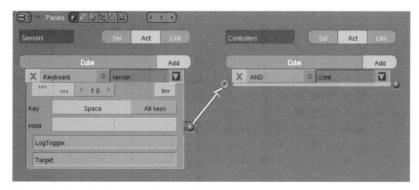

Figure 6.12 Connecting the sensor to the controller

9. Add an actuator by connecting the controller and the actuator in the same way you connected the sensor and the controller (see Figure 6.13). Set the value for the middle column of the dLoc row to **0.10**.

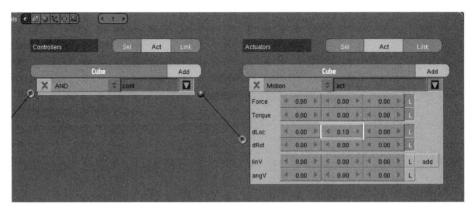

Figure 6.13 Adding an actuator

10. In the 3D viewport, press P again to enter Game Play mode. This time, try pressing the spacebar while in Game Play mode. You should now have some control over the movement of the cube. Giving the spacebar a good press will send the cube flying off the plane as in Figure 6.14. Press Esc to get out of this mode.

Figure 6.14 Enjoying an exciting game of "Push the Cube into the Abyss"

11. You can minimize and maximize the view of logic blocks by clicking the triangle in the upper-right corner of the logic block. In Figure 6.15, the blocks you just created are minimized, and two new sensors, two new controllers, and two new actuators have been added. The sensors are for the right-arrow and left-arrow keys, and the actuators represent right and left rotation around the local Z axis,

with –0.10 and 0.10 values, respectively, in the third column of the dRot rows. Set these logic blocks up as they are shown in Figure 6.15.

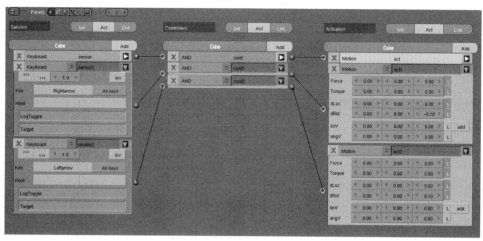

Figure 6.15 More controls

12. Add an Icosphere next to the cube, as shown in Figure 6.16. Using the Logic buttons, set the sphere as an actor with the same parameters as you set for the cube, except with Sphere selected under Bounds, as shown in Figure 6.17.

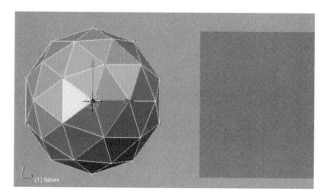

Figure 6.16 Add an Icosphere.

13. Press P again. Notice how the sphere and the cube interact. You can now drive the cube around by rotating right and left with the arrow keys and moving forward with the spacebar. Try pushing the sphere off the plane as in Figure 6.18. Press Esc to get out of this. Experiment with adding more objects with and without Actor enabled, and playing around with the angle and shape of the plane.

You now know most of what you need to know to get started with BGE. As you can see, setting up interactive logic is not too complicated. For the purposes of this book, minimal interactive logic is necessary, so this is all the detail I'm going to cover here. Much of the time, no interaction will be necessary—you'll just set up a physical situation and let the simulator take over. However, sometimes using interactive triggers can be very handy to get the effect you want.

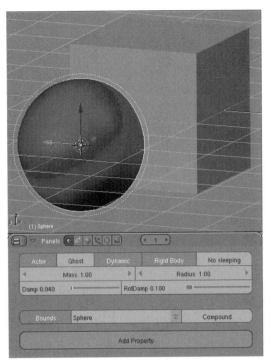

Figure 6.17 Parameters for the sphere

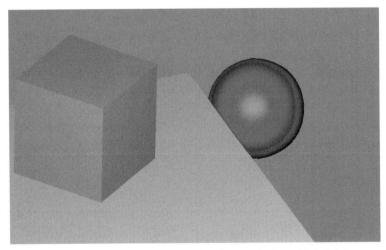

Figure 6.18 An even more exciting game of "Push the Sphere into the Abyss with the Cube"

Using Ipos and Actions in BGE

For people designing games, it's important to be able to have animated objects and armature motions accessible to the game logic. Mostly, animators are best off doing sophisticated animation in the ordinary Blender animation environment—animation in the game engine is far more restrictive than it is in Blender itself. Nevertheless, there are times when you will want to simulate physical reactions to hand-keyed animation. To do this with BGE, you use Ipo objects or actions in the game-play environment, as follows:

1. Start a fresh session of Blender and key the location and rotation of the default cube at frame 1.

2. Advance to frame 31 (click the Up button three times), move the cube up along the Z axis, and rotate it slightly to the left. Key this location and rotation as shown in Figure 6.19. Note that the figure shows the keyframe view in both the Ipo Editor and the 3D window. You can toggle the keyframe view by pressing the K key. The keyframe view in the 3D window is convenient for adjusting actual keyed objects' positions.

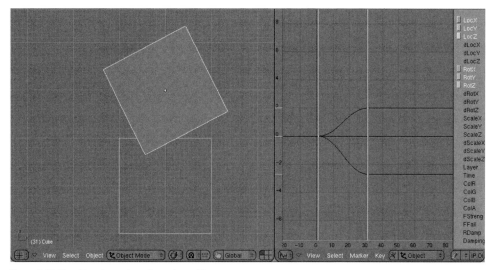

Figure 6.19 Keyed location and rotation at frame 31

3. In the Logic Buttons area, with the cube selected, set up a sensor, controller, and Ipo actuator as in Figure 6.20. In the setup, I have the sensor selected as Always, and the Ipo actuator type is Play. The Start and End frames of the Ipo to be played, in the Sta and End fields, are 0 and 30. When you press P, the cube will go through the motion of the active Ipo from frame 0 to 30 repeatedly. If you use a different sensor type, such as a keyboard action sensor, the Ipo motion will be triggered when you press a key. Also, if you change the Start and End frames of the Ipo actuator, a different (potentially longer or shorter) section of the Ipo will be played. Other Ipo actuator types can also be selected besides Play. (See if you can guess what the Ping Pong and Flipper types do.)

Figure 6.20 Sensor, controller, and Ipo actuator setup

4. Experiment with combining this setup with the setup from the previous section. Try to set up a flipper-style controller to swing at a falling cube, knocking it into space before it hits the plane. Note how the cube interacts with Rigid Body objects such as the sphere from the previous section's example.

Rigid Body Simulation and Ipos

You now know how to set up basic physics simulations in BGE. But if you're reading this book, chances are you're most interested in using these simulations in your rendered animations. What you want is not real-time simulation, but Ipo curves. There are two ways to get these Ipos into your animation environment: the hard way and the easy way.

The most common way up until now has been to do it the hard way, going directly into BGE and recording the game physics to Ipos. This method had various problems, mostly to do with differences between how Blender handles Ipos and how BGE handles real-time animation. There is now a better way to get the benefits of Bullet Physics in your animation without going into Game Play mode at all, by simply using the Ctrl+Alt+Shift+P key combination. I'm going to describe both approaches. For people with an interest in the game engine, there's a lot to be learned by going through the steps of the former, but the latter is the approach I recommend for actual use. If you're impatient to get your rigid body simulations underway, you can skip forward to the section on Ctrl+Alt+Shift+P for a complete demonstration of how to use that method.

Baking Game Ipos

You can save the movements of Dynamic objects in BGE by selecting Record Game Physics To IPO from the Game menu in the User Preferences/Information header at the top of your Blender workspace, as shown in Figure 6.21. After you exit from Game Play mode by pressing Esc, the Ipos will be associated with whatever objects were enabled as Dynamic objects in the physics simulation. You can press Alt+A or the Play button on the Timeline and play the animations like any other animation, and you can render it as you would anything else in Blender.

The animated shot shown in Figure 6.22 was created in this way. Six cubes were created and set up vertically in space along the lines of the first image in the sequence. Each cube was enabled as an actor and made Dynamic. Rigid Body was selected to enable the blocks to roll and tumble. Another cube was scaled to the shape of a book, and under that a shadow-only plane was added for the blocks to land on. After baking the Ipo from BGE, some image textures were added to the objects, a sky map was applied, and the animation was rendered in the ordinary way by using ray shadows.

Figure 6.21
Record Game Physics
To IPO menu option

Note: After you've selected Record Game Physics To IPO, a check mark will appear beside the option, and it will remain active until you deselect it. This means that every time you press P to enter Game Play mode, the game physics Ipos will be overwritten, so be careful. If you want to run a simulation and record it to a different Ipo than a previous simulation, select the object, and in the Ipo Editor window click the X beside the drop-down menu where the Ipo you want to save is shown. This disconnects the Ipo from the object, so that a new game physics Ipo object can be written without overwriting what you already have.

Frame Rate and Simulation Speed

If you try this with the first example of this chapter or with an example of your own, you will surely notice that when you press Alt+A or render your animation to a movie, the resulting simulation is in slow motion. This occurs because the game engine uses a default frame rate of 60 frames per second (fps). This is desirable for real-time graphics for several reasons, but it is much faster than is necessary for animated movies, which are usually somewhere around 25 fps (the default frame rate in Blender). This means that when you record Ipos from the game engine, the resulting Ipos will be normal speed when played back at 60 fps, but will be about half speed when played back at 25 fps. Furthermore, if you use hand-keyed Ipos in the animation in the form of Ipo actuators, as described in the second example in this chapter, you'll find that the resulting baked physics Ipos do not sync up properly with the hand-keyed Ipos in the animation because of mismatched frame rates.

Figure 6.22 Rigid body blocks in a rendered animation

To correct this in the game engine, you need to reset the BGE frame rate to match the frame rate of the animation you want to create, such as 25 fps. In order to do this, it is necessary to take a brief detour into Python scripting for BGE.

To see how scripts are called in BGE, repeat the first five steps of the first example in this chapter to set up a Dynamic Actor object falling onto a plane. When you press P, the cube falls onto the plane, and if you select Record Game Physics To IPO, you will see that the playback is in slow motion. To set up the Python script, follow these steps:

1. Open a Text Editor window by creating a new work area and selecting the Window Type menu item, as shown in Figure 6.23. From the header menu of the Text Editor window, select Text (see Figure 6.24). This is the name of the default text file in the editor.

Window type:
- Scripts Window
- File Browser
- Image Browser
- Node Editor
- Buttons Window
- Outliner
- User Preferences
- Text Editor
- Audio Window
- Timeline
- Video Sequence Editor
- UV/Image Editor
- NLA Editor
- Action Editor
- Ipo Curve Editor
- 3D View

Figure 6.23
Text Editor Window
Type menu item

Figure 6.24 Select Text from the header drop-down menu.

2. In the text area, type the following code, exactly as it is shown in Figure 6.25:

```
import GameLogic

GameLogic.setPhysicsTicRate (25.0)
GameLogic.setLogicTicRate (25.0)
```

Also, change the name of the script from the default Text to **framerate**, as shown in the highlighted area of the figure.

Figure 6.25 The framerate script

3. Now you need to set up the logic blocks to call the code from within the game engine. To do this, you will associate an Always sensor and a Python controller with an object in the game. The plane is a good choice for this. Select the plane and set up the logic as shown in Figure 6.26. Type **framerate** into the Script field, as shown in Figure 6.27.

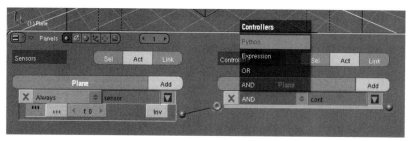

Figure 6.26 Python controllers

Figure 6.27 Enter the script name.

4. Make sure BGE is set to record game physics to Ipos by using the menu selection shown in Figure 6.21. Press P to run the simulation. The frame rate will be 25 fps, just as you specified in the script. Try changing the value in the script to see how other values change the speed of the resulting simulation. Higher values such as the default value of 60 will result in slower motion in the final animation.

Note: Remember, if you duplicate an object that has Ipos associated with it, the new object will have the same Ipos associated with it. In the case of a location Ipo, this means that no matter where you place the new object, it will jump back to where the Ipo places it, which will be the same place as the original object it was duplicated from. To make the new object act independently of the old object, it is necessary to disconnect the Ipo from the new object, so you can key a fresh Ipo to the object. It is also possible to make Blender create a new Ipo for duplicated objects. In the Edit Methods section of the User Preferences window, select Ipo from the Duplicate With Object options. In this case, a new Ipo will be created when you duplicate the object. However, the new Ipo will still be an exact copy of the original, so your new object will still jump to follow the original object unless you alter or delete the Ipo keys.

Ctrl+Alt+Shift+P

You can use the Ctrl+Alt+Shift+P key combination to record physics simulations straight from Bullet without entering Game Play mode at all. This method also enables you to bypass a number of issues relating to how BGE works, such as the mismatched frame rates in the previous section. In this method, you do all of your animation as you ordinarily would, keying values in Blender. You should not add

Ipo or Action actuators, and it is not necessary to use Python controllers. In fact, no logic blocks of any kind are used. The only thing you use in the Logic Buttons area is the Actor tab, where you set the parameters for Rigid Body dynamic objects.

In this section, you'll set up a complete rigid body simulation from scratch. The completed simulation can be found on the CD that accompanies this book in the file ballandcubes.blend.

Follow these steps to put the elements in place and run the simulation:

1. Set up a scene as shown in Figure 6.28, with the default cube in its original position. Add the following objects at the original cursor location, and move them along the Z axis while holding down the Ctrl key:

    •   A second cube located 6 Blender Units (BUs) under the first on the Z axis

    •   A floor plane scaled up to about 14 times its original size and located 8 BUs beneath the first cube on the Z axis

    •   An Icosphere located 3 BUs above the cube

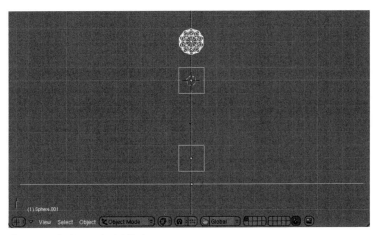

Figure 6.28 Setting up the rigid body scene

2. Add an armature at the original cube's location, as in Figure 6.29. In Object mode, translate the Armature object 3 BUs down the Z axis, as shown in Figure 6.30. In Edit mode, translate the tip of the armature downward to the middle of the second cube, as shown in Figure 6.31.

3. Bone-parent the cube to the bone. To do this, select the armature in Object mode and change to Pose mode. Select the cube (you will return to Object mode automatically). Hold down the Shift key and select the armature so that both the Cube object and the armature are selected in Pose mode, as shown in Figure 6.32. Press Ctrl+P and select Bone.

4. Key the motion of the topmost cube and the plane. The topmost cube will rotate counterclockwise. Key the rotation at frame 1, and then go to frame 11, rotate the cube to an angle of –45 degrees around the Y axis, and key the rotation at that frame. Choose Curve > Extend Mode > Extrapolation for the Ipo curve. For the plane, key its rotation at frame 61, and then advance to frame 81, rotate the plane around the Y axis 25 degrees, and key the rotation. Leave the curve's Extend mode at Constant.

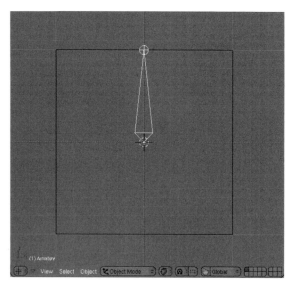

Figure 6.29

Add an armature.

CHAPTER 6: BULLET PHYSICS AND THE BLENDER GAME ENGINE ■

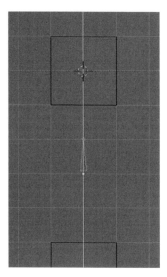

Figure 6.30

Translate the armature downward.

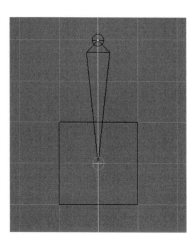

Figure 6.31

Translate the tip in Edit mode.

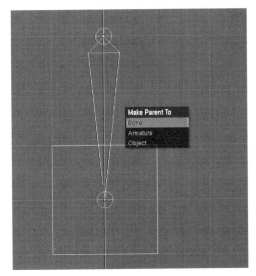

Figure 6.32 Bone-parent the cube.

5. Select the Icosphere. Go into the Logic buttons and make the sphere an actor with Dynamic and Rigid Body selected, as shown in Figure 6.33. Under Bounds, select Sphere. Next, select each of the Cube objects in the 3D viewport, go into the Logic buttons, and press the Bounds button to select Box. You do not need to make the Cube objects actors. I've also added a level 2 Subsurf modifier to the sphere and used Set Smooth. This is not necessary, but it will make your scene look a bit nicer.

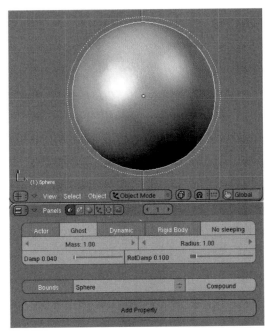

Figure 6.33 Making the sphere a Rigid Body object

6. Now's the big moment. Press Ctrl+Alt+Shift+P to record the physics simulation to Ipos. You won't see anything happen, but your system's standby icon may be displayed for a few moments. After this finishes, you can press Alt+A to run the animation. You'll see that it looks something like Figure 6.34.

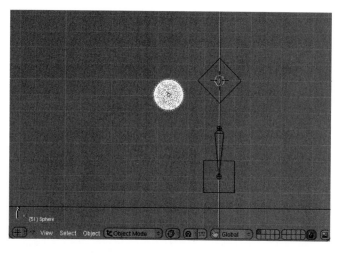

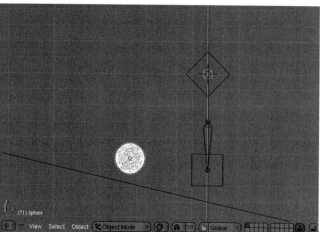

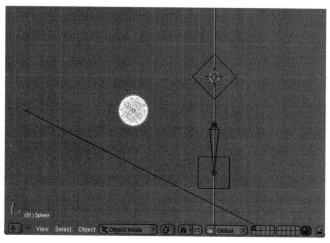

Figure 6.34 The animated simulation

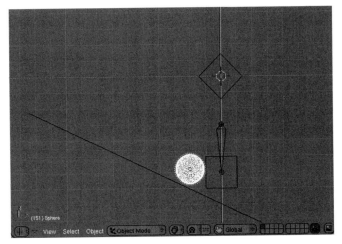

Figure 6.34 *(continued)*

7. As you can see, the sphere comes to rest against the second cube at about frame 131. Knowing this, it is possible to key the motion of the armature so that the second cube will "kick" the sphere at exactly the right moment. To do that, key the beginning and ending of the kicking movement about 20 frames before and after the point where the cube should impact the sphere, around frames 111 and 151, as shown in Figure 6.35.

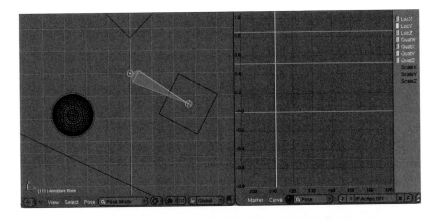

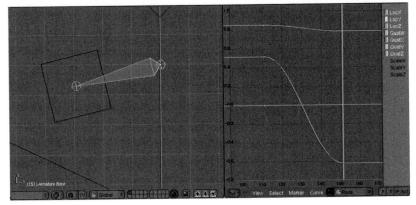

Figure 6.35 Keying the "kick"

8. Press Ctrl+Alt+Shift+P again, and run the animation with Alt+A again. The first part of the simulation will be the same, but instead of coming to rest, the sphere will be kicked off the plane as in Figure 6.36. Doing this enables you to skip entering the BGE and adjusting the frame rate with scripts.

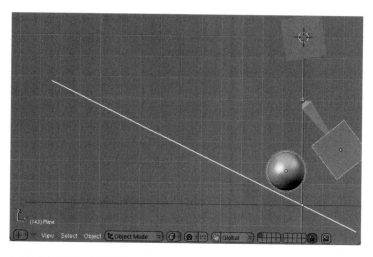

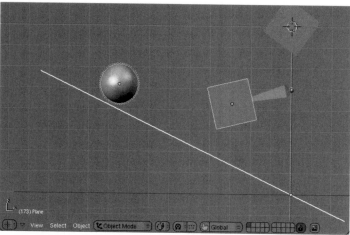

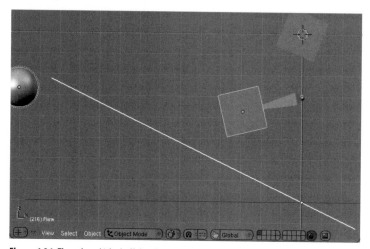

Figure 6.36 The sphere kicked off the plane

Actor Parameters, Boundaries, and Hull Types

There are several qualities that objects need to have in order to behave naturally in physics simulations. You've already come across several of these as you've been setting up objects for Bullet simulations. Now I'll discuss what the terms mean in a little more detail. The top row of the rigid body physics settings in the Logic Buttons context contains the following five options:

Actor enables the rest of the buttons so that physics parameters can be set for an object. If this is not selected, the object will be evaluated only as an obstacle. You can still set the collision Bounds for a nonactor.

Ghost enables in-game objects to *not* have physical interactions with others, so that they can be passed through like a ghost. Because ordinary animation does not have physics calculated automatically, this option is not usually needed in nongame simulations.

Dynamic enables the object to be moved by physical forces. Only objects with this option selected will have Ipos generated for them during a simulation.

Rigid Body enables spring-based collision behavior and rolling. This is a necessary option for convincing physical simulation of multiobject interaction.

No Sleeping disables BGE's default behavior of turning off physics on objects that have not been moved or touched for some time. If you find that an object is becoming unresponsive over the course of a long simulation, select this option. Don't select it if it is not necessary.

In the next row in the panel are the Mass and Radius parameters. The Mass value determines the mass of the object relative to other objects in the simulation. When an object with a greater mass collides with an object with less mass, the trajectory of the object with less mass is more affected. As in the real world, objects with greater mass have greater inertia. This means that they require more force to get moving and also that they are more difficult to slow down when they are moving, making them less subject to damping in the physics engine. Due to current limitations in the Bullet physics engine (and in fact all physics engines), simulations become unstable when objects with extremely different masses interact in certain ways. Objects in constraint chains should be within a few kilograms of each other, and very heavy objects should not be placed on top of very light objects. These kinds of interactions between objects with extreme differences in mass should probably be keyed by hand or simulated in another way, such as with particles.

The Radius parameter indicates the size of the sphere collision bounds. When you enable an object as a dynamic actor, the sphere is displayed as a dotted line representing the default collision boundary for the object (as shown in Figure 6.37). This is accurate only if your object is a sphere. If not, you will need to select a more-appropriate collision boundary type, and Radius is not pertinent (although the dotted circle will continue to display).

In the area below the Mass and Radius fields are the damping fields. Both Damp and RotDamp remove motion energy from the object over time—Damp from translation, and RotDamp from rotation. When these values are zero, no damping occurs and the movement of the object is unimpeded. With higher values, movement and rotation is diminished to mimic the effects of air friction.

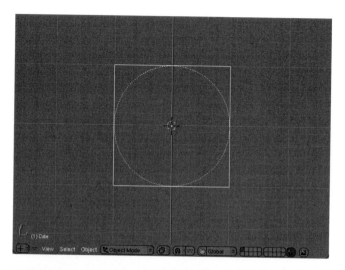

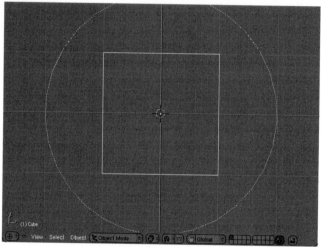

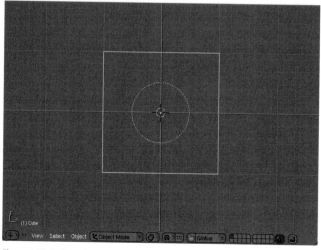

Figure 6.37 Radius values of 1.0 (default), 2.0, and 0.5

Collision Boundary Types

By default, a Rigid Body object behaves like a sphere, rolling on the boundary defined by its Radius value. For most shapes, this is not what you want. In order to have Bullet calculate the collision boundaries accurately for the object, you must select a collision boundary type by clicking Bounds and selecting one of the following options from the drop-down menu:

Box calculates the collision boundary as a cube-shaped box. If your object is a cube shape, this is the fastest and most accurate option.

Sphere calculates the collision boundary as a sphere. If your object is a sphere, this is the fastest and most accurate option.

Cylinder calculates the collision boundary as a cylinder. If your object is a cylinder, use this.

Cone calculates the collision boundary as a cone. If your object is a cone, use this.

Convex Hull Polytope calculates a "convex hull" around the shape of the object, yielding an accurate collision boundary for many complex shapes. There are two important qualities to note about the Convex Hull Polytope. The first is that it can represent only convex shapes; concavities, such as the inside of a cup or a bell, are not accurately simulated. The second point is that it must be a low poly mesh. Meshes of more than about 100 vertices should not be used as Convex Hull Polytopes. Ideally, Convex Hull Polytope meshes should be between 4 and 30 vertices.

Static Triangle Mesh can simulate highly accurate, high-poly shapes, including concavities. There are also two notable qualities of Static Triangle Meshes. The first is that they can be used only for static (nonmoving) objects (that is, the object should not move on its own; a static object can move as the child of a dynamic object). Static Triangle Mesh bounded objects will not receive Ipos from the physics simulation. The second notable quality is that two Static Triangle Meshes will not collide with each other. A Static Triangle Mesh will collide only with dynamic objects.

It is worth noting that there is no visual feedback for these boundary types. Regardless of which you choose, the dotted sphere will be shown. To the right of the drop-down menu is the Compound button. This button must be selected if the object has children. When you select this, the object and its children will be considered collectively as a single compound object. The Compound option enables you to add multiple collision shapes in a single Rigid Body object. The secret of doing more-advanced physics simulations is in cleverly combining Convex Hull Polytopes and Static Triangle Mesh bound objects as compound objects in such a way that all the objects appear to interact with each other in an accurate way.

Example: Glass and Ball

In this example, the solution uses several boundary types together. The goal is to create a rigid body simulation with a ball and a glass, in which the ball can fall into the glass in a natural way and the glass can interact with both the ball and the floor plane correctly, as shown in Figure 6.38.

Figure 6.38 The ball interacting with the glass and the floor

As you've seen in previous examples, the floor and the ball are simple to set up. The difficulty here is the glass. The glass must be a dynamic Rigid Body object in order to fall and tumble naturally, so simply making it a Static Triangle Mesh is not an option. It does not fit into one of the predefined shapes such as sphere or box, so those are also out. Finally, using a Convex Hull Polytope boundary is also not possible, because this boundary type cannot represent concavities. If the glass is a Convex Hull Polytope, the ball will settle on "top" of the glass, rather than falling into the mouth of the glass, as shown in Figure 6.39. To get around these problems, it will be necessary to create a compound object for the cup composed of several component objects of different boundary types.

Figure 6.39 If the glass is a Convex Hull Polytope, the ball sits on top.

To see how this can be done, first model a glass with geometry as shown in Figure 6.40, or else append the object glass from the .blend file glassandball.blend, included on the CD that accompanies this book. Before beginning the following process, make sure that any object-level rotation or scaling has been applied with Ctrl+A, and any translations cleared with Alt+G. Also make sure that any Ipos associated with the object at this point are disconnected by clicking the X button to the right of the Ipo drop-down menu in the Ipo Editor header.

As mentioned earlier, it is possible to have a Static Triangle Mesh move if it is parented to a moving object. This means that it is possible to have the glass itself be a Static Triangle Mesh in order to interact correctly with the ball. However, if this is the case, the glass cannot collide with the ground; two Static Triangle Meshes do not collide with each other. It is necessary to create a set of special collision meshes to do this.

To create the special collision meshes, select the vertices of the cup shown in Figure 6.41. Duplicate these vertices by pressing Shift+D, and then press P and choose Selected to create a new object with these vertices. You can see the new object in Edit mode in Figure 6.42. Note the four vertices shown in orange around the lip of the cup.

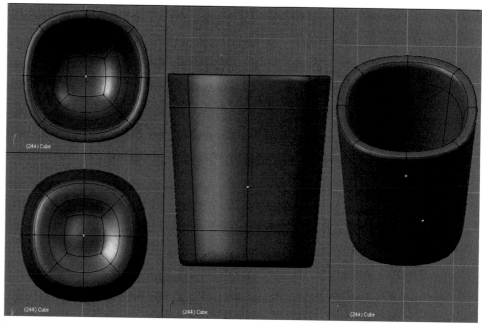

Figure 6.40 Model the glass with this geometry.

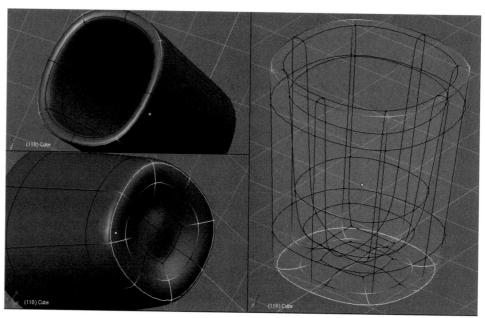

Figure 6.41 Separating the vertices

Eventually, this new collision mesh will use the Convex Hull Polytope collision bounds. Another quality of Convex Hull Polytopes is that only vertices that are part of faces contribute to the collision boundaries. So to make this collision mesh work, it is necessary to fill in some triangular faces between the vertices, as shown in Figure 6.43. Do this by pressing the F key while in Edit mode. Turn off subsurfing for this object. You can also delete the extra edges, because they don't do anything.

Figure 6.42 The separated collision mesh in Edit mode

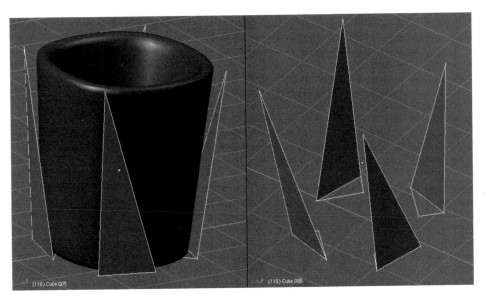

Figure 6.43 Filling in faces between vertices in the collision mesh

Because the model is subsurfaced, making its visible outline smaller than the actual mesh, the collision mesh should be reduced in size slightly. Reduce it along the X and Y axes (see Figure 6.44) by pressing the S key followed by Shift+Z. Then reduce it slightly less along the Z axis (see Figure 6.45) by pressing S followed by Z.

Now, separate each of the four corner segments of the mesh, one by one, by selecting their vertices, pressing P, and choosing Selected (see Figure 6.46). You should wind up with four objects. Name these objects *hull1*, *hull2*, *hull3*, and *hull4*. It doesn't matter which is which.

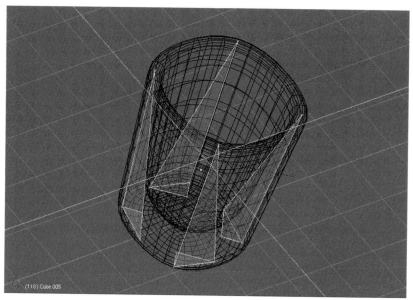

Figure 6.44 Scaling down along X and Y axes

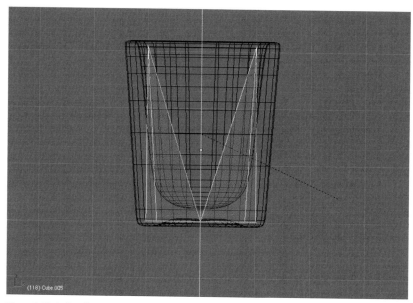

Figure 6.45 Scaling down along the Z axis

The object called hull1 is going to be the parent object for the compound Rigid Body object. In order for that to happen, each of the other objects (the other three hull objects *and* the glass mesh) all need to be parented to hull1. Furthermore, they need to be parented in a slightly special way. Parent each of the objects one by one to hull1 by selecting the child-to-be object, selecting hull1, pressing Ctrl+P,and selecting Make Parent (see Figure 6.47). Immediately after parenting each object, press Alt+P and select Clear Parent Inverse (see Figure 6.48). This step is easy to overlook, but it's necessary to make this setup work properly. Do this for each hull object and for the glass mesh.

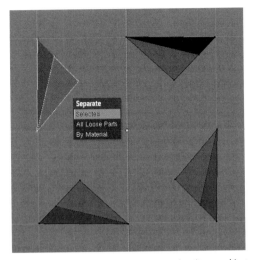

Figure 6.46 Separating one corner segment into its own object

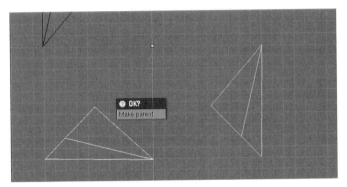

Figure 6.47 Parenting hull objects

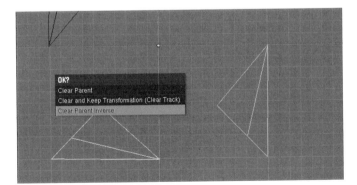

Figure 6.48 Clear parent inverse

After you have parented all the objects, set their boundary types. First, set hull1 as a Dynamic Rigid Body actor with boundary type Convex Hull Polytope and with Compound enabled (see Figure 6.49). Set hull2, hull3, and hull4 to have Convex Hull Polytope bounds. Finally, set the glass object to be a Static Triangle Mesh.

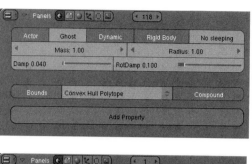

Figure 6.49 Settings for hull1, for hulls 2 through 4, and for glass

After you've set these values, set your ball and glass up where you want them at the beginning of the simulation. Use hull1 to move the glass object around. You can preview the simulation in the game engine quickly by pressing P, and press Esc when it finishes. Ctrl+Alt+Shift+P will create the Ipos.

Because you won't be rendering the Convex Hull Polytope collision meshes, either place them on an inactive layer or set them to not be renderable in the Outliner window, as shown in Figure 6.50.

Figure 6.50 Setting the collision meshes not to render

General Tips on Working with Bullet

There are several further points to keep in mind when working with Bullet:

- Avoid scaling rigid bodies. If you need to scale an object, disable the rigid body, scale the object, and apply the scale and rotation by pressing Ctrl+A.

- Avoid very small (<0.2 Blender Units in any direction) or very large rigid bodies.

- Avoid large mass ratios. Keep the ratio of masses between interacting rigid bodies less than 1:100.

- Avoid degenerate triangles. Degenerate triangles are extremely long, thin sliver-like triangles. Bullet will not handle these well.

- Make sure the center of the object is in the middle of the mesh.

- Don't make child objects in a Compound object dynamic.

Adjusting Simulation Quality with Python

It's possible to increase the quality of your simulations by increasing the number of internal simulation substeps. This can be done by simply running two lines of code, in the same way that you ran the Python script for adjusting the frame rate, described previously in this chapter. The code for changing the time steps is as follows:

```
import PhysicsConstraints
PhysicsConstraints.setNumTimeSubSteps(10)
```

The argument 10 in this example can be set to whatever value you want, with the default being 1, and higher numbers resulting in better-quality simulation.

Using Physics Visualization

You can see more information about how the physics is working by selecting Show Physics Visualization in the Game drop-down of the Information window header, shown in Figure 6.51. When this is selected, color-coded physics information will be visible in Game Play mode when you press P.

The example in Figure 6.52 shows a small chain of three objects that are constrained to each other by rigid body joins. The leftmost cube is not dynamic; the other two objects are Rigid Body objects. When P is pressed, the Rigid Body objects fall in a chain and their physics is highlighted as shown in Figure 6.53. Bounding boxes are shown in red. Physics is calculated on the structures displayed in white, which indicate the Rigid Body object's center of gravity, and when the simulation reaches a state of equilibrium, those structures turn green, indicating that the Rigid Body object is "sleeping." Sleeping increases the efficiency of the simulation and reduces the possibility of jitter for motionless objects. Physics visualization is helpful for seeing how objects are colliding with each other and also to make sure that Compound objects are set up correctly.

Figure 6.51
Show Physics Visualization

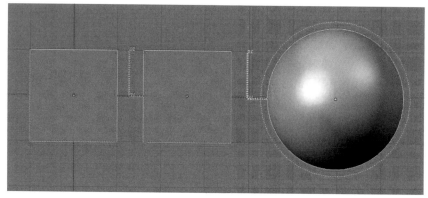

Figure 6.52 Objects with Rigid Body constraints

Joints, Ragdolls, and Robots

In 3D, as in the real world, joints are mechanisms that hold two solid objects together, allow certain freedoms in how the objects move in relation to each other, and restrict other kinds of movements. In 3D there are usually considered to be three fundamental types of joints that differ in the kinds of movement they allow. These are hinges, ball-and-socket joints, and slider joints.

Figure 6.54 illustrates the different ways that these joints behave. The hinge allows the objects to rotate on a specific axis around a common point with respect to each other. The ball-and-socket joint allows combinations of rotation around all three axes. The slider joint allows the objects not to rotate but to translate (move) along an axis with respect to each other.

Using Rigid Body Joint Constraints

In Blender, you can set up joints by using the Rigid Body Joint constraint found in the Constraints tab of the Object buttons context (F7). To get an idea of these, start up a fresh session of Blender and duplicate the default cube and move the new copy, Cube.001 along the X axis so that it is next to the original cube with a small space between them. With the new cube selected, select the Rigid Body Joint constraint from the Constraints drop-down menu, as shown in Figure 6.55.

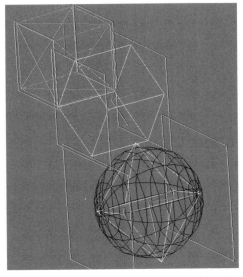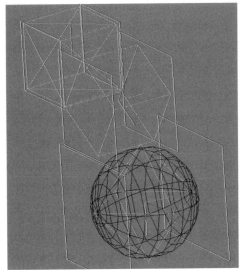

Figure 6.53 Visualizing the simulation in action and sleeping

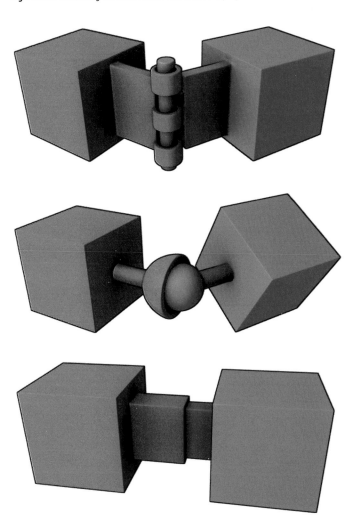

Figure 6.54 Hinge, ball-and-socket, and slider joints

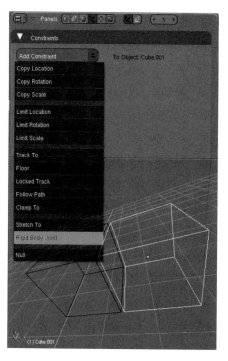

Figure 6.55
Rigid Body Joint constraint

The options for the type of joint are Ball, Hinge, and Generic (experimental). Ball and Hinge are ball-and-socket joints and hinges (respectively) along the lines of the earlier diagrams. The Generic joint option enables you to set numerical restrictions on six degrees of freedom, three axes of rotation and three axes of translation. This enables you to not only represent slider joints but also to lock or restrict movement to a specified range for each degree of freedom. For this example, select Hinge.

Set the Hinge parameters as shown in Figure 6.56. The toObject field is for the object that the hinge attaches to, in this case the first cube. ShowPivot makes the constraint's pivot point visible in the 3D viewport. Pivot X, Pivot Y, and Pivot Z locate the pivot in space with relation to the object's center (measured in Blender Units). The Ax X, Ax Y, and Ax Z rotate the constraint. The Hinge constraint rotates around its own X axis; therefore, to line the hinge up along the bottom edges of the cube, enter a Pivot X value of –1, a Pivot Z value of –1, and an Ax Z value of 90.

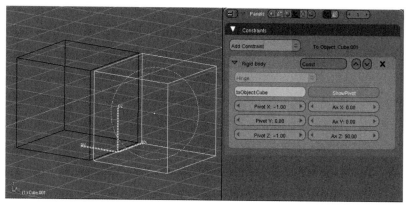

Figure 6.56 Hinge parameters

In the Logic buttons, set Cube.001 to be a dynamic rigid body actor. Leave Cube as it is. Press Ctrl+Alt+Shift+P to generate the physics simulation Ipos. When you play back the animation, it should look something like Figure 6.57. As an experiment, try switching the joint type to Ball and baking the Ipos again to see how the two joints behave differently.

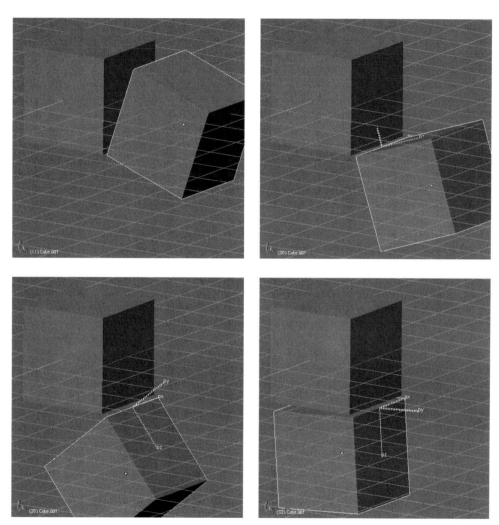

Figure 6.57 Hinge in action

Using Generic (6DoF) Joints

If you took the next logical step in the preceding example and experimented with switching the joint type to Generic (experimental), you may have gotten a little bit of a surprise when Cube.001 just dropped into oblivion with no apparent connection to Cube at all. By default, all six degrees of freedom in the Generic joint are unconstrained, which means that when you first set the joint, it has no effect at all. To constrain them, click the button corresponding to the degree of freedom you want to constrain, and set minimum and maximum values for their range. If you leave the default values of 0 and 0, the object will be fully constrained in that degree of freedom. For linear values, the units are Blender

Units. For rotation values, the possible range is from –5 (representing a 180-degree counterclockwise rotation) to 5 (representing a 180-degree clockwise rotation). For example, in the settings shown in Figure 6.58, all the buttons are depressed, so the object would be prevented from moving in any degree of freedom except rotating 36 degrees in either direction around the X axis.

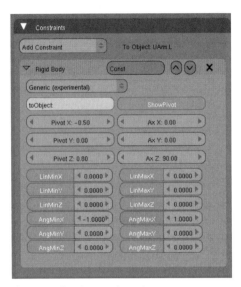

Figure 6.58 Generic constraint settings

Another joint type, the Cone Twist joint, is currently under development and may be ready to use in an official version by the time this book has gone to print. Check the resources listed at the end of this chapter for information on how to use this joint type.

Setting Up a Ragdoll Armature

Animators and game creators spend a lot of time with human figures, and for this reason a complete discussion of physics should touch on how to make it act on the human form. This approach to treating the human body as a purely physical collection of parts connected by joints is referred to as *ragdoll physics*.

In this section, you'll see how to use ragdoll physics to control a simple armature. In this way, you can use ragdoll physics to control the movements of mesh characters. If you don't yet know the basics of working with armatures and using them to deform meshes, you can find out everything you need to know in my book *Introducing Character Animation with Blender* (Sybex, 2007).

Ragdolls can be simple or complex. Likewise, they can be more or less restricted in their range of motions. A less-restricted ragdoll can more accurately mimic the range of positions of a human, but it is also more likely to get into impossible positions. Setting up a ragdoll is similar in some ways to setting up an armature, but with an important difference: An armature is intended to be posed by hand, so if it is more flexible than necessary, this is not usually a problem. A ragdoll is intended to be "posed" only by the forces that act on it; therefore, it must be very carefully constrained so as to avoid getting into unnatural positions. At present, constructing a very sophisticated ragdoll like this in Blender is a painstaking and difficult process, but improvements are planned for Bullet's constraint system that will make this process much easier within the next release or two. For now, though, I'll stick with a very simple ragdoll. When you create your own ragdoll, you can use whatever shapes you like: cylinders, spheres, or other convex polyhedrons. Don't use objects that are too small, though, as this can cause instability in the simulation. In this example, because I am using mainly the mesh objects to control the movement of empties and an armature, I will stick with the simplest possible construction of just boxes, most of which are approximately the scale of the default cube.

This ragdoll is composed of 11 separate Cube objects, scaled and positioned as shown in Figure 6.59. Rename these objects **Head**, **Torso**, **Midriff**, **UArm.L**, **UArm.R**, **LArm.L**, **LArm.R**, **ULeg.L**, **ULeg.R**, **LLeg.L**, and **LLeg.R**. When you have the objects scaled and placed as you want them, press Ctrl+A on each object to apply scale and rotation.

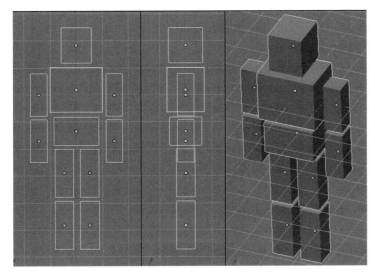

Figure 6.59 The objects that compose the ragdoll

The shoulders, elbows, and knees of this ragdoll will be joined by Hinge constraints. The constraints themselves have no built-in restrictions, but by placing the hinges correctly, it is possible to make the meshes restrict the way the joints bend. Begin with the left upper arm, object UArm.L. Add a constraint of type Hinge with a toObject value of Torso. Set the values as shown in Figure 6.60 so that the pivot is visible and positioned as in Figure 6.61. The only way to adjust the positioning of the pivots is through these numerical values. If you need to use slightly different values to get your pivot positioned correctly, that's no problem. Set the right shoulder pivot up as a mirror image of the left shoulder by following the same steps and setting the values as shown in Figure 6.62.

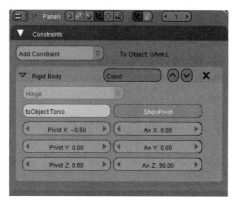

Figure 6.60 Hinge constraint values

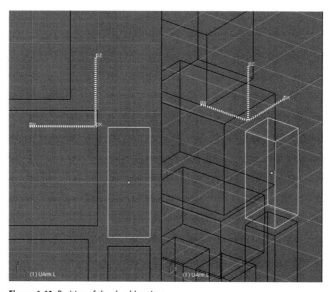

Figure 6.61 Position of the shoulder pivot

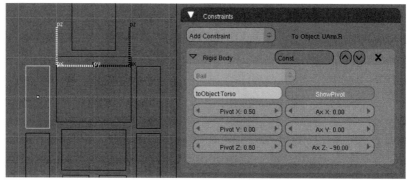

Figure 6.62 Right shoulder pivot

Create an elbow joint by adding a Hinge constraint on LArm.L targeted to UArm.L, as shown in Figure 6.63. Do the same on the right side.

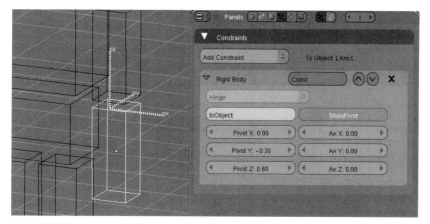

Figure 6.63 Left elbow

To see the constraints in action, go to the logic buttons and set Torso, UArm.L, UArm.R, LArm.L, and LArm.R as actors. Make them Dynamic Rigid Body objects and set their Bounds to Box. You can tell which objects are enabled as actors in the 3D viewport by whether their bounds radius is visible, as shown in Figure 6.64. Make sure that Record Physics To Ipos is *not* selected, and press P to take a look at the ragdoll physics so far. You should see the arms and torso dangle freely, as in Figure 6.65. They do not fall down, because they are being supported by nondynamic objects below the torso.

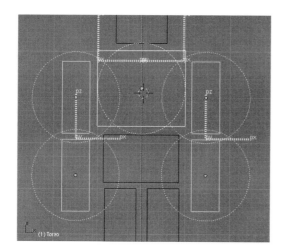

Figure 6.64 Torso, UArm.L, UArm.R, LArm.L, and LArm.R set as dynamic objects

Now set up the rest of the ragdoll. In this example, the head will not move freely—it will be fixed to Torso by parenting. To do this, parent Head to Torso as shown in Figure 6.66. Be sure to select Compound for the Torso Bounds.

The hinges at the hips should be placed flush with the front faces of the legs, so that the hinges bend forward, as shown in Figure 6.67. By contrast, the knee constraints should be flush with the back faces of the legs, as shown in Figure 6.68, so that the knees bend in the opposite direction. Note that all of these constraints are hinges. In real life, the human hip is a restricted ball-and-socket joint, but I'm opting for simplicity in this example.

Figure 6.65 Ragdoll physics for the arms and torso

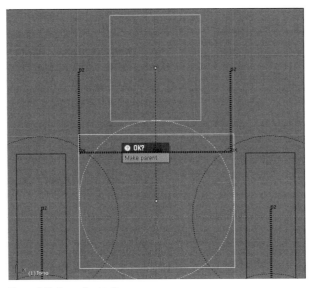

Figure 6.66 Parent Head to Torso

Add a Hinge constraint from Midriff to Torso, as shown in Figure 6.69. This will enable the body to bend slightly at the middle. Again, the movement is much more restricted than in a real human body, but this will be plenty for now. Finally, in the Logic buttons, set the rest of the objects up as dynamic rigid body actors.

If you press P now, your ragdoll should fall straight down into oblivion. If not, double-check to make sure that all the objects are set as dynamic rigid body objects. If parts of the body separate from others, double-check that the correct constraints are present and that they are targeted to the correct objects. If parts go haywire, make sure there are no parent-child relationships between meshes that are not part of Compound dynamic objects. Only Torso should be a compound object.

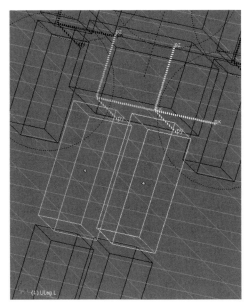

Figure 6.67 Hip joint placement

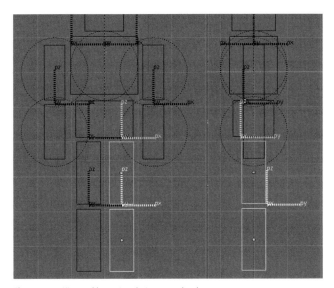

Figure 6.68 Hips and knees in relation to each other

Falling straight into oblivion isn't very interesting. Add a plane below the ragdoll and tilt it to one direction so that the ragdoll falls onto the plane and slides off. You can press P to see the action, and press Ctrl+Alt+Shift+P to bake the physics. After you render the ragdoll with some camera motion, you should see it take a tumble along the lines of Figure 6.70.

For slightly more realistic motion, you can adjust the masses of the various parts of the body to have more-accurate relative masses.

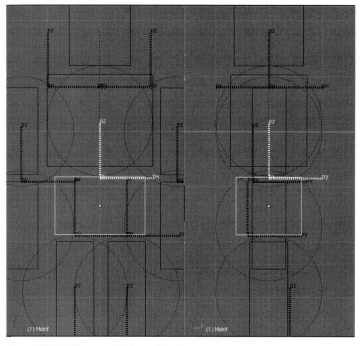

Figure 6.69 Midriff connected to Torso with a hinge

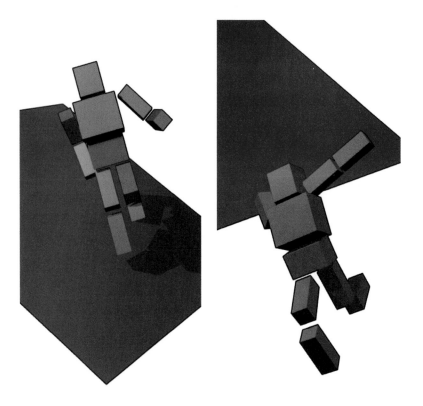

Figure 6.70 The ragdoll takes a fall.

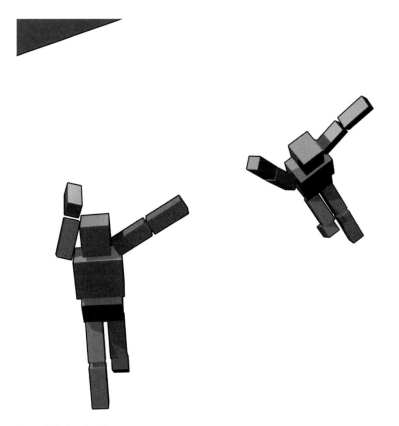

Figure 6.70 *(continued)*

Controlling an Armature

It would be nice to be able to use ragdoll physics to control an armature, in order to deform a mesh for animation. In this section, I'll show you a simple way to do this. The example is a little backward; ordinarily you would begin with a mesh character, create a ragdoll armature to fit the character, and then set up the ragdoll as in the previous section, so that the ragdoll's shape matches the character. In this case, the ragdoll came first. Nevertheless, the way to control the armature is the same.

The first thing to do is to add empties to key points, where the tips of the bones will be, as shown in Figure 6.71. An easy way to position empties is to select the vertices around where the empty should go and snap the cursor to selection by pressing Shift+S (as shown in Figure 6.72 for positioning the 3D cursor at the end of the left arm), and then add the empty in Object mode (Figure 6.73), and parent it to the body part that should control it (Figure 6.74). Parent the "hand" and "foot" empties to the lower arms and legs, respectively, the knee empties to the upper legs, the elbow empties to the upper arms, and the hip empties both to Midriff.

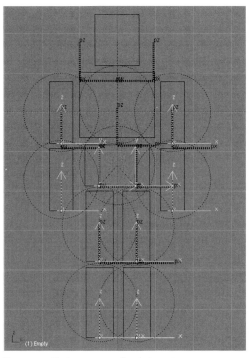

Figure 6.71 Placing empties at key posing points

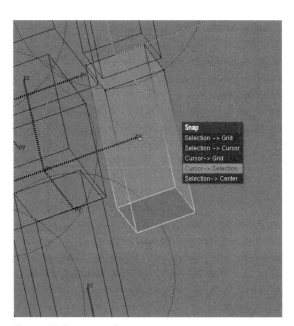

Figure 6.72 Snapping to a face

Now for the armature. In Object mode, select the Midriff object and snap the cursor to the selection. Add an Armature object and edit it as shown in Figure 6.75. Snap the bone tips to the empties you just added.

Finally, enter Pose mode and set up IK constraints on each of the bones shown in yellow in Figure 6.76. Enter the name of the empty at the bone's tip as the IK target, and make sure that chain length is set to 1 for each bone.

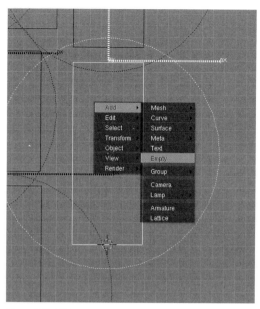

Figure 6.73 Add an empty.

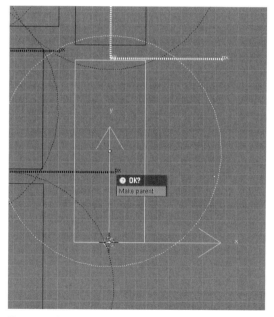

Figure 6.74 Parent the empty to the object.

Press Ctrl+Alt+Shift+P and run the animation again to see the ragdoll armature in action, as in Figure 6.77.

You'll find the full .blend file for this ragdoll (ragdoll.blend) on the CD that accompanies this book.

A Passive-Walking Robot

A current area of robotics research is *passive walking*. This is the study of the way that walking can be accomplished by means of a repetition of "controlled falls," where the walker simply follows the forces of physics at certain points in the walk cycle, and then exerts itself at key points to adjust its balance and ensure that it is in the right position to take the next step. In fact, this kind of passive walking is an important part of how humans actually walk, and a big reason why human walking is so fluid and smooth when compared to the way most current robots walk. Rather than controlling every movement with our muscles, a lot of what we do is to allow the forces of physics to work for us.

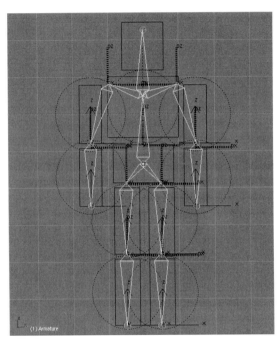

Figure 6.75 The armature

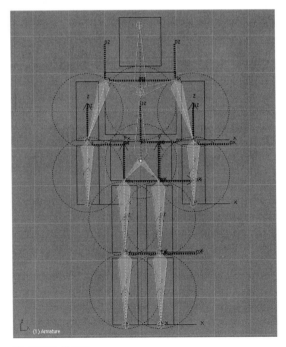

Figure 6.76 IK setup

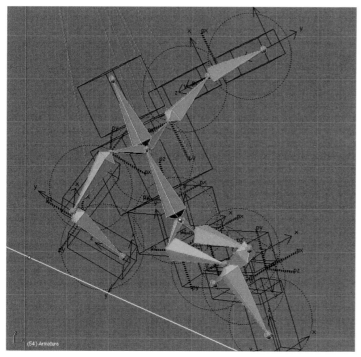

Figure 6.77 Ragdoll armature in action

Passive walking is closely related to ragdoll behavior, and it is possible to construct ragdoll-like walkers that can carry out passive walking in Blender. Yuta Fuji (Hans), a researcher who studies passive walking, has done just this with his intriguing Bullet/Blender passive-walking robot. You can find the simulation in the file KneeRoboWalk3pv.blend on the CD that accompanies this book.

This visualization uses a three-legged robot, as shown in Figure 6.78. As you can see in the figure, the robot's natural joints are represented by Hinge constraints, just as they were in the ragdoll example in the previous section.

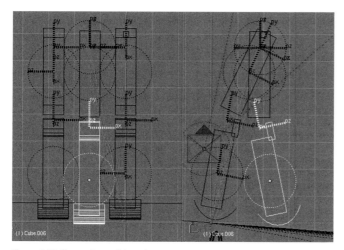

Figure 6.78 The passive-walking robot

Constraints are used in a few other interesting ways. The robot's right leg is made to follow its left leg's motion by means of two orthogonal Hinge constraints, as shown in Figure 6.79. The left leg is also constrained by a Generic constraint with no target, set to be unrestricted on all degrees of freedom except Y rotation, which it constrains fully (0 min, 0 max), as shown in Figure 6.80. This ensures that the object can move and rotate freely in any direction except twisting.

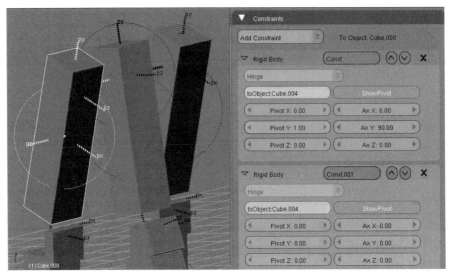

Figure 6.79 Hinge constraints

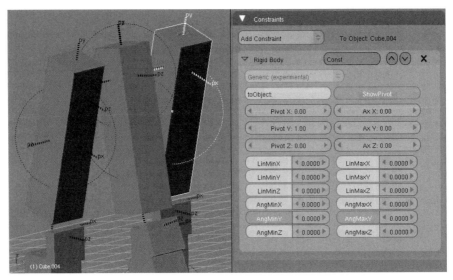

Figure 6.80 An untargeted Generic constraint

If you press P to run the game engine, you can watch the robot walk, as in Figure 6.81. Don't use Ctrl+Shift+Alt+P for this, though. The walker is sensitive to changes in any aspect of the environment; mass of objects, speed, relative distances, and the slope of the walking surface all need to be set just right. The simulation was set up with game engine parameters in mind, and because certain parameters (speed, in particular) are different when Ctrl+Shift+Alt+P is used, the robot's walk becomes unstable, and it takes a nasty tumble after only a step or two. Note also that the simulation was created in Blender 2.44, and may be unstable in other versions of Blender. It may also be unstable on operating systems other than Windows. On my Mac Pro, the robot stumbles at about the 4 marker.

You can watch the movie of the robot online at the following site:

```
http://video.google.com/videoplay?docid=-7369019972032648620
```

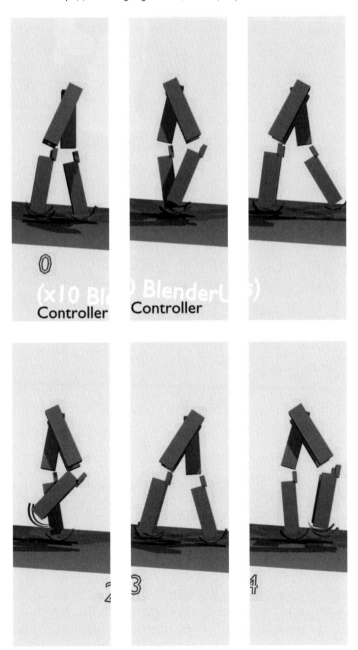

Figure 6.81 The walking robot in action

Erwin Coumans

Erwin Coumans wrote and integrated Blender's rigid body dynamics system. He is currently simulation team lead at Sony Computer Entertainment America. Since studying computer science at Eindhoven University, he has worked for Guerrilla Games, Blender, SCEE London, and Havok in Ireland doing collision detection and physics development. He actively promotes the sharing of ideas and technology through forum discussion, open standards and the use of open source software. He is the main author of the Bullet Physics Library, used by several game companies for games on XBox 360, PC, Wii and PS3. At the moment, he is writing a book on advanced game physics which will cover topics including continuous collision detection, iterative constraint solvers, and taking advantage of multi-threaded architectures like multi-core CPUs, GPGPU and Playstation 3 Cell. His book will be published by Morgan Kaufmann.

Further Resources

You can find out much more about the Bullet Physics Library at the project's website at http://bulletphysics.com. Documentation for new features and a forum devoted to Bullet can be found there. For general user support, go to the Game Engine forum at http://blenderartists.org/forum.

On the CD that accompanies this book, you'll find the physics regression test files for Bullet, which are a great source of examples for learning more about the features described in this chapter. You'll also find the .blend files for the top three winners of the Rube Goldberg machine competition. These Rube Goldberg machine files were created to work properly with Blender version 2.43, and because of the sensitivity of the physics simulations, they may not work properly in other versions, or on platforms other than the one they were created on. If the Rube Goldberg machines in the files are not working as you think they should, you might want to download and install Blender 2.43 from www.blender.org, where previous versions of Blender are always available.

Also on the CD, you'll find a file submitted by Blender user Kawl Nevina illustrating an interesting approach to making noncolliding joints. Nevina takes advantage of the fact that Static Triangle Mesh objects cannot collide with each other, and parents them to dynamic, jointed compound objects. Also in that file is an interesting example of an inner tube filled with balls. These you can find in the file ultraoll.blend. Change scenes in the file to see the different examples.

As you've seen by now, there are a variety of ways to use physics to bring the effect of life (or, in the case of ragdolls, lifelessness!) to inanimate objects. In the next chapter, you'll look at a totally different kind of simulation, not of physics, but of the very processes of life itself.

Imitation of Life: Simulating Trees and Plants

7

With a few exceptions, this book has been mainly concerned with simulating the physical behavior of nonliving things. In this chapter, we'll take a step up the food chain and look at a few tools that can be useful for creating trees and vegetation for your scene. These tools exploit the fact that plant growth can be simulated by adjusting parameters in some simple algorithms, which can save you a lot of work in modeling scenery. Although the exercises in this chapter represent only a small example of the uses of these tools, you should get a good sense of the possibilities available to you.

Chapter Contents
The Blender greenhouse: creating foliage with L-Systems and ngPlant
An open source ivy generator
A few more points to mention

The Blender Greenhouse: Creating Foliage with L-Systems and ngPlant

Like anything in the natural world, plant growth follows rules. In reality, these rules come about as the result of complex chemical and biological processes. However, as you saw in Chapter 2 in the discussion of boids, it is sometimes possible to model complex behaviors by adjusting specific parameters in a general algorithm. One interesting area in this field is the simulation of plant growth.

As in many other cases touched on in this book, simulation is not always what you want and should be used judiciously. For delicate, precise work intended to be seen close up, such as in Shigeto Maeda's lilies in Figure 7.1, it is best to do your modeling by hand. On the other hand, if you have a lot of foliage that is intended to be seen only in the background, the models that result from simulations may contain too many vertices to be rendered quickly. When you want high-polygon, realistic 3D models of foliage to be viewed in perspective at a medium distance, the tools described in this chapter can save you a lot of modeling time.

Figure 7.1 Hand-modeled lilies by Shigeto Maeda

There are many scripts and tools available to simulate plant growth. I've selected a few open source options for you to look at that I think are comparatively easy to use, flexible, and yield good results. Some other options are also mentioned later in the chapter.

L-Systems

L-Systems are a classic example of using computational methods to mimic living processes. People who have studied computer science are familiar with the idea of formal languages and grammars and the structures that these formalisms produce. These structures are typically referred to as *trees*, and the terminology here is no coincidence. An *L-System* is essentially a grammar which, given a set of parameters and a stochastic (random) component, produces a structure that is shaped like an organic tree or plant.

The L-System script by Armagan Yavuz is an automatic tree-generation script for Blender. It operates entirely within Blender, so it requires no importing or exporting to other file formats. It is also one of the simpler-to-use parameter-based tree-generation scripts available. More-powerful tools are available, but this is a good place to start in understanding parametric tree generation.

You can find the script on the CD in the packed .blend file called lsystem.blend.

Setting Parameters

To get started, open the .blend file in Blender. In the Text Editor window on the right, you will see the script itself. Press Alt+P to run the script. The Text Editor window will change to a Scripts window and display the interface shown in Figure 7.2. In your 3D viewport, you can see the beginning of a tree shown (from camera view) in Figure 7.3.

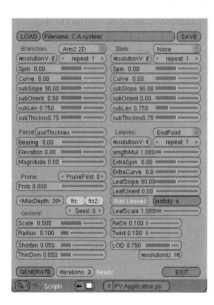

Figure 7.2

L-System script interface

The generator works recursively. You set the parameters to control how the branches will be generated at each iteration of the algorithm, and then click the Generate button at the lower left of the panel to create the tree. An iteration is a single cycle of generating sub-branches, and you can set the number of iterations in the field to the right of the Generate button. You can see the effect of the iteration values in Figure 7.4.

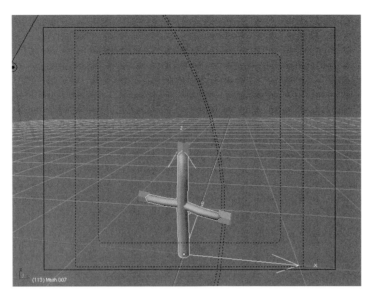

Figure 7.3
The default tree

Figure 7.4 Iterations set at 1, 2, 3, and 4

As you can see, there are a lot of parameters. As you experiment with them, it will become clearer what each does. Here, I'll give an overview of the most important parameters for getting started.

The General parameters at the lower left of the panel control certain overall characteristics of the tree. These are as follows:

Scale controls the overall size of the tree.

Radius controls the radius of the branches, with a possible range of 0 to 0.5, which is half the length of the branch. You can see the influence of the Radius parameter in Figure 7.5.

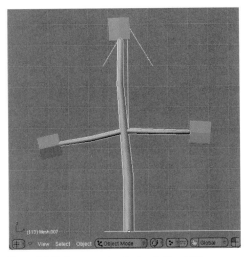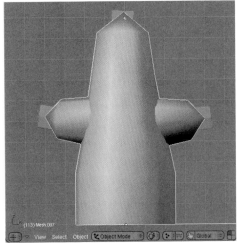

Figure 7.5 Radius parameter at values 0.05 and 0.5

Shorten controls the degree to which branches get progressively shorter over iterations.

ThinDwn controls the degree of tapering of the branches. You can see the effects of this in Figure 7.6.

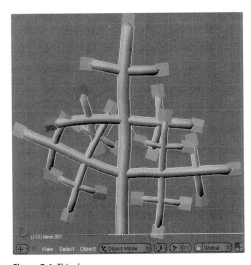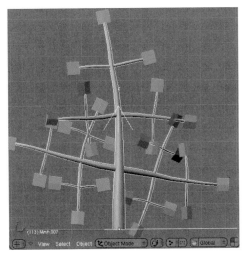

Figure 7.6 Thin down

The parameters for the branches are as follows:

Branches gives you the option of how the branches will diverge from each other; the Branches drop-down menu is shown in Figure 7.7. You can determine whether the branching is in arm style (new branches diverge from the main branch, leaving it intact) or in split style (the original branch splits into the new branches). Both styles are shown in Figure 7.8. In this drop-down menu, you can choose how many branches occur at each branch point, and whether the branching is constrained to a 2D plane or occurs in 3D space.

ResolutionV controls the number of edge loops between branchings. Higher resolutions increase the vertex count but enable smoother and more accurately controlled branch shapes.

Spin controls the degree to which the branches twist. The effect of this parameter can be seen clearly in Edit mode, as shown in Figure 7.9.

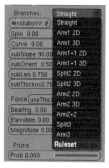

Figure 7.7 The Branches drop-down menu

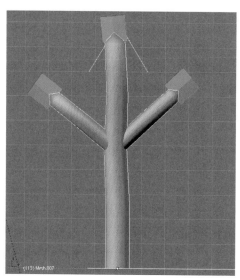 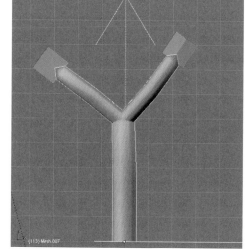

Figure 7.8 Arm branching and split branching

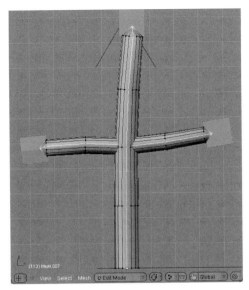
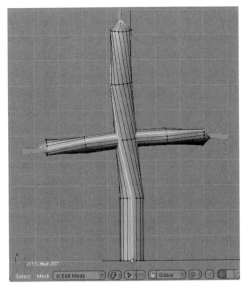

Figure 7.9 The effect of the Spin parameter

Curve controls how much the branches bend toward the ground, as shown in Figure 7.10.

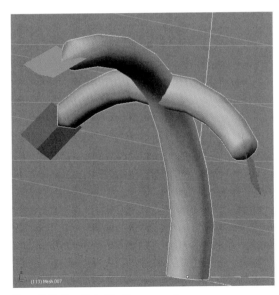

Figure 7.10 The effect of the Curve parameter

subSlope controls the angle at which child branches diverge from the parent branch, as shown in Figure 7.11.

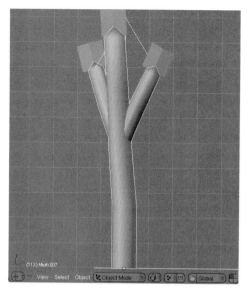

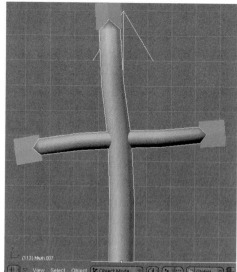

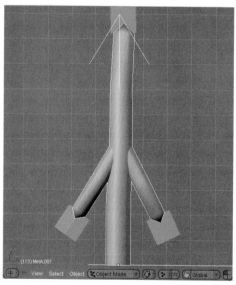

Figure 7.11
subSlope at values 20, 90, and 160

subOrient controls the angle at which the child branches grow with respect to the axis of the parent branch, as shown in Figure 7.12, viewed from above.

subLen controls the length of sub-branches as compared to their parent branch. A value of 1 means that the sub-branch will be the same length as the parent branch, and a value of 0.5 means that each branch is half the length of its parent.

subThickness controls the thickness of sub-branches as compared to their parent branch, and the values are analogous to those of subLen.

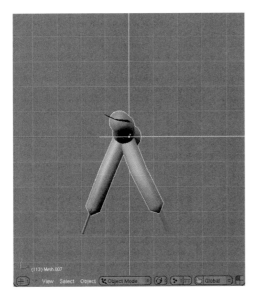

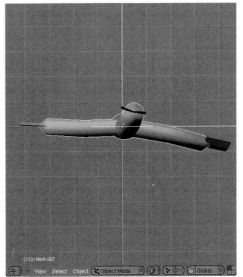

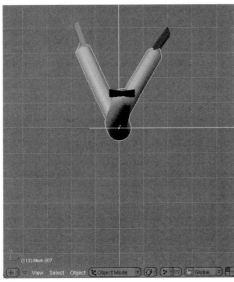

Figure 7.12
The effect of subOrient as seen from above at values
0.1, 0.5, and 0.9

The Stem parameters are mostly analogous to the Branches parameters. The Stem drop-down menu enables you to have one main stem that has different parameter settings from the branches that extend off of it. Not all trees and plants require separate parameter settings for the stem, so you can often choose None from this drop-down. In the example I give in this section, I do not use a stem.

The Leaves parameters enable you to add length, spin, or curvature to branches that carry leaves, and also to determine how and where leaves connect to branches, according to the options shown in Figure 7.13.

Figure 7.13 Leaves drop-down menu

Force settings enable you to apply a force such as wind to a tree. The Bearing value determines the direction of the force on the XY plane in 360 degrees around the tree. The Elevation value determines whether the force is pushing the branches upward or downward, and the Magnitude is the strength of the force. The Use Thickness value enables you to apply the force with greater intensity to narrower branches, in the same way that wind has a greater effect on weaker branches. In Figure 7.14, you can see the effects of a downward (< 0) Elevation force applied to a tree, with the Use Thickness value maximized. The bearing value is 270, making the force push along the Y axis. Note that these are not dynamic, animated forces—they only cause the tree to be formed as though it had been subject to those forces during the process of its growth.

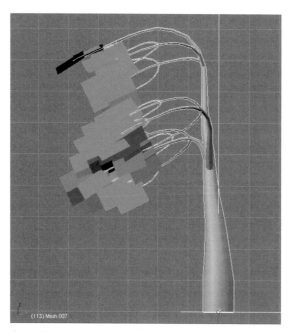

Figure 7.14 Tree with force applied

The Prune settings are just what the name suggests. Thick foliage can be randomly pruned with the probability determined by the Prob value of the Prune settings. Finally, the two buttons Frz and Frz2 can be used to freeze a specific tree so that the same tree is generated for the same parameters every time. If you do not use this, each time you generate a tree, the randomization of the algorithm will create a totally new tree.

Creating a Tree

The process of making a tree is simple with the L-System script. Simply set the parameters and click Generate. In this example, I've created a simple tree by using the parameter settings in Figure 7.15. I have not used any stem, so the value in that drop-down is None. Branching is with two arms extending in 3D space, and I have added some spin to keep the branches from lining up too directly. The subSlope value is 36, which yields quite narrowly angled branchings. Other important values are the Radius setting and the ThinDwn setting, for getting the branches to taper. The Iterations value is set to 5.

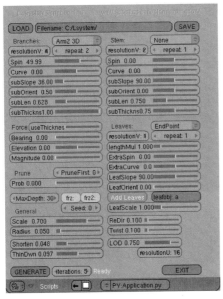

Figure 7.15 Parameter settings for a simple tree

When I click the Generate button with the values set in this way, the tree shown in Figure 7.16 is generated in the 3D viewport. Your tree will not look identical to this, even if your parameters are the same, because of the random aspect of the generator. You can click Generate several times until you are happy with the resulting tree. You can set up your lights and camera to render this tree immediately. The render I made turned out as shown in Figure 7.17.

You'll notice when you render the image that the texture for the leaves is already in place. You can choose from several leaf objects in the LeafObj parameter field in the parameters panel. In this example, I left it with the default value of *a*. If you rotate your view around the 3D space, you will see where these leaf objects reside, more or less below the camera, as shown in Figure 7.18. Each of these objects represents a different leaf type, and each is UV-mapped to a different part of a single leaf texture image, which is packed with the .blend file. If you look at these objects in Face Select mode with a UV/Image Editor window open, you can see specifically which leaf object is mapped to which leaf texture in that image file, as shown in Figure 7.19, where leaf object *a* is selected.

Figure 7.16 The generated tree

Figure 7.17 The rendered tree

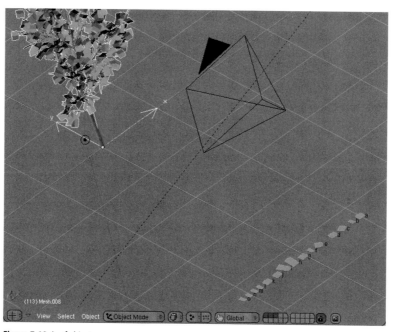

Figure 7.18 Leaf objects

Figure 7.19 Texture mapping of leaf objects

You can of course create your own leaf textures by simply creating a new image similar to the default texture image and UV-mapping the leaf objects accordingly. I also recommend having a look at J.M. Soler's tutorial at http://marief.soler.free.fr/Monsite/ lsystem_en.htm for further information about how to add objects such as fruits to L-System-generated trees.

ngPlant

L-Systems build a tree or plant randomly, making all the decisions about branching, shape, and size based on the parameters you enter to begin with. You may want more control than this, however. ngPlant is a free-standing open source application by Sergey Prokhorchuk that is somewhat less oriented toward automatic simulation and thus enables you to have more freedom in controlling how your plants and trees look. It is still a far cry from modeling meshes by hand, because it incorporates many of the same kinds of parameters as other plant simulators, albeit in a more-interactive way. There is a random element to trees created in ngPlant, but this too is something that can be easily accessed interactively by adjusting the random seed. Although it is not as easy to create an accurate tree of a specific type just by feeding in a set of parameters, ngPlant more than makes up for this by giving you more freedom than most other tree-generation scripts and applications. As you can see from the images in Figure 7.20, ngPlant is capable of producing some very nice results. ngPlant is presently available as a Windows binary, and you can compile it from the source for Macintosh or Linux.

Figure 7.20 Jungle images created using ngPlant, by Yorik van Havre

Figure 7.20 *(continued)*

Interface Overview

When you first launch ngPlant, you will see the interface shown in Figure 7.21. On the left is the 3D viewport, on the upper right are the parameters panels, and on the lower right is the tree structure window.

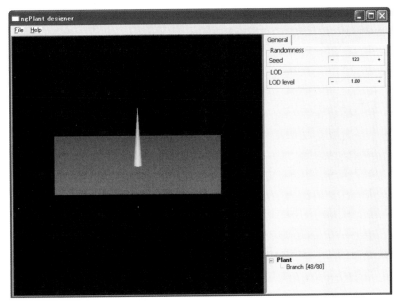

Figure 7.21 Starting up ngPlant

The ngPlant 3D viewport can be navigated by using the MMB. Rotate the view by holding the MMB and dragging the mouse. Pan the view by holding Shift+MMB and dragging the mouse. You can zoom by using the mouse wheel. If you do not have a three-button mouse, you will be stuck in the default view. This isn't an especially big problem for what you will be doing with ngPlant, but it's a little annoying. Still, if you've come this far as a Blender user without a three-button mouse, I'm sure you can make do!

There are several ways to input information for the various parameters. Some parameters take numeric inputs via a numeric edit field. You can click the plus (+) and minus (−) symbols to increase and decrease values in these fields, or drag your mouse across the field to the right or left to quickly increase or decrease the values, respectively. Alternately, you can double-click the field to input numeric values directly.

Other kinds of parameter values are inputted by using a curve editor like the one shown in Figure 7.22. You can alter the curve by left-clicking the red control points and dragging them. If you left-click on the curve in a place where there is no control point, a new control point will be created. You can delete control points by right-clicking them.

Figure 7.22
Curve editor

In some cases, the curves represent a literal visual interpretation of the values they control. For example, the Branch Profile curves determine the profile of the branch they describe, as shown in Figure 7.23. Likewise, the Offset Influence curves for a branch represent the offset of that branch's child branches in a literal way, as shown in Figure 7.24. In other cases, the relationship between the curve is slightly more abstracted. For example, the Phototropism value refers to the degree to which a branch or part of a branch tends toward the sun. The length of the curve in this case represents the branch from the base to the tip, and the height of the curve represents the degree to which that part of the branch is tending upward, as you can see in Figure 7.25. In general, the meaning of the curves tends to be quite intuitive.

Figure 7.23 Branch Profile curves

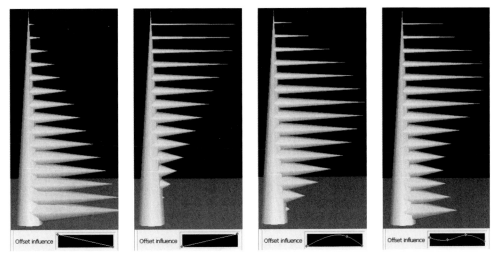

Figure 7.24 Offset Influence curves

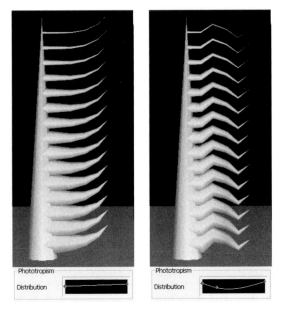

Figure 7.25 Phototropism curves

To set parameters for a branch, click on the entry for the correct branch level in the tree structure window at the lower right. When you select a branch, four tabs appear in the parameters area in the upper right: Stem, Material, Branching, and General. In the next section, you will look more closely at how to create a palm tree by setting parameters in these tabs.

Yorik van Havre

Yorik is the owner of the Blender Greenhouse website (http://yorik.orgfree.com/green-house.html), a resource for Blender models created mostly by using ngPlant. Yorik uses Blender professionally to create 3D architectural visualizations, and has worked on projects in countries throughout Europe, Asia, North America, and South America. Architectural visualization is an area especially well suited for using simulated vegetation, particularly when fly-throughs and animation demand fully three-dimensional foliage, which explains Yorik's interest in ngPlant. He is also a contributor to the Blender for Architecture wiki page (http://blender-archi.tuxfamily.org/Main_Page), and his personal website (http://yorik.orgfree.com/) contains many useful resources for people interested in architectural visualization with Blender. Yorik's jungle images created in ngPlant are featured in this chapter.

Creating a Palm Tree in ngPlant

To create a palm tree in ngPlant, follow these steps:

1. Start up ngPlant. Select the item Branch in the tree structure window in the lower right. This will be the trunk of the palm tree. The numbers beside the Branch entry in the tree structure window indicate the number of faces and vertices that make up the model up to this level of branching. Set the parameters in the Stem tab as shown in Figure 7.26. The main parameters to take note of are the Axis parameters and the Cross-section parameters. The shape of the trunk tapers slowly until the top, and then tapers sharply, as determined by the Profile curve. Place the two red control points by clicking the LMB on the curve and dragging.

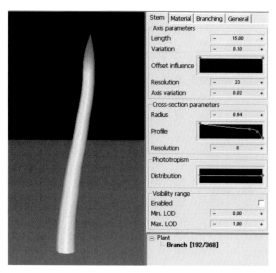

Figure 7.26 Stem parameter values for the trunk

2. Add sub-branches by right-clicking the Branch entry in the tree structure window and selecting Append Branch, as shown in Figure 7.27. Set the Stem parameters as shown in Figure 7.28. Because these branches are smaller than the trunk (and they will also be a bit more concealed), it is not necessary for them to have the resolution set as high. Also, the ends of the branches will hang down slightly, which is accomplished by moving the right endpoint of the Phototropism curve downward very slightly.

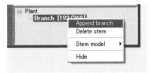

Figure 7.27 Adding another level of branches

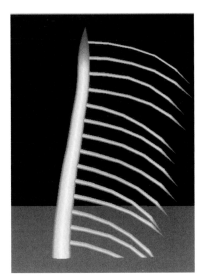

Figure 7.28 Stem parameters for branches

3. The number of sub-branches per a given length of the branch is determined by the Density value in the Branching tab. Set this value to 32. The result will be something like Figure 7.29. Of course, you don't want branches extending all the way up the trunk for a palm tree. Set Min Offset to 0.89 and Max Offset to 0.96 to determine the minimum and maximum points (in terms of percentage of the total length of the trunk) from which branches will extend. This results in the tree shown in Figure 7.30.

4. Set the remaining Stem parameters for this Branch level as shown in Figure 7.31. Set the RevAngle at 35 and set a small Variation value to avoid uniformity. Set the RotAngle to 90. The Declination curve controls the angle and curvature of the branches. Set it in a way that looks good to you.

Figure 7.29 Density value set at 32

Figure 7.30 With Min and Max Offset values set

Figure 7.31 Stem parameters for branches

5. Now is a good time to add a little bit of color. Go to the Material tab and click the Base Color button to open up a color picker, and then set the color for these branches. Do the same for the trunk by selecting the appropriate branch level in the tree structure window and setting a color in the Material tab, as shown in Figure 7.32.

Figure 7.32 Setting the base colors

6. One more level of branching is necessary to create the leaves. Append another branch level to the branches of the palm tree in the same way you appended them to the trunk. Select the new branch level, right-click, and choose Stem Model > Quad as shown in Figure 7.33 to make these branches quads.

Figure 7.33 Setting the Stem Model to Quad

7. Set the Stem parameters for the leaves as shown in Figure 7.34 and the Branching parameters as shown in Figure 7.35. The RevAngle is set at 180 so that the leaves form a canopy on each branch by extending directly off of opposite sides of the branch. At this point, however, note that each leaf quad is visible from only one side. For this reason, the 180-degree-rotated leaves cannot be seen in the figure, because their normals are pointing in opposing directions. If you rotate the view around, you will see that they are there.

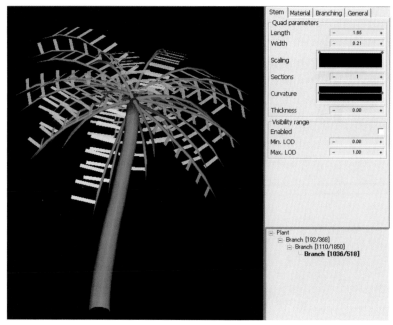

Figure 7.34 Stem parameters for leaves

Figure 7.35 Branching parameters for leaves

8. Go to the Material tab and set the parameters as shown in Figure 7.36. Add a base texture by clicking the Texture button and selecting **greenleaf.tga** from the textures directory in the ngPlant installation directory. Select the Double-Sided and Transparent check boxes.

Figure 7.36 Material parameters for leaves

9. The tree is complete now. If you want a different tree that conforms to the same parameters, you can change the random seed in the General tab at whichever branch level you want it to apply to. To export the file, go to the File menu and choose Export > Alias Wavefront OBJ, and export the file to the directory you want it in. Save the ngPlant file and quit ngPlant.

10. Open Blender and import the object by choosing Import > Wavefront (.obj). After you have located and selected your palm tree .obj file, a dialog box will appear like the one shown in Figure 7.37. Deselect Image Search and click OK. You now have your completed palm tree in Blender as shown in Figure 7.38, which you can texture and render as you like. An ngPlant (.npg) file of a palm tree similar to this one, as well as several other sample trees, can be found in the **samples** directory in your ngPlant installation.

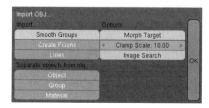

Figure 7.37
Import dialog box in Blender

Figure 7.38 Palm tree in Blender

Other Software

This section gave some examples of commonly used tree- and plant-generation tools for Blender. There are others, with different strengths and weaknesses.

Sergey Prokhorchuk, the creator of ngPlant, has also written a parametric tree generator called Gen3, which is available for download at www.geocities.com.nyud .net:8080/bgen3/. Gen3 requires considerably more knowledge to use than ngPlant. Getting started with Gen3 can be difficult if you don't have some background knowledge of the underlying algorithm. (This algorithm was based on the paper "Creation and Rendering of Realistic Trees" by Jason Weber and Joseph Penn, which can be found in the SIGGRAPH '95 conference proceedings.) Nevertheless, Gen3 is a powerful tool if you prefer to do your tree generation in a parametric, recursive way.

Another more-accessible option that comes highly recommended is Arbaro, a widely used cross-platform tree generator written in Java and available at http://arbaro .sourceforge.net/. Arbaro is an intuitive and easy-to-use alternative that has the nice added benefit of containing several preprogrammed tree types. Arbaro runs well on any platform and produces high-quality results. If you have worked with the plant generators described in this chapter, you should find Arbaro easy to use.

Finally, a new script-based method of creating trees within Blender itself is under development for use on the Peach Project, and is likely to be included in the official 2.46 release. This method will be accessible from the Scripts menu in the Scripts Window Header, by selecting Wizards > Tree From Curves and running the script on selected Curve objects. This method is quite different from the approaches described in this chapter and will enable a considerable amount of control for artists that other methods lack. This method will be particularly useful for creating cartoon-styled, exaggerated, or otherwise unrealistic trees. Check the official online documentation for the 2.46 release to learn more about using that script.

An Open Source Ivy Generator

Thomas Luft's Ivy Generator is a little different from the tree and plant generators described previously in that it specializes in simulating ivy growth on and around objects. Using this tool can yield quite impressive results and can produce ivy models that would be painstaking to model by hand. You'll find the software on the CD that accompanies this book.

Like ngPlant, the Ivy Generator is a free-standing application that interfaces with Blender via exported and imported 3D objects in .obj format. In this tutorial, I'll cover all the steps in growing ivy on a mesh object modeled in Blender.

To make the ivy, follow these steps:

1. Begin with the object you want to grow the ivy on. In this case, I'm using the model of a broken pillar shown in Figure 7.39, which you can find in the column.blend file from the CD for this book. You can use this object or use an object of your own, but keep it low-poly to begin with. The program works much slower as polygons increase.

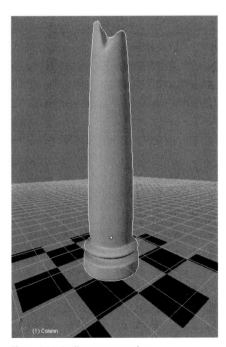

Figure 7.39 A pillar to get started on

2. To use the mesh in the Ivy Generator, it is necessary to export it as an .obj file. In the case of the column I'm using, the object is subsurfaced. Remove the subsurface modifier before exporting the object. You can put the subsurface modifier back on later, but it's not necessary for the purposes of ivy generation, and the mesh you will use in the Ivy Generator should be as simple as possible. Select all objects that you want to export, in this case the column and the floor objects, and then export them by accessing the script from the Information window header at File > Export > Wavefront (.obj), as shown in Figure 7.40. Select the destination file in the file browser and click Export Wavefront Obj. When you do this, the dialog box shown in Figure 7.41 appears. Select Triangulate then click OK. This is necessary because the Ivy Generator requires meshes to be made up of triangles.

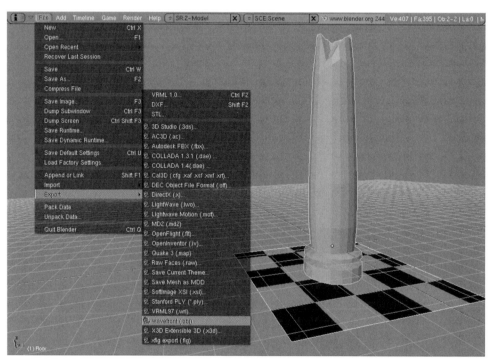

Figure 7.40 Running the .obj export script

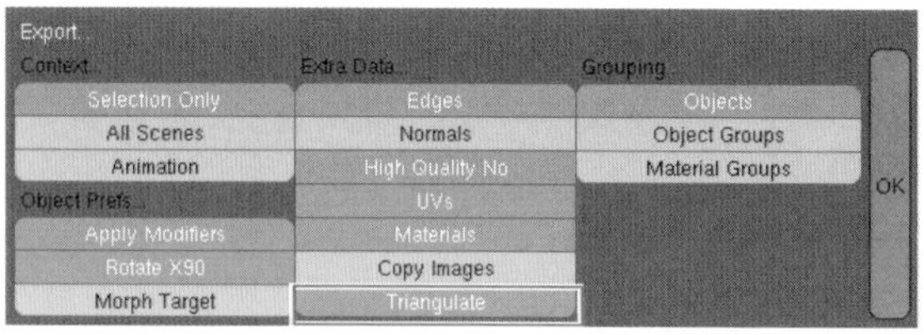

Figure 7.41 The Obj Export dialog box

3. After you have exported the objects to an .obj file, you can set Blender aside and start up the Ivy Generator. The interface is simple. On the right is a panel with the buttons and parameters you will use to create the simulation, and on the left is the 3D viewport. Click Import Obj+Mlt and find the .obj file that you just created. After you've imported it, you will see the pillar in the 3D viewport, as shown in Figure 7.42. You can zoom the view with the RMB, and translate the view with the LMB (or, for more Blenderlike movement, Shift+LMB), and rotate the view with Ctrl+LMB. The default translation and rotation directions are actually the opposite of Blender's, which takes a bit of getting used to, but there is very little translation and rotation necessary to do what you need to do in this software, so this isn't a big problem.

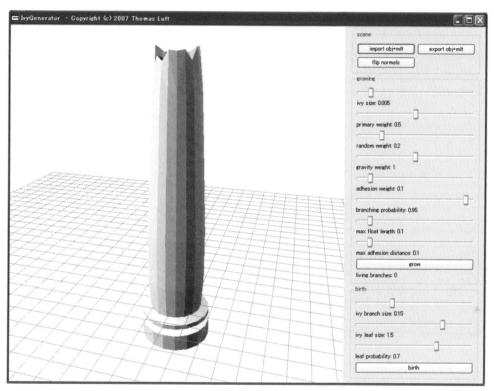

Figure 7.42 The Ivy Generator with the pillar imported

4. Creating the ivy itself happens in two steps. In the grow step, the branches are created that cling to the surface of the object. In the birth step, leaves are created. Both of these steps have a random component so that the results are never the same twice. Before you begin these steps, however, it is necessary to specify the point from which you want the ivy to grow. Do this by double-clicking the LMB anywhere on the object. This creates a green dot at the point from which the ivy will begin to grow. In this example, I wanted the ivy to grow up onto the pillar and also onto the ground. After a little experimentation I found a point near the base of the pillar that achieved this, shown circled in red in Figure 7.43. Of course, you won't get this exactly the same, but with a few tries you will eventually find a point that gives the results you're after.

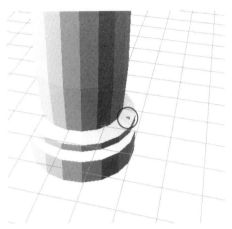

Figure 7.43 The starting point for the ivy

5. In the Growing panel, you'll find the parameters that control the growth of the ivy. The parameters are as follows:

Ivy Size controls the scale of the ivy in relation to the object. A large Ivy Size value will be more spread out, and a small value will be more compressed and bunched together.

Primary Weight controls the degree to which the ivy branches want to continue growing in the direction they are already going.

Random Weight controls the degree to which the ivy branches want to grow in random directions.

Gravity Weight controls the influence of gravity on the branches, causing them to tend downward.

Adhesion Weight controls the degree to which the ivy branches want to cling to the object they are growing on. Branches that don't adhere tend to die without creating new branches.

Branching Probability controls the probability that the branch will split at each time step.

Max Float Length controls the distance that a branch can continue to grow before losing adhesion and being considered dead.

Max Adhesion Distance controls the distance from the object that the program will consider the ivy still attached to the surface and viable for continued branching and growth.

The values I decided on for this object are shown in Figure 7.44. Set your values at something close to these.

Figure 7.44
Grow parameters

6. Click the Grow button to grow the ivy and watch the vines begin to emerge from the start point. You can stop the growth of the ivy whenever you are happy with the effect by clicking Grow again. The grown ivy should look something like that in Figure 7.45. You can control the growth interactively while the ivy is growing by changing parameter values or by setting a new start point (by double-clicking the LMB on a new spot on the object). If you find that the ivy is growing on the inside of your mesh instead of the outside, click the Flip Normals button at the top of the buttons panel.

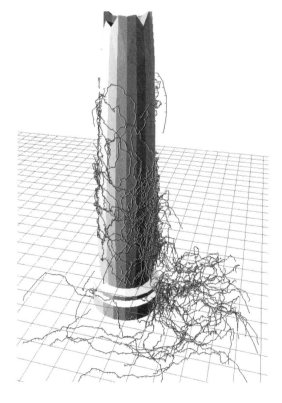

Figure 7.45
Grown ivy

7. When you are satisfied with the pattern of the ivy, set the Birth parameters to values similar to those in Figure 7.46. The Birth parameters are pretty self-explanatory. They are as follows:

Ivy Branch Size controls the thickness of the branches.

Ivy Leaf Size controls the size of the leaves.

Leaf Probability controls the density of the leaves. For some reason, however, this value seems to be the reverse of what one would expect. A lower value yields denser foliage.

After you've set these parameters, click the Birth button. The result should look something like Figure 7.47.

8. This is all for the ivy generation. Click the Export Obj+Mlt button to export the ivy to an .obj file. After you've done this, you can close the Ivy Generator.

9. Bring Blender back up. Follow a similar procedure to import the .obj file as you did to export previously: Choose File > Import > Wavefront(.obj). The Import dialog box is shown in Figure 7.48. Deselect Image Search to speed the process up a little bit.

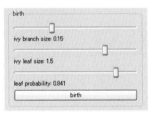

Figure 7.46
Birth parameters

Figure 7.47
The birthed ivy

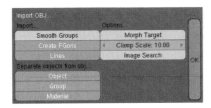

Figure 7.48
The Import dialog box

10. The ivy will import as three separate objects, each of which has a single material associated with it, called None_leaf_adult, None_leaf_young, and None_branch. These objects are shown selected in Figure 7.49.

Figure 7.49
Three parts of the ivy

11. All that remains to be done is to set the values and textures for each of these materials. Unpack the ivy_generator_Textures.zip file from the CD that accompanies this book. Select the object None_leaf_adult. The material for this object is called leaf_adult. Set the Alpha value to 0 and enable ray transparency. Select Oren-Nayar as the diffuse shader and set Rough to 0.5. Set Spec at 0.05 and Hard at 100. Select TraShadow. The texture images for this material are efeu1.tif, efeu1_Bump.tif, efeu1_Norm.tif, efeu1_rough.tif, and efeu1_trans.tif, shown in Figure 7.50. Create a separate Image texture on the material for each of these. For each one, select UV in the Map Input tab. Map efeu1.tif to Col and Csp. Map efeu1_Bump.tif to Nor. For efeu1_Norm.tif, select Normal Map in the Map Image tab in the Textures buttons, and map this to Nor also. Map efeu1_rough.tif to Spec. Finally, map efeu1_trans.tif to Alpha. (Because this image happens to be black on white, click the Alpha button twice to invert the mapping.) You can find the completed model with ivy in the file ivy_column.blend on the CD.

12. The textures for leaf_young and branch can be found in the same directory. The leaf_young texture filenames begin with efeu0, and the textures for the branch begin with efeu_branch. For leaf_young, follow the same steps as you did for leaf_adult. For branch, the steps are the same, except that transparency is not enabled and Alpha is left at 1.

13. Add the Subsurf modifier to the pillar, set up your lights, and render. You can check the file column-ivy.blend to see the settings and light placement I used to do the render in Figure 7.51.

Figure 7.50 Textures for adult leaves

Figure 7.50 *(continued)*

Figure 7.50 *(continued)*

Figure 7.51 Final render with ivy

A Few More Points to Mention

After reading this chapter, you now have a good idea of how to build convincing plants and trees by using automatic generation tools. As with the other simulations I have discussed in this book, these methods are only as effective as the use you put them to. In this section, I will give a few general suggestions for making the most of your simulations.

Tips for Creating an Outdoor Scene

Integrating the trees that you create by using a tree-generation script or application into a completed outdoor scene can be a challenge, and there is no single right answer to how to do it.

The approach to sky maps discussed in Chapter 1 is a good way to create your sky. Distant backgrounds can be accomplished by using textured planes. Think in terms of layers and building up depth by multiple textured planes, and try to work with the least amount of actual geometry you can get away with. If parts of your scene will not be seen in perspective, don't use 3D models for them. For trees and plants that need not be in full perspective but are close enough to need to be seen from multiple camera angles, you can use a rendered image of the tree mapped to nonmoving particles in Billboard mode. Static particles are also an excellent way to create grass, as you've seen elsewhere in this book.

For trees and plants that must be rendered in perspective, you can use generated models as described in this chapter. Several standard Python scripts can be useful in positioning such objects in a random way. The Randomize Loc Size Rot script can take a collection of selected objects and randomize their location, scale, and rotation within limits that you set. Select the items you want to randomize, and then from the header menu choose Object > Scripts > Randomize Loc Size Rot. The image in Figure 7.52 was created by setting each of the parameters Loc, Size, and Rot to a value of 1, and selecting the Link Axis option to maintain the proportions of the objects. Another handy script is the Drop Onto Ground script, which enables you to snap a collection of objects to a ground object. Simply select the objects you want to place, Shift-select the ground object last (it needs to be the active object, so order is important here), and run the script by choosing Object > Scripts > Drop Onto Ground. The results of running this script can be seen in Figure 7.53.

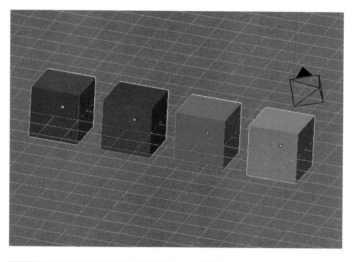

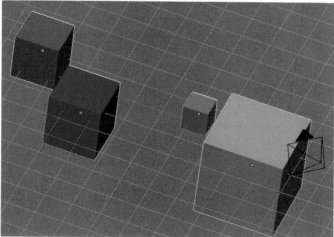

Figure 7.52 Randomize Loc Size Rot script

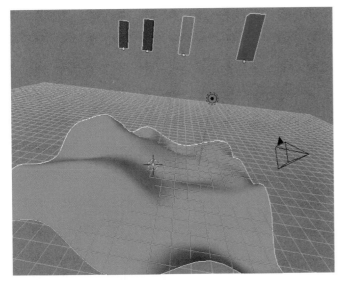

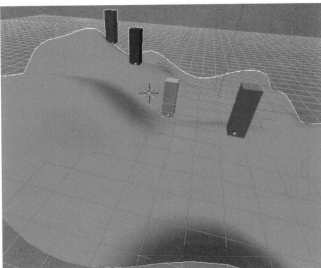

Figure 7.53 Drop Onto Ground script

The Importance of Observation

In this chapter and throughout the book, I have focused on how to accomplish simulation-related tasks by using Blender and other open source tools. It has been far beyond the scope of this book to do more than scratch the surface of discussing the science behind these methods. Nevertheless, some understanding of the underlying processes can be useful even to artists who simply want to make the most of the available tools. For this reason, I've tried to include references enabling you to find out more about the original research from which the methods derive.

For plant and tree generation, the Weber and Penn paper mentioned previously is an excellent place to start. Of course, if you have an interest in contributing code, I strongly urge you to investigate the areas in which Blender's simulation capabilities still have room for improvement and to study the current research in those areas. The accelerating pace of Blender development has resulted in Blender pulling well ahead of many proprietary applications in terms of simulation functionality, and it is energetic, knowledgeable volunteer coders who will ensure that it will continue to push the envelope.

For artists, however, understanding the technical underpinnings of the tools is secondary to having the ability to observe the world, and a clear vision of how you want to represent it in your artwork. In this chapter, for example, you learned how to create trees based on a set of parameters controlling branching angles, spin, and taper. The next step is to keep your eyes open to the way that these parameters manifest themselves in the world around you. Everything in nature follows rules, and plant life in particular is subject to rigid geometrical constraints. Observe the trees and take note of the angles of their branches and the way their leaves connect. With a sharp eye and attentive observations, you will develop the ability not only to create trees that are convincing and authentic, but to use all of the various tools at your disposal to create effects of all kinds that are truly evocative.

In addition to observing the world, you need to consider how you will be representing it and what the needs are of the artwork. Are you creating stills or animations? Are you working in a photorealistic style or in a cartoony style? Will objects be seen in perspective, or can they be faked with textures or billboards? What are your time and computing constraints? Do you need a simulation, or is there a simpler way to get the effect you want? In all cases, remember that a result that looks good *is* good. Do what it takes to achieve a good-looking result with the resources you have.

This book was intended to help you better understand what your software is capable of and how to exploit it. There's a lot of terrain to explore, and I hope this book proves to be a useful guide through the wilderness of Blender's powerful simulation capabilities. I am certainly hoping to see more art and animation that makes use of these features cropping up in the Blender.org gallery and BlenderArtists.org forums.

Happy Blendering!

About the Companion CD

A

In this appendix:
What you'll find on the CD
System requirements
Using the CD
Troubleshooting

What You'll Find on the CD

The following sections are arranged by category and provide a summary of what you'll find on the CD. If you need help with installing the items provided on the CD, refer to the installation instructions in the "Using the CD" section of this appendix.

Note that *trial, demo,* or *evaluation* versions of software are usually limited either by time or functionality (such as not letting you save a project after you create it).

Chapter Files

All the files provided in this book for completing the tutorials and understanding concepts are located in the Chapter Files directory, and further divided into directories corresponding to each chapter. In order to open .blend files you will need to have an up-to-date installation of Blender on your computer. For the purposes of this book, you should use Blender version 2.46, which is also included on the CD.

Blender 2.46 Software

Executable installation files for Blender 2.46 are provided for Windows and Mac OS X, both Intel and PPC architectures. The source code is provided in an archive for users of Linux and other Unix-like systems. Users of these systems who would like an executable build specific to their system and architecture can find many available in the downloads section at www.blender.org.

System Requirements

Make sure that your computer meets the minimum system requirements shown in the following list. If your computer doesn't match up to most of these requirements, you may have problems using the software and files on the companion CD. For the latest and greatest information, please refer to the ReadMe file located at the root of the CD-ROM.

- A PC running Microsoft Windows 98, Windows 2000, Windows NT4 (with SP4 or later), Windows Me, Windows XP, or Windows Vista.
- A Macintosh running Apple OS X or later.
- A PC running a version of Linux with kernel 2.4 or greater.
- An Internet connection
- A CD-ROM drive

Using the CD

To install the items from the CD to your hard drive, follow these steps.

1. Insert the CD into your computer's CD-ROM drive. The license agreement appears.

2. Read through the license agreement, and then click the Accept button if you want to use the CD.

The CD interface appears. The interface allows you to access the content with just one or two clicks.

> **Note:** Windows users: The interface won't launch if you have autorun disabled. In that case, click Start > Run (for Windows Vista, Start > All Programs > Accessories > Run). In the dialog box that appears, type **D:\Start.exe**. (Replace *D* with the proper letter if your CD drive uses a different letter. If you don't know the letter, see how your CD drive is listed under My Computer.) Click OK.

> **Note:** Mac users: The CD icon will appear on your desktop, double-click the icon to open the CD and double-click the Start icon.

Troubleshooting

Wiley has attempted to provide programs that work on most computers with the minimum system requirements. Alas, your computer may differ, and some programs may not work properly for some reason.

The two likeliest problems are that you don't have enough memory (RAM) for the programs you want to use, or you have other programs running that are affecting installation or running of a program. If you get an error message such as "Not enough memory" or "Setup cannot continue," try one or more of the following suggestions and then try using the software again:

Turn off any antivirus software running on your computer. Installation programs sometimes mimic virus activity and may make your computer incorrectly believe that it's being infected by a virus.

Close all running programs. The more programs you have running, the less memory is available to other programs. Installation programs typically update files and programs; so if you keep other programs running, installation may not work properly.

Have your local computer store add more RAM to your computer. This is, admittedly, a drastic and somewhat expensive step. However, adding more memory can really help the speed of your computer and allow more programs to run at the same time.

Customer Care

If you have trouble with the book's companion CD-ROM, please call the Wiley Product Technical Support phone number at (800) 762-2974. Outside the United States, call +1(317) 572-3994. You can also contact Wiley Product Technical Support at http://sybex.custhelp.com. John Wiley & Sons will provide technical support only for installation and other general quality control items. For technical support on the applications themselves, consult the program's vendor or author.

To place additional orders or to request information about other Wiley products, please call (877) 762-2974.

Index

Note to the Reader: Throughout this index **boldfaced** page numbers indicate primary discussions of a topic. *Italicized* page numbers indicate illustrations.